Red Hat Enterprise Linux (RHEL) 7 Server Installation and Administration

Training Manual: Covering CentOS-7 Server, Cloud Computing, Bind9 DNS Server, Fedora 23 Server and Astaro Firewall

Kefa Rabah

To my beloved family:
Jackline Okinyi, Briner Milan, Nigel Rabah

About the Author

Kefa Rabah is the founder of Global Open Versity, Vancouver Canada. Kefa has vast experience with Open Source Technology and Application including High Performance Computing (HPC) Clusters, Hypervirtualization, and Cloud Computing. Kefa is also an expert in Cryptography, IT Security, Cybercrime investigation and Digital Forensics; Information Security Compliance and Project Management. He is also knowledgeable in the areas of Science & Technology, and Renewable Energy Systems. He is also the founder of Global Technology Solutions Institute (Vancouver Canada) a place to enhance your educating and career goals using the latest innovations and technologies. Founder Serengeti Systems Consulting & Training; and Mara Publishing the publisher of Mara Research Journals.

Red Hat Enterprise Linux 7 Server Installation and Administration
Training Manual: Covering CentOS-7 Server, Cloud computing
Seafile & OwnCloud, Bind9 DNS Server and Fedora 23 Server

Table of Contents   Page No.

CHAPTER V   265

STEP-BY-STEP GUIDE USING WEBMIN AND BIND9 ON CENTOS-7 SERVER TO SETUP ROBUST DNS SEVER   265

Chapter I

Introduction

1.0 Background

Today, the Open Source IT community is growing more comfortable with the open-source development model, reporting that open source will dominate as their Web server application platform and server operating system in five years. The majority (64%) of companies surveyed in 2011 are using open source, most frequently as a server operating system and for Web development, and application servers. CIOs say the greatest benefits from using open source are lower total cost of ownership, lower capital investment and greater reliability and uptime compared to their existing systems. IT executives report that open source provides greater flexibility, control and faster, cheaper application development. All things equal, the majority of IT executives surveyed said they would choose open source for a new implementation over a proprietary vendor solution.

Red Hat Enterprise Linux (RHEL) is a Linux distribution produced by Red Hat and targeted toward the commercial market, including mainframes. Red Hat Enterprise Linux is released in server versions for x86, x86_64, Itanium, PowerPC and IBM System z, and desktop versions for x86 and x86_64. All of Red Hat's official support and training, and the Red Hat Certification Program center on the Red Hat Enterprise Linux platform.

The very nature of the GNU Public License (GPL) ensures that any project, company or organization which builds products based on GPL licensed software has to release the source for that derivative work. Red Hat has been a pillar of the open source community for more than twenty years. Its own distributions, and the distributions to which it contributes, play a major role in the Linux eco-system. One of those distributions is Red Hat Enterprise Linux (RHEL). It is a commercial distribution aimed primarily at large businesses. As a commercial product, there is no free version. If you want to run RHEL, you need to buy a license.

The long-awaited Red Hat Enterprise Linux (RHEL) 7 delivers improvements including KVM and improved scalability. However, Xen is no longer supported. Red Hat Enterprise Linux (RHEL) is a commercial Linux OS that is designed for businesses that need full support and the highest amount of reliability possible for mission critical applications. Historically, RHEL has been a derivative of the Fedora Linux project with features and release cycles that meet the requirements of Red Hat's commercial customers.

Red Hat has demonstrated its commitment to continuously delivering the value and innovation that make Red Hat Enterprise Linux the strategic operating system platform for long-term IT deployments. Dramatic improvements in reliability, performance, and scalability make Red Hat Enterprise Linux 7 the platform of choice for physical, virtual, and cloud infrastructures and the most demanding workloads.

Furthermore, on one certified platform, Red Hat Enterprise Linux offers your choice of: (i) **Applications** - Thousands of certified ISV applications; (ii) **Deployment** - Including standalone or virtual servers, cloud computing, or software appliances; (iii) **Hardware** - Wide range of platforms from the world's leading hardware vendors. This gives IT departments' unprecedented levels of operational flexibility. And it gives ISVs unprecedented market reach when delivering applications. Certify once, deploy anywhere. All while providing world-class performance, security, and stability. And unbeatable value. This is why today Red Hat continues to be the platform of choice.

Xen has been dropped and instead KVM is in place. KVM (Kernel-based Virtual Machine) replaced Xen as the virtualization product of choice. KVM is a bare metal hypervisor that runs directly on x86 hardware instead of on top of an operating system. It was distributed in RHEL 5.4 in a package called Red Hat Enterprise Virtualization Hypervisor (RHEV-H). With a memory footprint of only 128MB, it can easily be started from flash or a network drive.

Red Hat Identity Management with IPA Directory Services: The IPA (now simply called Identity Management) is an acronym for Identity, Policy, and Auditing.. The latest Red Hat Enterprise Linux 7 boasts being a great OS to run your identity management infrastructure. As of 2014 FreeIPA uses 389 Directory Server for its LDAP implementation, MIT's Kerberos 5 for authentication and single sign-on, the Apache HTTP Server and Python for the management framework and Web UI, and (optionally) DogTag for the integrated CA, and BIND with a custom plugin for the integrated DNS. Since version 3.0.0, FreeIPA also uses Samba to integrate with Microsoft's Active Directory by way of Cross Forest Trusts (source Wikipedia)". FreeIPA aims to provide support not just for Linux- and Unix-based computers, but ultimately for Microsoft Windows and Apple OS X computers." The 389 Directory Server key features include: Multi-Master Replication, to provide fault tolerance and high write performance. Scalability: thousands of operations per second, tens of thousands of concurrent users, tens of millions of entries, hundreds of gigabytes of data. It has extensive documentation, including helpful Installation and Deployment guides. It's capable of Active Directory user and group synchronization. Excellent security with secure authentication and transport (SSLv3, TLSv1, and SASL). It support for LDAPv3 compliant. It has on-line, zero downtime, LDAP-based update of schema, configuration, management and in-tree Access Control Information (ACIs). And the cool part is has graphical console for all facets of user, group, and server management.

Chapter III: Covers CentOS 7 Server: is a community-supported, free and open source operating system based on Red Hat Enterprise Linux. It exists to provide a free enterprise class computing platform and strives to maintain 100% binary compatibility with its upstream distribution .CentOS stands for "Community ENTerprise Operating System". CentOS is the perfect server for people who need an enterprise class operating system stability without the cost of certification and support and pocket burning baggage that comes with proprietary software. And the beauty is CentOS is free.

CentOS-7.0 is based on the upstream release of Red Hat EL 7.0 and includes packages from all variants. All upstream repositories have been combined into one, to make it easier for end users to work with. It exists to provide a free enterprise class computing platform and strives to maintain

100% binary compatibility with its upstream distribution, in this case RHEL 7. To-date, CentOS simply remains the unrivaled champion of rock solid, and with excellent and modern capabilities, good performance and ultra-long support.

CentOS 7 is the first version to be released after the nominally independent CentOS and Red Hat brokered a deal to work together more closely, in away for CentOS to become a staging ground for future features for RHEL, akin to Fedora Project's former status. This could be a plus for Red Hat to reach out more directly to CentOS's vast customer base - the enterprises, service providers, ISPs, and other outfits using CentOS to keep cost low gain on ROI.

Chapter IV: covers Mastering Virtualization with VirtualBox & Cloud Computingon CentOS-7 Infrastructure Server starting with how install and manage Oracle VirtualBox virtualization with phpVirtualBox, followed by installation of owbCloud, Sealfile secure cloud storage, Pydio file sharing server.

Oracle VirtualBox is a powerful x86 and AMD64/Intel64 virtualization product for enterprise as well as home use. VirtualBox is a general-purpose full virtualizer for x86 hardware. Targeted at server, desktop and embedded use, it is now the only professional-quality virtualization solution that is also Open Source Software. It supports a large number of guest operating systems, Linux distros, Windows OSes, Solaris, OpenSolaris, and OpenBSD.

ownCloud is a web application that can store and serve content from a centralized location, much like Dropbox. The difference is that ownCloud 8 allows you to host the serving software on your own machines, taking the trust issues out of putting your personal data someone else's server. The ownCloud also provides access to your data through a web interface or WebDAV while providing a platform to easily view, sync and share across devices—all under your control. ownCloud's open architecture is extensible via a simple but powerful API for applications and plugins and works with any storage.

The Seafile Secure Cloud Storage is an open source cloud platform. In this section you'll lean how to install, configure and Seafile cloud storage which you can use to synchronize your files and data with PC and mobile devices or access via web interface for managing your data files from home, workplace or just anywhere or as ago about your business. Thus, its ideal for small Storage solution mostly for small to medium business purposes, eLearning, joint project management - i.e., a place where you have the flexibility of group sharing and multiple projects, with no need for a public server provision, and has complete security provided by the client-side encryption of the data. You can choose to host your data on the Seafile cloud or provision it through your local Seafile server which you'll have gained expertise to setup after undertaking the Tech Training Series provision using RHEL 7 / CentOS 7 server.

Pydio is an alternative to Dropbox and box.com, for enterprise. You need to access your documents across multiple devices, and regularly share documents (weblinks) and folders with your contacts and teams. Still, using a consumer SaaS box or drive service is neither practical nor safe. And enterprise SaaS box or drive services are expensive and come with Disk Storage that you already have on your servers or private cloud. Pydio file sharing & sync includes applications for web, desktop and mobile assuring that your end users can easily manage their critical documents everywhere. Pydio is hosted exclusively on your private server or cloud so you can rest assured that files are securely managed under company control.

Cloud storage is nothing but an enterprise-level cloud data storage model to store the digital data in logical pools, across the multiple servers. You have the option to deploy your own on-premise private cloud solution or you can use public cloud from hosting company such as Amazon, Google, Rackspace, Dropbox and others for keeping your data available and accessible 24/7/365. You can access data stored on cloud storage via API or desktop/mobile apps or web based systems.

Chapter V: Fedora Linux is well known for its innovative features and for incorporating cutting-edge technology in every major release version. **Fedora** (formerly **Fedora Core**) is an operating system based on the Linux kernel, developed by the community-supported Fedora Project and sponsored by Red Hat. Fedora contains software distributed under a free and open source license and aims to be on the leading edge of such technologies. Fedora Server is a powerful, flexible operating system that includes the best and latest datacenter technologies. It puts you in control of all your infrastructure and service. Finally, Fedora Cloud provides a minimal image of Fedora for use in public and private cloud environments. It includes just the bare essentials making it very light on resources, but you get enough to run your cloud application.

Fedora Workstation is a polished, easy to use operating system for laptop and desktop computers, with a complete set of tools for developers and makers of all kinds. It's a reliable, user-friendly, and powerful operating system for your laptop or desktop computer. It supports a wide range of developers, from hobbyists and students to professionals in corporate environments. The latest release includes quite a few improvements thanks to GNOME and other upstream projects. Fedora's developers are also on the cusp of switching to the new Wayland graphical server by default, with a stable, optional Wayland session available in Fedora 23. Finally, Fedora 23 provides you with the balance most tech and ICT infrastructure designers looks for – a leading edge operating system with enterprise-level tools for fast provisioning and configuration.

Chapter VI: Project: *Deploy secure enterprise network defense solution using Astaro Security Gateway (ASG).* (Astaro Security Gateway is Trademark of Astaro AG.) The ASG is all in One – The Unified Threat Management (UTM) appliance that brings enterprise-class Network, Web and Mail Security to organizations for all sizes. You have the option to use Home Use Edition, fully free for home use; the Essential Edition, fully free for Business Use; and the Professional Edition, which you can purchase for commercial use; however, you have the possibility to test it free for 30 day trial. In this IT Security & Network Defense Hands-on Training session, we're going to use the Professional edition for training purposes.

Chapter II

Step-By-Step Install Guide RHEL7 Server Installation & Administration

Introduction

Red Hat Enterprise Linux (RHEL) is a Linux distribution produced by Red Hat and targeted toward the commercial market, including mainframes. Red Hat Enterprise Linux is released in server versions for x86, x86_64, Itanium, PowerPC and IBM System z, and desktop versions for x86 and x86_64. All of Red Hat's official support and training, and the Red Hat Certification Program center on the Red Hat Enterprise Linux platform.

The very nature of the GNU Public License (GPL) ensures that any project, company or organization which builds products based on GPL licensed software has to release the source for that derivative work. Red Hat has been a pillar of the open source community for more than twenty years. Its own distributions, and the distributions to which it contributes, play a major role in the Linux eco-system. One of those distributions is Red Hat Enterprise Linux (RHEL). It is a commercial distribution aimed primarily at large businesses. As a commercial product, there is no free version. If you want to run RHEL, you need to buy a license.

The long-awaited Red Hat Enterprise Linux (RHEL) 7 delivers improvements including KVM and improved scalability. However, Xen is no longer supported. Red Hat Enterprise Linux (RHEL) is a commercial Linux OS that is designed for businesses that need full support and the highest amount of reliability possible for mission critical applications. Historically, RHEL has been a derivative of the Fedora Linux project with features and release cycles that meet the requirements of Red Hat's commercial customers.

Red Hat has demonstrated its commitment to continuously delivering the value and innovation that make Red Hat Enterprise Linux the strategic operating system platform for long-term IT deployments. Dramatic improvements in reliability, performance, and scalability make Red Hat Enterprise Linux 7 the platform of choice for physical, virtual, and cloud infrastructures and the most demanding workloads.

Furthermore, on one certified platform, Red Hat Enterprise Linux offers your choice of: (i) **Applications** - Thousands of certified ISV applications; (ii) **Deployment** - Including standalone or virtual servers, cloud computing, or software appliances; (iii) **Hardware** - Wide range of platforms from the world's leading hardware vendors. This gives IT departments' unprecedented levels of operational flexibility. And it gives ISVs unprecedented market reach when delivering applications. Certify once, deploy anywhere. All while providing world-class performance, security, and stability. And unbeatable value. This is why today Red Hat continues to be the platform of choice.

Xen has been dropped and instead KVM is in place. KVM (Kernel-based Virtual Machine) replaced Xen as the virtualization product of choice. KVM is a bare metal hypervisor that runs directly on x86 hardware instead of on top of an operating system. It was distributed in RHEL 5.4 in a package called Red Hat Enterprise Virtualization Hypervisor (RHEV-H). With a memory footprint of only 128MB, it can easily be started from flash or a network drive.

Hands-on Lab Session

In this Hands-on Labs module, you will learn how to install RHEL7 from DVD ISO. You'll also learn how to perform post-installation configuration e.g., upgrade the system with new patches and bug fixes, configure static IP address from dynamic one, change the computer hostname, modify hosts file, perform ping test among others. You'll also learn Webmin as part of your arsenal. In this Hands-on Lab assignment you'll have an opportunity to install LAMP: Apache2 (httpd), MySQL (MariaDB) server, PostgreSQL server PHP. This also include: vsFTP server, NFS server, JDK8, Tomcat 9 and Ant. You'll also learn how to install WildFly AS 9.0 and the bundled option JBoss-Portal. Setup backup server with Bacula Backup server. Finally you'll be to install and configure IPA (Identity Management). The entire lab training was performed on VMware, however, do feel free to use any other virtual machine as desired for your lab session.

Part 1: Installing and Updating Red Hat Enterprise Linux (RHEL) 7

Step 1: Install RHEL 7 Server

1. Point your browser to www.redhat.com and download DVD ISO Server, RHEL 7

2. Once you have downloaded the RHEL 7 ISO specific to your distribution, you have the option of burning it to CD or just using the ISO package to install it from your virtual machine, in our case VMware.

3. Fire-up a new virtual machine and perform the initial configuration and setup to use ISO package.

4. Start the virtual machine, and you should be able to see the first RHEL 7 installation screen.

5. From Fig. 1, and hit **Enter** key to start installation.

Fig. 1

6. From Fig. 2, The system will perform some initial tasks, just relax while it does so.

Fig. 2a

Fig. 2b

7. From Fig. 3, **WELCOME TO RED HAT ENTERPRISE 7.2** screen, accept the default selection, or change as desired and then click on **Continue** button.

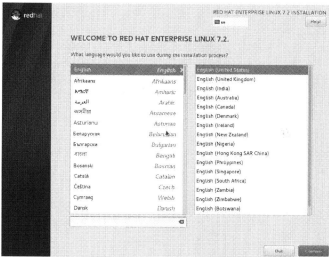

Fig. 3

8. On the next screen the **INSTALLATION SUMMARY** screen, here you can customize your installation by using other **Installation Sources** than your local DVD/USB media, such as a network locations using **HTTP, HTTPS, FTP** or **NFS** protocols and even add some additional repositories, but use this methods only if you know what you're doing. So leave the default **Auto-detected installation media** and hit on **Done** to continue

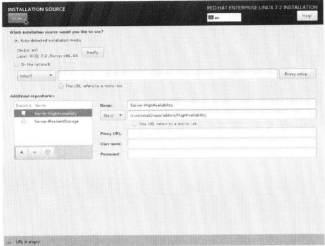

Fig. 4

9. From Fig. 5, **INSTALLATION SUMMARY** screen, click on the INSTALLATION DESTINATION to take you to the **INSTALLATION DESTINATION** screen, accept the default selection "Auto-configure partitioning" or change as desired, click on **Done** to continue.

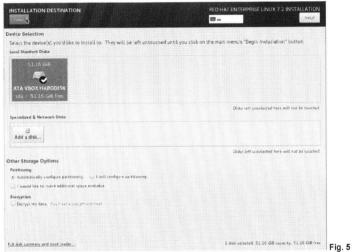

Fig. 5

10. From Fig. 6, **INSTALLATION SUMMARY** screen, click on the INSTALLATION DESTINATION to take you to the **NETWORK & HOST NAME** screen, accept the default selection or change as desired, in our case " `rhel7.systemhost.com`" click on **Done** to continue.

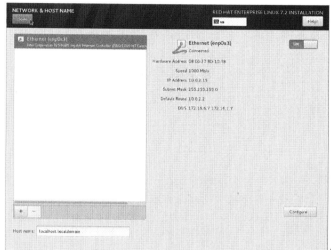

Fig. 6

11. From Fig. 7, **INSTALLATION SUMMARY** screen, you're now ready to begin installation once you're satisfied with your settings, click on **Continue** to continue.

Fig. 7

12. From Fig. 8, **CONFIGURATION** screen, here we're required to set the root password and also add a user as shown. Click on individual icon to perform the task.

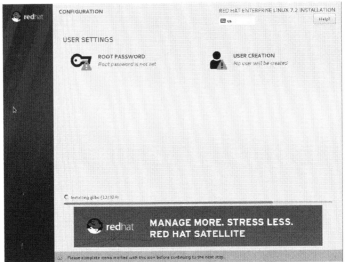

Fig. 8

13. From Fig. 9, **CONFIGURATION** screen, Click on the ROOT PAASWORD to set it as shown, click Done to continue.

Fig. 9

14. From Fig. 10, **CREATE USER** screen, add the desired user as shown, click Done to continue.

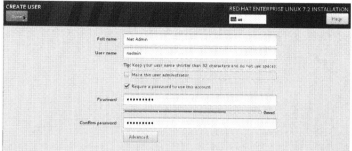

Fig. 10

15. From Fig. 12, **CONFIGURATION** screen, when done click on **Finish Configuration** to continue.

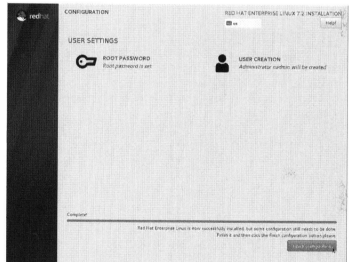

Fig. 11

16. From Fig. 11, **CONFIGURATION** screen, wait for the system configure root user password and the adding of user.

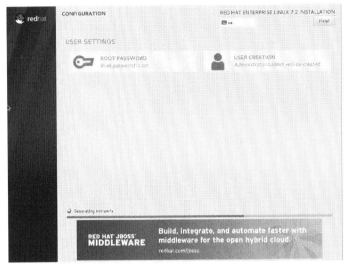
Fig. 12

17. From Fig. 13, **CONFIGURATION** screen, wait for the systems to complete the task, when done click on **Reboot** button to continue. (**Note**: the license agreement notification)

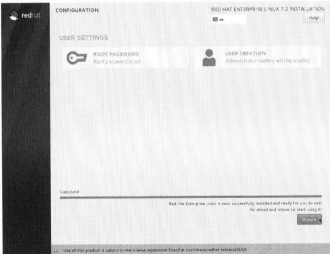
Fig. 13

18. From Fig. 14, the system will go through rebooting as shown, just relax for it to take to the login screen.

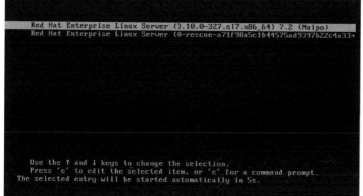

Fig. 14

19. From Fig. 15, **INITIAL SETUP** screen, click on the LICENSING icon to access the licensing acceptance screen.

Fig. 15

20. From Fig. 16, **Licensing Agreement** screen, read and accept the agreement, the click on the Done button to continue.

14

Fig. 16

21. From Fig. 17, **INITIAL SETUP** screen, click on the FINISH CONFIGURATION button to continue.

Fig. 17

22. From Fig. 18, you should be presented with the login screen as shown.

Fig. 18

23. From Fig. 19, login with the username and password entered earlier, change to suit, and the click on Sign In button.

Fig. 19

24. From Fig. 20, you should be presented with the RHEL 7 Desktop. Take your time to wonder around to get formalized with your newly minted server.

Fig. 20

25. You're done with RHEL-7 server installation. In the next section, we're going to perform other post-installation work like system upgrade etc.

Part 2: Post Installation Configurations.

Step 1: Perform System Upgrade

For best practices in IT, it's important to always perform systems upgrade after initial installation is completed. To do this, perform the following procedures:

1. From Fig. 20 above click on **Applications** → **Favorites** → **Terminal** as shown below.

Fig. 21

2. From Fig. 22, you should be presented with Terminal window, type "ifconfig" command and hit Enter, you should be able Network card information. Note here "eth0" is shown as "enp0s3" with IP address "10.0.2.15". Go ahead and ping it to check if its active.

```
[nadmin@rhel7 ~]$ ifconfig
enp0s3: flags=4163<UP,BROADCAST,RUNNING,MULTICAST>  mtu 1500
        inet 10.0.2.15  netmask 255.255.255.0  broadcast 10.0.2.255
        inet6 fe80::a00:27ff:fe49:98a7  prefixlen 64  scopeid 0x20<link>
        ether 08:00:27:49:98:a7  txqueuelen 1000  (Ethernet)
        RX packets 86  bytes 10332 (10.0 KiB)
        RX errors 0  dropped 0  overruns 0  frame 0
        TX packets 125  bytes 12754 (12.4 KiB)
        TX errors 0  dropped 0 overruns 0  carrier 0  collisions 0

lo: flags=73<UP,LOOPBACK,RUNNING>  mtu 65536
        inet 127.0.0.1  netmask 255.0.0.0
        inet6 ::1  prefixlen 128  scopeid 0x10<host>
        loop  txqueuelen 0  (Local Loopback)
        RX packets 4  bytes 340 (340.0 B)
        RX errors 0  dropped 0  overruns 0  frame 0
        TX packets 4  bytes 340 (340.0 B)
        TX errors 0  dropped 0 overruns 0  carrier 0  collisions 0

virbr0: flags=4099<UP,BROADCAST,MULTICAST>  mtu 1500
        inet 192.168.122.1  netmask 255.255.255.0  broadcast 192.168.122.255
        ether 52:54:00:70:55:9e  txqueuelen 0  (Ethernet)
        RX packets 0  bytes 0 (0.0 B)
        RX errors 0  dropped 0  overruns 0  frame 0
        TX packets 0  bytes 0 (0.0 B)
        TX errors 0  dropped 0 overruns 0  carrier 0  collisions 0
```

Fig. 22a

```
[nadmin@rhel7 ~]$ ping 10.0.2.15
PING 10.0.2.15 (10.0.2.15) 56(84) bytes of data.
64 bytes from 10.0.2.15: icmp_seq=1 ttl=64 time=0.112 ms
64 bytes from 10.0.2.15: icmp_seq=2 ttl=64 time=0.081 ms
64 bytes from 10.0.2.15: icmp_seq=3 ttl=64 time=0.066 ms
^C
--- 10.0.2.15 ping statistics ---
3 packets transmitted, 3 received, 0% packet loss, time 1999ms
rtt min/avg/max/mdev = 0.066/0.086/0.112/0.020 ms
[nadmin@rhel7 ~]$
```
.... **Fig. 22b**

1. From **Terminal** window, issue the command "yum update -y" as shown in Fig. 23: This enables the system to get the latest patches and bug fixes.

```
[nadmin@rhel7 ~]$ su -
Password:
Last login: Mon Dec 21 10:41:47 EST 2015 on pts/0
[root@rhel7 ~]# yum update -y
```
.... **Fig. 23**

2. You're now down with system update. In the next section we're going to learn how to change NIC adapter configuration from dynamic IP address to static IP address.

Step 3: Check Computer Hostname

Note 1: The old way of changing hostname by modifying the "/etc/sysconfig/network"; no longer works and if you do so, it did not take an effect of the modification. That is, even do so, after you reboot the server, the hostname will still remains "localhost.localdomain". The procedure to change the hostname in RHEL 7 is now totally different from the previous version, this section will help you to setup the hostname on both the RHEL 7.

Note 2: RHEL 7 Supports three class of Hostnames

1. **Static** - The static hostname is the traditional host which can chosen by the user and is stored in "/etc/hostname" file
2. **Transient** - The transient hostname is maintained by the kernel and can be changed by DHCP and mDNS.
3. **Pretty** - It is a free UTF-8 hostname for the presentation to the user.

Note 3: Hostname can be
- 64 character in length
- Recommend to have FQDN
- Consists of: a-z, A-Z, 0-9, "-", and "." only.

In this section we're going to change the computer hostname. But first let's check the current hostname.

1. To check the hostname issue "hostname" command, as shown in Fig. 24. which shows the current hostname is: : "rhel7.govsystemhost.com"

```
[root@rhel7 ~]# hostname
rhel7.govsystemhost.com
[root@rhel7 ~]#
```
Fig. 31

2. You're done with this section.

2. Using nmtui tool to Change Hostname on RHEL 7

3. The NetworkManager tool is used to set the static hostname in "/etc/hostname". From the Terminal window issue the command "nmtui" to ass the NetworkManager dialogue box as shown in Fig. 32. From here you can do three things: Edit a connection; Activate a connection, and Set system hostname. Move to Set system hostname and hit **Enter** key or OK.

Fig. 25

4. Now in case, for example, you're interested in changing the hostname to, say: "server01.mydomain.org". Now you can modify your hostname as desired and then hit Enter key.

Fig. 26

5. In case you any modification to the hostname, then you'll need to restart the hostname to force the "hostnamectl" to notice the change in static hostname.

```
[root@rhel7 ~]# systemctl restart systemd-hostname
```

6. You can verify the change in the hostname as shown in Fig. 27:

```
[root@rhel7 ~]# cat /etc/hostname
rhel7.govsystemhost.com
[root@rhel7 ~]# cat /etc/sysconfig/network
NISDOMAIN=govsystemhost.com
[root@rhel7 ~]#
```
Fig. 27

7. You're done with this section.

3. Using `hostnamedctl` command to Change Hostname on RHEL 7

Hostnamectl is used to change the hostname. With this tool we can change all three classes of hostname, however, here we are only interested with the static hostname.

1. First, and as usual, we need to check the current hostname, as shown in Fig. 28:

```
[root@rhel7 ~]# hostnamectl status
```

```
[root@rhel7 ~]# hostnamectl status
   Static hostname: rhel7.govsystemhost.com
         Icon name: computer-vm
           Chassis: vm
        Machine ID: 044e020008604b22bcbf5dd4287fbf31
           Boot ID: 8c04b81b8b194501b9d18c0327b13be0
    Virtualization: vmware
  Operating System: Red Hat Enterprise Linux
       CPE OS Name: cpe:/o:redhat:enterprise_linux:7.2:GA:server
            Kernel: Linux 3.10.0-327.el7.x86_64
      Architecture: x86-64
[root@rhel7 ~]#
```
Fig. 28

2. Next, if desired, you can change the hostname, as follows:

```
[root@rhel7 ~]# hostnamectl set-hostname server01.mydomain.com
```

3. You can also use the hostnamectl command on its own.

```
[root@rhel7 ~]# hostnamectl
```

4. You're done with this section.

3. Using nmcli tool to Change Hostname on RHEL 7
The nmcli tool can be used to query and setup the static hostname in "/etc/hostname" file.

1. To check the hostname:

```
[root@rhel7 ~]# nmcli general hostname
```

2. To change the hostname:

```
[root@rhel7 ~]# nmcli general hostname server01.mydomain.com
```

3. To restart the hostname to force hostnamectl to notice the change in static hostname

```
[root@rhel7 ~]# nmcli restart system-hostnamed
```


4. Edit "/etc/hostname" to Change Hostname on RHEL 7
Note: this is the simplest but requires a reboot of the server to in order to take effect

4. You are done with this section.

22

Part 3: Installing Linux, Apache, Mariadb (MySQL), PHP (LAMP) Stack on RHEL 7 Server

The LAMP stack forms the basic core components for a dynamic, database-driven web site. We'll use "yum" to handle all the required packages. LAMP stack is nothing but software bundle or a platform consisting of Linux operating system, Apache web-server, MySQL (now MariaDB) database server and PHP (or Perl/Python) scripting language. The LAMP stack is used for building heavy duty dynamic websites entirely out of free and open-source software. In this section of the Hands-on guide, we are going to go through on how to install and run LAMP stack. This same guide can be used on CentOS 7.

This section will present us the opportunity to install Apache2 (httpd), PHP, MySQL (server and client), and the component that allows PHP to talk to MySQL database.

Step 1: Install Apache on RHEL 7 Server

1. From the Terminal window, run the following yum command to install Apache web-server:

```
sudo yum install httpd -y
```

Note: Troubleshooting: In case you encounter dependencies problem, then you can perform yum command with "—skip-broken" option, as follows:

1. Next, we now need to enable the httpd service to start automatically at the boot time, type:

```
sudo systemctl enable httpd.service
```

Note: to disable the httpd service at boot time, issue:

```
sudo systemctl disable httpd.service
```

2. Now, we need to start the httpd service, type:

```
sudo systemctl start httpd.service
```

3. Test your httpd functionality, go to http://localhost or http://your-domain or http://ip-address, and if all works well, it should display **RHEL7 Test Page,** as shown in Fig. 29.

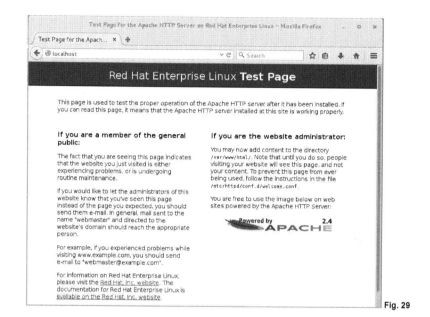

Fig. 29

Note: to stop `httpd` service, run:

```
sudo systemctl stop httpd.service
```

4. To restart `httpd` service, run:

```
sudo systemctl restart httpd.service
```

5. To verify the `httpd` service status, enter:

```
sudo systemctl is-active httpd.service
```

6. To gracefully restart `httpd` service status, enter:

```
sudo apachectl graceful
```

7. To test `httpd` configuration file for errors, enter:

```
sudo apachectl configtest
```

Sample output:

```
Syntax OK
```

8. You're done with Apache2 server setup and testing.

9. You're with this section.

1. The httpd (Apache) service default configuration
- Default config file: `/etc/httpd/conf/httpd.conf`
- Configuration files which load modules: "`/etc/httpd/conf.modules.d/`" directory (e.g., PHP).
- Select MPMs (Processing Model) as loadable modules [worker, prefolk (default)] and event
  "`/etc/httpd/conf.module.d/00-mpm.conf`
- Default ports: `80` and `443` (SSL)
- Default log files: "`/var/log/httpd/{access_log, error_log}`"

10. You're with this section.

Step 2: Install MariaDB (MySQL) Database Server
MariaDB is an enhanced, drop-in replacement for MySQL server. RHEL/CentOS 7.x has shift from MySQL to MariaDB for its database management systems needs.

1. Install MariaDB
1. To install MariaDB run the `yum` command as follows:

```
sudo yum install mariadb-server maraidb -y
```

2. Start Mariadb (`mariadb`) daemon service, if you haven't done so, run:

```
sudo systemctl start mariadb.service
```

3. To make sure Mariadb (`mariadb`) daemon service start automatically at boot time, type:

```
sudo systemctl enable mariadb.service
```

4. To stop/start and disable mariadb service use the following commands:

```
sudo systemctl stop mariadb.service          # Stop mariadb server
```

```
sudo systemctl restart mariadb.service      # Restart mariadb server
sudo systemctl disable mariadb.service      # Disable mariadb server
sudo systemctl is-active mariadb.service    # Is mariadb server
running
```

5. You're done with this section.

2. Securing MariaDB

IMPORTANT! Set up the MySQL database root password. Without a password, ANY user on the box can login to mysql as database root. The mysql root account is a separate password from the machine root account.

Now that our MySQL (Mariadb) database is running, we want to run a simple security script that will remove some of the dangerous defaults and also allow us to lock down access to our database a little bit. To do this, from the Terminal window type:

```
sudo mysql_secure_installation
```

The prompt will ask you for your current root password. However, since we have just installed MySQL, you most likely won't have one, so leave it blank by pressing enter. On the next prompt you will be asked if you want to set a root password. Go ahead and enter Y, and follow the instructions as below:

```
Enter current password for root (enter for none):
OK, successfully used password, moving on...

Setting the root password ensures that nobody can log into the MariaDB
root user without the proper authorization.

New password: password
Re-enter new password: password
Password updated successfully!
Reloading privilege tables..
 ... Success!
```

Note: for the rest of the questions, you should simply hit **"ENTER"** key through each prompt to accept default values, or change as desired. This will remove some of the sample users and databases, disable remote root logins, and load these rules, so that MySQL immediately respects the changes we have made. However, since this is a non production server, which are only using for training, we have left some of the settings as is. (**Note:** for production server please do ensure that the server full locked-down).

1. We can now login into our database as follows (enter the password set above):

```
$ mysql -u root -p

$ mysql -u root -p
Welcome to the MariaDB monitor.  Commands end with ; or \g.
Your MariaDB connection id is 3
Server version: 5.5.44-MariaDB MariaDB Server

Copyright (c) 2000, 2015, Oracle, MariaDB Corporation Ab and others.

Type 'help;' or '\h' for help. Type '\c' to clear the current input statement.

MariaDB [(none)]>
```

2. You're with this section.

3: Creating a Test Database on MariaDA

1. Now we need to create a sample database and database user for a sample application. You will use this database and username in your database connection string. The "GRANT" statement actually creates a new MariaDB/MYSQL user account.

```
MariaDB> GREATE DATABASE webdb;
MariaDB> GRANT ALL PRIVILEGES ON webdb.* TO 'webuser'@'localhost'
IDENTIFIED BY 'webpass';
MariaDB> FLUSH PRIVILEGES;
MariaDB>exit
```

```
MariaDB [(none)]> CREATE DATABASE webdb;
Query OK, 1 row affected (0.00 sec)

MariaDB [(none)]> GRANT ALL PRIVILEGES ON webdb.* TO 'webuser'@'localhost' IDENT
IFIED BY 'webpass';
Query OK, 0 rows affected (0.03 sec)

MariaDB [(none)]> FLUSH PRIVILEGES;
Query OK, 0 rows affected (0.41 sec)

MariaDB [(none)]>
```
Fig. 30

2. You can check if your "webdb" database has been successfully created, using "show databases" command.

```
MariaDB [(none)]> SHOW DATABASES;
+--------------------+
| Database           |
+--------------------+
| information_schema |
| mysql              |
| performance_schema |
| webdb              |
+--------------------+
4 rows in set (0.12 sec)

MariaDB [(none)]>
```
Fig. 31

3. You're done with MySQL (MariaDB) setup, configuration and testing.

4. You're done with this section

Step 3: Install PostgreSQL Database on RHEL 7

This will install the PostgreSQL database server and the component required to write PHP scripts that communicate with postgresql. Do this if you didn't initially install it. We use yum to handle dependencies and gather all of the required packages. For more information on PostgreSQL, see http://www.postgresql.org

1. To install PostgreSQL and the component that allows PHP to talk to it, run:

```
# yum -y install postgresql postgresql-server php-pgsql
```

2. We need to initialize PostgreSQL database, Run:

```
# service postgresql initdb
```
```
[nadmin@rhel7 ~]$ su -
Password:
Last login: Mon Dec 21 12:48:52 EST 2015 on pts/0
[root@rhel7 ~]# service postgresql initdb
Hint: the preferred way to do this is now "postgresql-setup initdb"
Initializing database ... OK

[root@rhel7 ~]#
```
Fig. 32

3. Configure the new service to start automatically on boot:

```
# /sbin/chkconfig --level 345 postgresql on
# /sbin/service postgresql start
```

```
[root@rhel7 ~]# /sbin/chkconfig --level 345 postgresql on
Note: Forwarding request to 'systemctl enable postgresql.service'.
Created symlink from /etc/systemd/system/multi-user.target.wants/postgresql.serv
ice to /usr/lib/systemd/system/postgresql.service.
[root@rhel7 ~]#
[root@rhel7 ~]# /sbin/service postgresql start
Redirecting to /bin/systemctl start  postgresql.service
[root@rhel7 ~]#
```

Fig. 33

Note: when you start postgresql for the first time, it'll initialize the database.

4. Start the `postgresql` interactive shell and create your first user and database.

```
# su - postgres            \\The dash "-" is important!
```

4. Next, issue the command, `"psql template1"`, to enter the default postgresql database

```
-bash-3.2$ psql template1
```

The whole sequence is as shown in Fig. 34.

```
[root@rhel7 ~]# su - postgres
Last failed login: Mon Dec 21 12:58:24 EST 2015 on pts/1
There was 1 failed login attempt since the last successful login.
-bash-4.2$ psql template1
psql (9.2.13)
Type "help" for help.

template1=#
template1=# help
You are using psql, the command-line interface to PostgreSQL.
Type:  \copyright for distribution terms
       \h for help with SQL commands
       \? for help with psql commands
       \g or terminate with semicolon to execute query
       \q to quit
template1=#
```
—— Fig. 34

Note: `"template1"` is the database that is included by default with PostgreSQL.

5. Check the `version` of your `postgresql` database:

```
template1=# select version();
                    version
------------------------------------------------------------------
PostgreSQL 9.2.13 on x86_64-redhat-linux-gnu, compiled by
GCC gcc (GCC) 4.8.3 20140911 (Red Hat 4.8.3-9), 64-bit
```

29

```
(1 row)
template1=# \q
-bash-4.2$ exit
```

6. Now create dbase user "webadmin" and make him a superuser:

```
-bash-4.2$ createuser -P webadmin
Enter password for new role:
Enter it again:
Shall the new role be a superuser? (y/n) y
-bash-4.2$
```

7. Next create the database "webdb"

```
-bash-4.2$
-bash-4.2$ createdb -O webadmin webdb
-bash-4.2$
```

8. Now connect into your newly created database:

```
-bash-4.2$ psql webdb
Psql (9.2.13)
Type "help" for help.
web_db=#
```

9. Logout of your dbase:

```
webdb=# \q
-bash-42$ logout
[root@rhel7 ~]#
```

10. Edit the **postgres** host based access "pg_hba" configuration file:

```
# vi /var/lib/pgsql/data/pg_hba.conf
```

11. Modify the local line to use "md5" based authentication rather than "peer". Please review the PostgreSQL documentation before making this change and take the security

```
local          all          all          md5
```

12. Restart the postgresql database service.

```
# /sbin/service postgresql reload          \\ restarts postgresql
```

13. Log back into the server

```
# su - postgres
```

14. Test your connection.

```
# psql -U webadmin webdb          \\ or psql webdb
```

```
[root@rhel7 ~]# psql -U webadmin webdb
Password for user webadmin:
psql (9.2.13)
Type "help" for help.

webdb=>
```

Fig. 35

15. You're on installing and configuring PostgreSQL database.

16. Hooray! – Enjoy LAMP + PostgreSQL

Step 4: Install & Test PHP Installation on RHEL 7

3. To install PHP and modules such as gd/myql type the following yum command:

```
sudo yum install php php-mysql php-pgsql php-gd php-peer -y
```

4. Next you must restart the httpd (Apache) service, type:

```
sudo systemctl restart httpd.service
```

5. Now we need to search all other PHP modules, enter:

```
sudo yum search php-
```

See sample below:

31

```
[root@rhel7 ~]# yum search php-
Loaded plugins: langpacks, product-id, search-disabled-repos, subscription-
          : manager
============================ N/S matched: php- ============================
php-cli.x86_64 : Command-line interface for PHP
php-common.x86_64 : Common files for PHP
php-gd.x86_64 : A module for PHP applications for using the gd graphics library
php-ldap.x86_64 : A module for PHP applications that use LDAP
php-mysql.x86_64 : A module for PHP applications that use MySQL databases
php-odbc.x86_64 : A module for PHP applications that use ODBC databases
php-pdo.x86_64 : A database access abstraction module for PHP applications
php-pear.noarch : PHP Extension and Application Repository framework
php-pecl-memcache.x86_64 : Extension to work with the Memcached caching daemon
php-pgsql.x86_64 : A PostgreSQL database module for PHP
php-process.x86_64 : Modules for PHP script using system process interfaces
php-recode.x86_64 : A module for PHP applications for using the recode library
php-soap.x86_64 : A module for PHP applications that use the SOAP protocol
php-xml.x86_64 : A module for PHP applications which use XML
php-xmlrpc.x86_64 : A module for PHP applications which use the XML-RPC protocol
```
Fig. 36

6. Following the above steps for Apaache2 setup, the document root for Apache is "/var/www/hmtl/"

7. Create a test PHP script file called "/var/www/html/test.php" and place it in the documents root. A useful test script sample:

```
sudo vi /var/www/html/test.php
```

and appended the following code:

```
<?php
   phpinfo(INFO_GENERAL);
?>
```

8. Now fire-up your browser and point it to: http://localhost/test.php and you should the browser rendered as shown in Fig. 37.

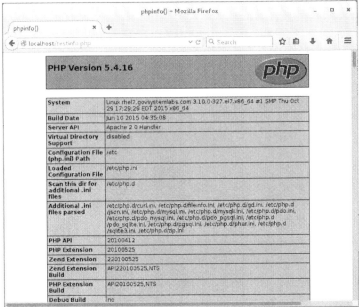

Fig. 37

9. You're done with PHP5 setup and testing.

Step 5: Install & Configure phpMyAdmin

phpMyAdmin 4.5 Released. It is web-based client written in php for managing MySQL and MariaDB databases. It provides a user friendly web interface to access and manage your databases. To ease usage to a wide range of people, phpMyAdmin is being translated into 72 languages and supports both LTR and RTL languages

1. Install phpMyAdmin

Now, we are ready to install the phpMyAdmin package. This software is not available in the RHEL / CentOS 7 default repositories. However, it is available in the EPEL repos (Extra Packages for Enterprise Linux).

1. We can add access to the EPEL repositories to our system by typing:

```
sudo yum install epel-release  -y
```

33

2. After accepting the new repository, you can install the phpMyAdmin package by typing:

```
sudo yum install phpmyadmin -y
```

3. You're done with section

2. Configure Apache & phpMyAdmin

phpMyAdmin by default allowed to access from localhost only. If you want to make it accessible from remote computers edit /etc/httpd/conf.d/phpMyAdmin.conf and update all 127.0.0.1 with your network like below or enable phpMyAdmin access for everyone.

4. To do this, open the file /etc/httpd/conf.d/phpMyAdmin.conf using your favorite text editor:

```
# nano /etc/httpd/conf.d/phpMyAdmin
```

locate and change the parts marked in red font, that is the IP address and the Network address.

```
<Directory /usr/share/phpMyAdmin/setup/>
   <IfModule mod_authz_core.c>
     # Apache 2.4
     <RequireAny>
       Require ip 192.168.6.10
       Require ip ::1
     </RequireAny>
   </IfModule>
   <IfModule !mod_authz_core.c>
     # Apache 2.2
     Order Deny,Allow
     Deny from All
     Allow from 192.168.6.0/24
     Allow from ::1
   </IfModule>
</Directory>
```

5. After updating phpMyAdmin Apache configuration file, restart Apache service to reload new settings.

```
# systemctl restart httpd.service
```

6. You're done with this section.

3. Accessing phpMyAdmin in Browser

7. Now you can access phpMyAdmin by pointing your browser http://mydomain.com/phpadmin or with your server IP/FQDN, as shown in Fig. 38

Fig. 38

8. Login with same credential you use to login to MariaDB database, see Fig. 39.

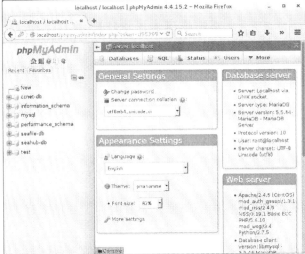

Fig. 39

9. You're done with this section.

10. Hooray! – Enjoy working with LAMP server.

Part 4: Install and Configure Webmin on RHEL 7

Administering Linux and Unix-based servers does not need to be the scourge of your work day. With a handy tool called **Webmin** as part of your arsenal, you can regain full control of your servers' setup and configuration via the Web browser.

Webmin is the most powerful administration tool in its nature. You can use it, for example, to setup DNS Server, but I will not go over it in detail because you will learn more about it in the coming modules. It is not difficult to use Webmin because it is web based, in any event, you should also know that you can use it remotely to administrate your network servers.

Step 1: Install Webmin

Now we need to install Webmin to ease your server administration pain!

1. To Install Webmin and get started, drop by www.webmin.com and download the latest release. You can use RPMs for RHEL and related systems that support binary installations or you can build Webmin from source. Webmin also supports a large number of UNIX variants, including Mac OS X.

2. Now download the latest Webmin using the following command or from here. Or use the "wget" command download from the terminal. (Note: at the time of the writing: "webmin-1.770-1.noarch.rpm") file:

```
wget http://prdownloads.sourceforge.net/webadmin/webmin-1.770-1.noarch.rpm
```

3. To install the **rpm**, simply open a terminal session, change to the download directory, and type in: "rpm -ivh webmin*", i.e.,:

```
# rpm -ivh webmin*
```

    • When done, open you Web browser and go to: http://localhost:10000 or in our case
      http://mydomain.com:10000

4. Your browser will be promise you with "**Error –Bad Request**", as shown in Fig. 40. Click on the link to proceed and accept the Untrusted certificate.

Fig. 40

5. From Fig. 41, login with root user credentials and click on Login.

Fig. 41

6. Login with root user name and you should be able to access the Webmin admin page as shown in Fig. 42. You may be prompted to update Webmin! Take your time to hand around to acquaint yourself with the tool. Noticed some of the Servers installed from the left hand pane.

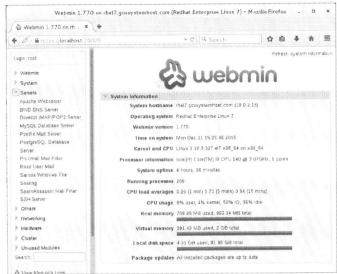

Fig. 42

7. Click **Logout** to exit Webmin

8. You're done with this section.

Part 5: Install and Configure vsFTPD Server on RHEL 7

The Very Secure FTP Daemon (vsftpd) is designed from the ground up to be fast, stable, and, most importantly, secure. Its ability to handle large numbers of connections efficiently and securely is why vsftpd is the only stand-alone FTP distributed with Red Hat Enterprise Linux.

Step 1: Install and Configure vsFTPD Server

1. First, let's verify if vsftpd is installed on your system:

```
# yum list installed | grep ftp
```
```
[root@rhel7 ~]# yum list installed | grep ftp
vsftpd.x86_64                          3.0.2-10.el7                @anaconda/7.2
[root@rhel7 ~]#
```
Fig. 43

Note: if nothing shown, then standard RHEL packages seem not have vsftp and proftp, then you can install these with very easily (via yum or rpm utility to install)

2. To install vsftpd using YUM, run:

```
# yum install vsftpd ftp -y
```

Note: you can also use "rpm -iUVh vsftpd*.rpm" (in your RHEL 7 DVD ISO under rhel folder). You can also grab it from DVD.

3. You can now edit "vsftpd.conf" file which is the main configuration file for vsFTP and make the necessary changes.

4. But, for best practices, first we need to take backup copy before making any changes to it.

```
# cp /etc/vsftpd/vsftpd.conf /etc/vsftpd/vsftpd.conf.Bkup
```

5. To start vsftpd service, type:

```
sudo systemctl start vsftpd.service
```

6. Let's enable vsftpd to auto start at boot-time, issue the command:

```
sudo systemctl enable vsftpd.service
```

7. Now check if `ftp` client is running, using either one of these:

```
# netstat -nap | grep 21
```

or:

```
# ps -ef | grep -i ftp
```

```
[root@rhel7 ~]# ps -ef | grep -i ftp
root      5819      1  0 14:13 ?        00:00:00 /usr/sbin/vsftpd /etc/vsftpd/v
sftpd.conf
root      5827   5599  0 14:13 pts/0    00:00:00 grep --color=auto -i ftp
[root@rhel7 ~]#
```

Fig. 44

8. You're done with this section.

Step 2: Securing vsFTPD Server

Before we can make our vsFTP server fully functional, we first need to do some house keeping to make it secure against hacking etc.

1. Now using the favorite text editor, let's open the `conf` file to make some changes:

```
# nano /etc/vsftpd/vsftpd.conf
```

Note: find the "`anonymous_enable=YES`" and change the value to "`NO`" to disable anonymous FTP access.

```
anonymous_enable=NO
```

2. Next, uncomment the below line (Line no: 100) to restrict users to only their home directory. Local user will be **'chroot jailed'** and thus denied access to any other parts of the server.

```
chroot_local_user=YES
```

Others:

```
## Uncomment ##
ascii_upload_enable=YES
ascii_download_enable=YES
```

```
## Uncomment - Enter your Welcome message - This is optional ##
ftpd_banner=Welcome to GOVSYSTEMLABS FTP Service
```

3. Allow local user to be able to login by changing the `"local_enable"` setting to `"YES"`

```
local_enable=YES
```

4. Next, if you want local user to be able to write to a directory, then change the `"write_enable"` setting to `"YES"`:

```
write_enable=YES
```

5. Finally, add lines below at the end of the file to enable passive mode and allow `chroot` writable

```
allow_writeable_chroot=YES
user_localtime=YES
pasv_enable=Yes
pasv_min_port=40000
pasv_max_port=40100
```

9. Save and exit the file.

10. Restart `vsftpd` service:

```
sudo systemctl restart vsftpd.service
```

6. Next, you should that ensure your firewall is not blocking (you might temporary disable firewall to diagnose first). Alternatively, you can open `port 21` on the firewall.

```
firewall-cmd --permanent --add-service=ftp
firewall-cmd --reload
```

Note: alternatively, you can also use port number to allow port 21 through instead as follows:

```
firewall-cmd --permanent --add-port=21/tcp
firewall-cmd --reload
```

7. Let's now login with Net Admin credentials that set during initial installation, changes desired.

```
# ftp localhost
```

```
[nadmin@rhel7 ~]$ ftp localhost
Connected to localhost (127.0.0.1).
220 (vsFTPd 3.0.2)
Name (localhost:nadmin):
331 Please specify the password.
Password:
230 Login successful.
Remote system type is UNIX.
Using binary mode to transfer files.
ftp> ls
227 Entering Passive Mode (127,0,0,1,188,164).
150 Here comes the directory listing.
drwxr-xr-x    2 1000     1000            6 Jan 05 19:21 Desktop
drwxr-xr-x    2 1000     1000            6 Jan 05 19:21 Documents
drwxr-xr-x    2 1000     1000            6 Jan 05 19:21 Downloads
drwxr-xr-x    2 1000     1000            6 Jan 05 19:21 Pictures
drwxr-xr-x    2 1000     1000            6 Jan 05 19:21 Public
drwxr-xr-x    2 1000     1000            6 Jan 05 19:21 Templates
drwxr-xr-x    2 1000     1000            6 Jan 05 19:21 Videos
226 Directory send OK.
ftp> exit
221 Goodbye.
[nadmin@rhel7 ~]$
```
.... Fig. 45

Note: you'll be required to login with appropriate username credentials. In case you get login failure , then check troubleshooting notes at the end of this training manual.

8. You can also test `vsftpd` from your browser: ftp://localhost or http:/domain-name or http://ip-address, and browse to the desired folder.

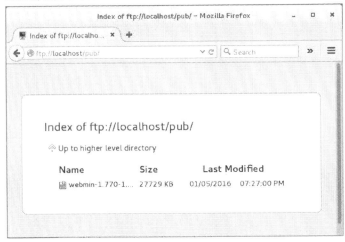

.... Fig. 46

41

Note: the `pub` folder is located under "`/var/ftp`" directory, and as you can see I have one file listed in it.

9. The `condrestart` (conditional restart) option only starts `vsftpd` if it is currently running. This option is useful for scripts, because it does not start the daemon if it is not running. To conditionally restart the server, as root type:

```
sudo condrestart vsftpd.service
```

10. You should be able to upload and download files as we had allowed earlier.

Fig. 47

11. To stop `vsftpd` service:

```
sudo systemctl stop vsftpd.service
```

12. You're done with this section.

1 Login to FTP as a Particular User

1. If you wish to login to FTP using a particular user, then fire-up browser and then navigate to "`ftp://username@FTP-Server-IP-address`". You be asked to enter the password of user, and then you be logged in, as shown in Fig. 48.

42

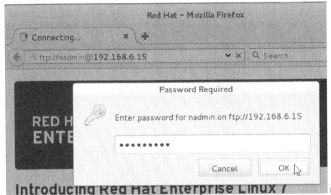

Fig. 48a

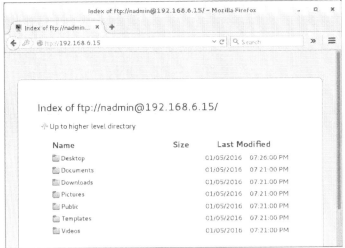

Fig. 48b

2. You're done with this section.

Step 3: Secure FTP Server

In order to support secure remote connections to your server, you will need to install the OpenSSH package. This package will come in handy in the future to support administrative tasks on the system. Secure File Transfer Protocol (SFTP) is used to encrypt connections between clients and the FTP server. It's highly recommended to use SFTP because data is transferred over encrypted connection using SSH-tunnel on port 22. By default this package is already installed in the RHEL 7 server option.

1. Install and Configure openSSH-Server on RHEL 7

Basically openSSH-server package to enable SFTP to work.

1. To install OpenSSH, issue the following command (skip if you have installed it!):

```
sudo yum install openssh-server -y
```

2. Start and enable sshd service, type:

```
sudo systemctl start sshd
```

```
sudo systemctl enable sshd
```

3. Your SFTP server is configure and ready at your service.

4. To log into a remote computer that is running OpenSSH, you use the ssh username@hostname command, replacing username with a valid user name on the computer you are trying to log into, and replacing hostname with either the fully qualified host name (e.g. example.com) of your server, or it's IP address (e.g., 192.168.6.15).

5. For example, let's login remotely to server via SSH as user nadmin with password xxxxx and IP address 192.168.6.15, run:

```
ssh nadmin@192.168.6.15
```

Note: you'll be asked to respond to yes/no and also enter root's password. And as you can observe we have successfully remotely logged in as user root. Now you can use your usual Linux commands to remotely manage your Linux server.

```
[root@rhel7 ~]# ssh nadmin@192.168.6.15
nadmin@192.168.6.15's password:
Last login: Tue Jan  5 14:21:27 2016
[nadmin@rhel7 ~]$ ls
Desktop  Documents  Downloads  Music  Pictures  Public  Templates  Videos
[nadmin@rhel7 ~]$ logout
Connection to 192.168.6.15 closed.
[root@rhel7 ~]#
```
Fig.
49

6. You're done with this section

2. FTP User Creation

1. Create user mjones (Mary Jones) with "/sbin/nologin" shell and also add ftpaccess group

```
# groupadd ftpgroup

# useradd -m mjones -s /sbin/nologin -g ftpgroup

# passwd mjones
```

2. Assign root ownership for the home for chroot access and modify permission as follows:

```
# chown root /home/mjones
# chmod 750 /home/mjones
```

3. Next, create a directory www inside mjones home directory for writing and modify ownership:

```
# mkdir /home/mjones/www
# chown mjones:ftpgroup /home/mjones/www
```

4. Finally, mjones should now be able to use both ftp and sftp. He can also upload files in www directory.

5. You're done with this section.

3. Adding existing users to ftpgroup

6. To add the existing users to our ftpgroup group, perform the following actions:

```
# usermod nadmin -g ftpgroup
# chown root /home/szulu
# chmod 750 /home/szulu
# mkdir /home/szulu/www
# chown szulu:ftpgroup /home/szulu/www

ssh szulu@192.168.6.15
```

```
[root@rhel7 ~]# ssh szulu@192.168.6.15
szulu@192.168.6.15's password:
[szulu@rhel7 ~]$ ls
www
[szulu@rhel7 ~]$ logout
Connection to 192.168.6.15 closed.
[root@rhel7 ~]#
```
_____ Fig. 50

Note: for those using Windows based systems, they can install PuTTY: a free telnet/ssh client.

7. You're done with section.

4. Allowing FTP Access to Files Outside the Home Directory Chroot

Occasionally once we have setup an FTP server software (e.g., proFTP, vsFTP etc.), we might at times be faced with dilemma, i.e., we want to **restrict** the access that ftp users will (in this case limit access to files normally in their home directory), but also we may want to allow them access to **another** directory that is normally in a different location (e.g., in case of a project development files for whatever work they are doing).

1. As you have seen above, if configure the **chroot restriction** for the ftp users, then as expected they will be **locked in the chrooted folder** (e.g., in their home directory or as in the earlier example the www directory we created, and which is shown below). If try to go around this restriction by creating a symlink to the other directory that they need access to, it will not allow to change into that directory (i.e., break out of the chroot) and this very normal.

```
[root@rhel7 ~]# ssh szulu@192.168.6.15
szulu@192.168.6.15's password:
[szulu@rhel7 ~]$ ls
www
[szulu@rhel7 ~]$ logout
Connection to 192.168.6.15 closed.
[root@rhel7 ~]#
```
_____ Fig. 51

2. Now let's look at an hypothetical situation, and consider a case where we are using **vsftpd** and one user "ftp_user". Further, chroot restriction is enabled on the ftp accounts and his home is in "/home/ftp_user". However, we need to provide the user access to another directory "/var/www/swdev". This concept is also applicable to other ftp server software not just **vsftpd**.

3. As was mentioned earlier the key important point here is to ensure that under **vftpd** configuration file, we have:

```
chroot_local_user=YES
```

46

Note: alternatively one way to overcome this limitation is to disable chroot and allow the **ftp** users full access to all the system files. However, for best practice, this is not at all recommended. The solution to this problem, is to **mount the needed directory using the -bind parameter**.

To achieve this, from your terminal enter:

```
mkdir /home/ftp_user/www_swdev
mount --bind /var/www/swdev /home/ftp_user/www_swdev
```

Note: now the **ftp** users should now be able to see the needed files in home directory and use them in his ftp clients as if they were local files.

4. Finally, in case you need to make this configuration permanent, then you can either add the mount command in some startup script or you can just include a line "/etc/fstab" as follows:

```
/var/www/swdev  /home/ftp_user/www_swdev        none  bind  0      0
```

Note: the vsftpd configuration file can look like:

```
/etc/vsftpd.con
listen=YES
anonymous_enable=NO
Local_enable=NO
write_enable=YES
dirmesaage_enable=YES
xferlog_enable=YES
connect_from_port_20=YES
chroot_local_users=YES
ssecure_chroot_dir=/var/run/vsftpd
pam_service_name=vsftp
rsa_cert_file=/etc/ssl/certs/vsftpd.pem
```

5. You're done with section.

Step 4. Install FileZilla FTP Client on RHEL 7

FileZilla is arguably the most popular FTP client in the world, and the good thing,, it is a free and platform independent i.e., it can be installed on both Linux, Windows and Mac OS. However, FileZilla does not come with the default RHEL repository, so we need to use Fedora EPEL repository instead. Installation is very simple, all we need to do is to first install the EPEL repository and then install FileZilla suing the yum command.

47

1. Install the extra EPEL repositories from dl.fedoraproject.orgon RHEL 7

1. The command is as follows to download `epel-release` for CentOS and RHEL 7.x using `wget` command (This was earlier installed!):

```
wget https://dl.fedoraproject.org/pub/epel/epel-release-latest-7.noarch.rpm
```

2. You can now extract the rpm file:

```
sudo rpm -ivh epel-release-latest-7.noarch.rpm
```

3. You now can simply install `filezilla` using yum command as follows:

```
sudo yum install filezilla
```

4. Now ensure that SELinux is disabled or is set to permissive in the `"/etc/selinux/config"` file:.

```
SELINUX=disabled
```

5. Now ensure to open port 21 and 22.

```
firewall-cmd --permanent --add-port=21/tcp
firewall-cmd --permanent --add-port=21/tcp
firewall-cmd --reload
```

6. Now to open the Filezilla client system click **Applications → Internet → FileZilla**, as shown in Fig. 52.

Fig. 52

7. From Fig. 53, enter the FTP server hostname address, username, password and port number. Click "**Quickconnect**" to login.

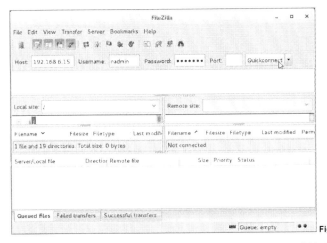

Fig. 53

8. If all is OK, you should now be presented with Fig. 54 showing successful login.

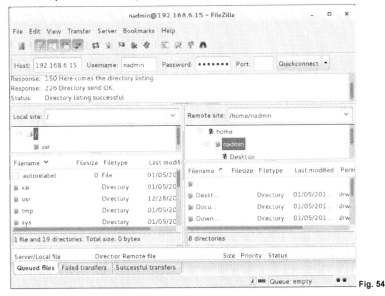

Fig. 54

9. You are done with this section.

Step 5: Users Login

10. Let's login using **ftp** client, as user `nadmin` with password `xxxxxx`, as follows:

```
[nadmin@rhel7 ~]$ ftp localhost
```

```
[nadmin@rhel7 ~]$ ftp localhost
Connected to localhost (127.0.0.1).
220 (vsFTPd 3.0.2)
Name (localhost:nadmin):
331 Please specify the password.
Password:
230 Login successful.
Remote system type is UNIX.
Using binary mode to transfer files.
ftp>
```

Fig. 55

11. While still logged in as user `Net Admin (nadmin)`, try to change to "`/var/ftp/pub`" directory, and you should be able to access all files and folder under this directory.

```
ftp> cd /var/ftp/pub
```

```
ftp> cd /var/ftp/pub/
250 Directory successfully changed.
ftp> ls
227 Entering Passive Mode (127,0,0,1,200,137).
150 Here comes the directory listing.
-rwxr--r--    1 0        0        28393526 Jan 05 19:27 webmin-1.770-1.noarch.rp
m
226 Directory send OK.
ftp>
```

Fig. 56

12. Now let's change to "`/home`", and although you can see all the other users' home folders, you should **only** be able to access files and folder under only you home directory.

```
ftp> cd /home
```

50

```
ftp> cd /home/
250 Directory successfully changed.
ftp> ls
227 Entering Passive Mode (127,0,0,1,144,117).
150 Here comes the directory listing.
drwxr-x---    4 0        1001            84 Jan 05 19:39 mjones
drwx------   18 1000     1001          4096 Jan 05 20:13 nadmin
drwxr-x---    4 0        1002            84 Jan 05 19:42 szulu
226 Directory send OK.
ftp>
```
Fig. 57

- Now try to change into user szulu home directory:

```
ftp> cd /home/szulu
550 Failed to change directory.
ftp>
```

- Now try login to your own home directory:

```
ftp> cd /home/nadmin
250 Directory successfully changed.
ftp
```

13. When done, close the ftp connect and exit, as follows:

```
ftp> exit
ftp> close
221 Goodbye.
ftp> quit
[root@rhel7 ~]#
```

14. You're done with this section.

Part 6: Install JDK8 on RHEL 7

The RHEL 7 / CentOS-7 now comes pre-installed with OpenJDK, which you can verify by typing:

```
]# java -version
```

```
[root@rhel7 ~]# java -version
openjdk version "1.8.0_65"
OpenJDK Runtime Environment (build 1.8.0_65-b17)
OpenJDK 64-Bit Server VM (build 25.65-b01, mixed mode)
[root@rhel7 ~]#
```
Fig. 58

Note: however, in case you wish to install the Sun Java, now Oracle, you can perform the following procedure:

1. To download Java SE SDK 8 just go to http://www.oracle.com/technetwork/java/javase/downloads/jdk8-downloads-2133151.html , and follow the instructions to download a file called: "jdk-8u65-linux-x64-rpm", and save it in /usr/java directory. You may have to create the java directory if it's not there.

1. Create directory "/usr/java" directory.

```
sudo mkdir /usr/java
```

2. Copy "jdk-8u65-linux-x64.tar.gz" to "/usr/java" directory and untar it.

```
sudo cp jdk-8u65-linux-x64.tar.gz /usr/java

cd /usr/java

sudo tar -xvzf jdk-8u65-linux-x64.tar.gz

rm jdk-8u65-linux-x64.tar.gz
```

3. Insert the following lines inside /etc/profile or /root/.bashrc.

```
export JAVA_HOME=/usr/java/jdk1.80_65
export PATH=$JAVA_HOME/bin:$PATH
```

4. Next, execute the following command to update the changes made without having to reboot the system::

```
source /etc/profile
```

5. Before we begin, we will need to ensure that JAVA_HOME is correctly set. To do this, open a terminal and type the following:

```
# echo $JAVA_HOME

# java -version
```

```
[root@rhel7 java]#  echo $JAVA_HOME
/usr/java/jdk1.8.0_65
[root@rhel7 java]#
[root@rhel7 java]# java -version
java version "1.8.0_65"
Java(TM) SE Runtime Environment (build 1.8.0_65-b17)
Java HotSpot(TM) 64-Bit Server VM (build 25.65-b01, mixed mode)
[root@rhel7 java]#
```
Fig. 59

6. You're done with this section

Part 7: Install Apache Ant Package on RHEL 7

Apache Ant is a Java library and command-line tool whose mission is to drive process described in build files as targets and extension points dependent upon each other. That main known usage of Ant is the build of Java applications. Ant supplies a number of built-in tasks allowing to compile, assemble, test and run Java applications,. Ant can be used effectively to build non Java applications, e.g., C or C++ applications. More generally, Ant can be used to pilot any type of process which can be described in terms of targets and tasks. That is Apache Ant builds a Java project from its source code and libraries by using a similar XML file.

1. To download Apache Ant, just go to http://ant.apache.org/bindownload.cgi, and follow the instructions to download a file called: "apache-ant-1.9.6-bin.tar.gz", and save it in /usr/ directory.

   Note: you can also use "wget" command to down it as follows

   ```
   sudo mkdir /usr/ant

   wget http://www.eu.apache.org/dist//ant/binaries/apache-ant-1.9.6-bin.tar.gz

   sudo tar -xvzf apache-ant-1.9.6-bin.tar.gz

   sudo cp -arp * /usr/ant
   ```

2. Add Apache Ant to the profile file "/etc/profile", type:

   ```
   sudo nano /etc/profile
   ```

   so that it now look like:

   ```
   export JAVA_HOME=/usr/java/jdk1.8.0_65
   export ANT_HOME=/usr/ant
   export PATH=$JAVA_HOME/bin:$ANT_HOME/bin:$PATH
   ```

53

3. Use the `source` command for the changes to take effect (**Note**: you may need to reboot the system):

```
# source /etc/profile
```

4. Before we begin, we will need to ensure that `"ANT_HOME"` is correctly set. To do this, we open a terminal and type the following:

```
# echo $ANT_HOME
/usr/ant
```

5. Verify that Apache Ant is successfully installed

```
# ant -version
Apache Ant(TM) version 1.9.6 compiled on June 29 2015
```

6. You're done with this section

Part 8: Install Apache Tomcat 9 Application Server on RHEL 7

1. To download Apache Tomcat 9, just go to http://tomcat.apache.org/, and follow the instructions to download a file called: **apache-tomcat-9.0.0.M1.tar.gz**, and save it in /usr/ directory.

2. Next, we are going to install tomcat in /usr directory, run:

```
# cd /usr
# tar -xvzf apache-tomcat-9.0.0.M1.tar.gz
```

3. While still under "/usr" directory, issue the following command to create a symbolic link to the tomcat directory.

```
# ln -s /usr/apache-tomcat-7.0.5 tomcat
```

4. Add Ant to the profile file /etc/profile, so that it now look like:

```
export JAVA_HOME=/usr/java/jdk1.8.0_65
export ANT_HOME=/usr/ant
export CATALINA_HOME=/usr/tomcat
export PATH=$JAVA_HOME/bin:$CATALINA_HOME/bin:$ANT_HOME/bin:$PATH
CLASSPATH=$CLASSPATH:.
```

5. issue the following command to update "/etc/profile" file:

```
# source /etc/profile
```

6. Before we begin, we will need to ensure that `CATALINA_HOME` is correctly set. To do this, we open a terminal and run:

```
# echo $CATALINA_HOME
/usr/tomcat
```

7. If everything is fine, you can start Tomcat with the following command.

```
# $CATALINA_HOME/bin/startup.sh
```

```
[root@rhel7 tomcat]# $CATALINA_HOME/bin/startup.sh
Using CATALINA_BASE:    /usr/tomcat
Using CATALINA_HOME:    /usr/tomcat
Using CATALINA_TMPDIR:  /usr/tomcat/temp
Using JRE_HOME:         /usr/java/jdk1.8.0_65
Using CLASSPATH:        /usr/tomcat/bin/bootstrap.jar:/usr/tomcat/bin/tomcat-juli
.jar
Tomcat started.
[root@rhel7 tomcat]#
```
Fig. 60

8. Logout and login again for the environment setup to take effect:

9. To verify that the Tomcat installation is complete, open a Web browser, and type in following URL: http://<your-tomcat_IP>:8080, DNS, or you can also simply use http://localhost:8080. If everything is fine, you should be able to see a web page such as one shown in Fig. 61.

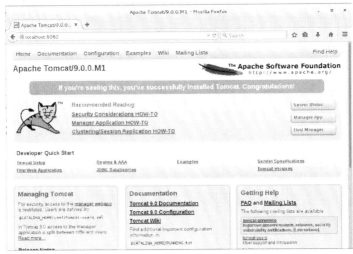

Fig. 61

10. To stop Tomcat, type:

```
# $CATALINA_HOME/bin/shutdown.sh
```

2. You're done with section.

11.1 Accessing Apache Tomcat 9 manager and host-manager webapps

In this section you'll learn how to setup Tomcat 9 manager role in order to access http://localhost:8080/manager/html, which will prompt for a username and password.

To do this, you'll need to modify "/usr/tomcat/conf/tomcat-users.xml" file to add the roles and user as follows:

1. Using your favorite Text editor, open:

```
# vi /usr/tomcat/conf/tomcat-users.xml
```

and you need to add he following text (Note: change as desired!)

```
<tomcat-users>
<role rolename="admin-gui"/>
<role rolename="admin-scrip"/>
<user username="tomcat" password="s3cret1" roles="admin-gui,admin-script"/>
<user username="user1" password="mypassword" roles="standard, managerscript"/>
</tomcat-users>
```

2. Now restarted tomcat service, run:

```
# $CATALINA_HOME/bin/startup.sh
```

3. Using appropriate user credentials you should be able to access http://localhost:8080/manager/html, or http://ip-address:8080/manager/html.

11.2 Moving around Apache Tomcat 9 under command-line
1. Open anew Terminal widow and change to /usr/tomcat/ folder which is writeable and run:

```
ls /usr/tomcat/
```

Note: you should see these directories bin, conf, lib, logs, webapps, temp, and work
    a. **webapps** - is where your servlets will go (or at least a xml file that points to them) as a test download this war file http://simple.souther.us/SimpleServlet.war

  b. Once you have `.war` file, then you can use the tomcat management page and select war file to deploy (in the deploy section) to upload this file to your server.

2. Optionally you can download the `.war` files directly to your the `webapps` folder

```
cd /usr/tomcat/weapps/
wget http://simple.souther.us/SimpleServlet.war
```

tomcat should recognize the war file and expand it with everything you need

3. Point your browse to http://serverip:8080/SimpleServlet/

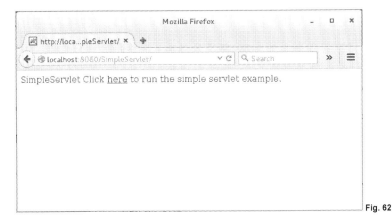
Fig. 62

4. You're done with this section.

Part 9: How to Install & Configure Backup Server using Bacula and Webmin on RHEL 7

In this section you're going to learn how to install and configure a Backup server using Bacula and Webmin on RHEL 7 which also should work on CentOS 7, Fedora 23 and Scientific Linux distros too. Bacula is an open source, network backup software, used to all Systems Administrators to manage backup, recovery and send the verification of data from any system in any location across network. Thus, its very flexible and robust, which makes it, while slightly cumbersome to configure, suitable for backups in many situations. It's important to note, that a backup system is an important component in most server infrastructures, as recovering from data loss is often a critical part of disaster recovery plans, and a critical component on how an enterprise manages risks to company data.

In this section of the hands-on tutorial, you will learn how to install and configure the server components of Bacula on a RHEL 7 server. We will configure Bacula to perform a weekly job that creates a local backup (i.e., a backup of its own host). This, by itself, is not a particularly compelling use of Bacula, but it will provide you with a good starting point for creating backups of your other servers, i.e., the backup clients. Finally, you also learn how to create backups of your other, remote, servers by installing and configuring the Bacula client, and configuring the Bacula server.

1. Prerequisites for Bacula Backup Server

1. One must have a superuser (sudo) access on your RHEL 7 / CentOS 7 server. The server must have adequate disk space for all of the backups that you plan on retaining at given time.

2. It's important that you configure Bacula to use the private FQDN of the server or its IP address. In case you don't have a DNS setup, then instead its recommended to use the appropriate IP addresses. In case you don't private networking enabled, then you can replace all the network connection information given here with network addresses that are reachable by the server in question (e.g., public IP addresses or VPN tunnels).

3. It's also assumed that SELinux is disabled or you are able to troubleshoot SELinux related issues on your own.

2. Overview of Bacula Components

Bacula backup server is compost of several software components, and it follows the server client backup model, with main components, which we concentrate on, being the **backup-server** and the **backup clients**. However, we will mention them here. The Bacula server (or backup server), is made up of the following components:

- **Bacula Director (DIR):** is the software that controls the backup and restore operations, which are performed by File and Storage daemons

- **Storage Daemon (SD):** is the software which performs reads and writes on the storage devices used for backups.

- **Catalog:** is the services that maintain a database of files that are backed up. The database is stored in an SQL database e.g., MySQL (MariaDB) or PostgreSQL.

- **Bacula Console:** is a command-line interface that allows the backup administrator to interact with, and control, Bacula Director.

A Bacula backup client, i.e., the server that will be backed up, runs the **File Daemon (FD)** component. The File Daemon is the software that provides the Bacula server (i.e., Director) access to the data that is to be backed up. We will also refer to these servers as (backup clients) or clients. In this hands-on tutorial, we are going to configure the backup server to create a backup of its own filesystem. That is, the backup server will also be a backup client, and will run the File Damon component. Once you acquire the skills you can then go ahead and set the clients backup.

Step 1: Install Bacula Backup Server

To install a Bacula backup server, we'll be using MySQL (MariaDB) for database, one can also use PostgreSQL database, with server's info shown below (changes as desired):

Backup Server Hostname: rhel7.govsysthost.com
IP Address: 192.168.6.15

1. Use yum command to install Bacula server, as follows:

```
# yum install bacula-director-mysql bacula-console bacula-client
bacula-storage-mysql mysql-devel -y
```

2. Now we need to run the following sets of commands to create database and necessary tables for Bacula server:

```
# /usr/libexec/bacula/grant_mysql_privileges -u root -p
# /usr/libexec/bacula/create_mysql_databse -u root -p
# /usr/libexec/bacula/make_mysql_tables -u root -p
# /usr/libexec/bacula/grant_bacula_privileges -u root -p
```

3. Next set bacula user password on MySQL. To do this, login to MySQL server, enter:

```
# mysql -u root -p
```

and set password, as follows:

```
Welcome to the MariaDB monitor.  Commands end with ; or \g.
Your MariaDB connection id is 3
Server version: 5.5.44-MariaDB MariaDB Server

Copyright (c) 2000, 2015, Oracle,  MraiDB Corporation Ab and Others.

Type 'help;' or '\h' for help. Type '\c' to clear the current input
statement.

mysql> UPDATE mysql.user SET password=PASSWORD("baculapass") WHERE
user='bacula';
Query OK, 2 rows affected (0.00 sec)
Rows matched: 2  Changed: 2  Warnings: 0

mysql> FLUSH PRIVILEGES;
Query OK, 0 rows affected (0.01 sec)
mysql> exit
Bye
```

4. You're done with this section.

Step 2: Set Bacula to use MySQL Library

By default, Bacula is set to use the PostgreSQL library, and since we are using MySQL (MariaDB), we need to set it to use the MySQL library instead.

1. To switch from the default PostgreSQL to MySQL database, run:

```
sudo alternatives --cnfig libbaccats.so
```

Note: you should see the following prompt. Enter 1 (MySQL):

```
There are 3 programs which provide 'libbaccats.so'.

  Selection    Command
-----------------------------------------------------
     1         /usr/lib64/libbaccats-mysql.so
     2         /usr/lib64/libbaccats-sqlite3.so
*+ 3          /usr/lib64/libbaccats-postgresql.so

Enter to keep the current selection[+], or type selection number: 1
```

2. The Bacula server (and client) components are now installed and set to use MySQL. In the next step we'll create the backup and restore directory.

3. You're done with this section.

Step 3: Create Backup and Restore Directories

The Bacula server requires a backup directories, for storing backup archives; and a restore directory, where restored files are placed. In case your system has multiple partitions, then do ensure to create the directories on one that has sufficient disk space.

1. To create the new directories for both purposes, enter:

```
sudo mkdir -p /bacula/backup  /bacula/restore
```

2. Next, we need to change the file permissions so that only `bacula` process (and a superuser) can access these locations:

```
sudo chown -R bacula:bacula /bacula

sudo chmod -R 700 /bacula
```

3. Now we're ready to configure the Bacula Director

4. You're done with this section.

Step 4: Configure Bacula Components

1: Configure Bacula Director

As earlier mentioned Bacula components now needs to be configured independently in order for it to function correctly. The configuration files are all located in the "/etc/bacula" directory.

First and foremost, we now need to update all Bacula configuration files with the new password and addresses for each Bacula component, each one at a time.

1. To configure Bacula Director, type:

```
# nano /etc/bacula/bacula-dir.conf
```

Note: here we need update Bacula server hostname, bacula mysql user password, Bacula console password, Bacula file daemon password etc. (**Note**: its important that you should use a FQDN name for adding clients or simply use the IP address instead).

```
[...]
Director {                          # define myself
  Name = bacula-dir
  DIRport = 9101                    # where we listen for UA connections
  QueryFile = "/usr/libexec/bacula/query.sql"
  WorkingDirectory = "/var/spool/bacula"
  PidDirectory = "/var/run"
  Maximum Concurrent Jobs = 1
  Password = "baculapass"           # Console password
  Messages = Daemon
[...]
# Client (File Services) to backup
Client {
  Name = bacula-fd
  Address = 10.0.2.15
  FDPort = 9102
  Catalog = MyCatalog
  Password = "baculapass"           # password for FileDaemon
  File Retention = 30 days          # 30 days
  Job Retention = 6 months          # six months
  AutoPrune = yes                   # Prune expired Jobs/Files
}
[...]
# Definition of file storage device
Storage {
  Name = File
# Do not use "localhost" here
  Address = 10.0.2.15               # N.B. Use a fully qualified name
here
  SDPort = 9103
```

61

```
Password = "baculapass"
Device = FileStorage
Media Type = File
}
[...]
# Generic catalog service
Catalog {
  Name = MyCatalog
# Uncomment the following line if you want the dbi driver
# dbdriver = "dbi:sqlite3"; dbaddress = 127.0.0.1; dbport =
  dbname = "bacula"; dbuser = "bacula"; dbpassword = "baculapass"
}
[...]
Console {
  Name = bacula-mon
  Password = "baculapss"
  CommandACL = status, .status
}
```

2. You're done with this section.

2. Configure Bacula Console

1. To configure Bacula Console, type:

```
sudo nano /etc/bacula/bconsole.conf
```

change the console password:

```
Director {
  Name = bacula-dir
  DIRport = 9101
  address = localhost
  Password = "baculapass"
}
```

2. You're done with this section.

3. Configure Bacula Storage Daemon

3. To update Storage Daemon, open "/etc/bacula/bacula-sd.conf" using your favorite text editor:

```
sudo nano /etc/bacula/bacula-sd.conf
```

4. Now update the sections marked in red font i.e., the Password and Archive Device, change to suit your settings:

```
[...]
```

```
Director {
  Name = bacula-dir
  Password = "baculapass"
}

# Restricted Director, used by tray-monitor to get the
#   status of the storage daemon
#
Director {
  Name = bacula-mon
  Password = "baculapass"
  Monitor = yes
}

[...]

Device {
  Name = FileStorage
  Media Type = File
  Archive Device = /bacula/backup
  LabelMedia = yes;                    # lets Bacula label unlabeled
media
  Random Access = Yes;
  AutomaticMount = yes;                # when device opened, read it
  RemovableMedia = no;
  AlwaysOpen = no;
}
[...]
```

5. Save and exit.

6. You're done with this section.

4. Configure File Daemon

7. To update the File Daemon, open "/etc/bacula/bacula-fd.conf" using your favorite text editor:

```
sudo nano /etc/bacula/bacula-fd.conf
```

now update the sections marked in red font i.e., the Password, change to suit your settings:

```
# List Directors who are permitted to contact this File daemon
#
Director {
Name = bacula-dir
Password = "baculapass"
}

# Restricted Director, used by tray-monitor to get the
#   status of the storage daemon
```

```
#
Director {
Name = bacula-mon
Password = "baculapass"
Monitor = yes
}
```

8. Finally, when done with updating the respective configuration, we now need to restart all the bacula daemons and make them to automatically start on boot.

9. You're done with this section.

5. Start Bacula Components

1. We need to start the Bacula Director, Storage Daemon, and local File Daemon with the following commands:

```
sudo systemctl start bacula-dir
sudo systemctl start bacula-sd
sudo systemctl start bacula-fd
```

2. Finally, if all is well then lets enable them to start automatically on boot:

```
sudo systemctl enable bacula-dir
sudo systemctl enable bacula-sd
sudo systemctl enable bacula-fd
```

3. Once Bacula has been successfully installed and configured. You can now add clients, jobs and volumes by updating the bacula config files

4. You're done with this section and ready to test that Bacula works by running a backup job.

6. Adjust Firewall/Router

5. Before testing the Bacula server, we first need to open the Webmin port "10000" and Bacula communication ports "9101", "9102", "9103", in order to be able access bacula server remotely, as follows:

```
firewall-cmd --permanent --add-port=9101/tcp
firewall-cmd --permanent --add-port=9102/tcp
firewall-cmd --permanent --add-port=9103/tcp
firewall-cmd --permanent --add-port=10000/tcp
firewall-cmd --reload
```

6. You're done with this section.

7. Manage Bacula with Webmin

You may recall that we had earlier installed Webmin which is extremely useful for system administration for Unix.

7. To access Bacula server via Webmin, point your browser to **"http://server-ip-address:10000"**, and login to access the Webmin admin page.

8. You should now be able to locate the Bacula Backup System in the left pane of the Webmin console i.e., **System → Bacula Backup System**. (**Note**: if not listed, then click on the `Refresh Modules` link at the bottom of the left-pane to update the Webmin console, followed by clicking on **Module Configuration** link on the right of the "**Bacula Backup System**" page).

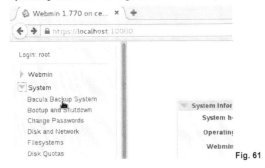

Fig. 61

9. This should bring up the page shown in Fig. 62. Select the database i.e., "MySQL" in this case, and enter `bacula` database user password, as set earlier. Then click on the **Save** button.

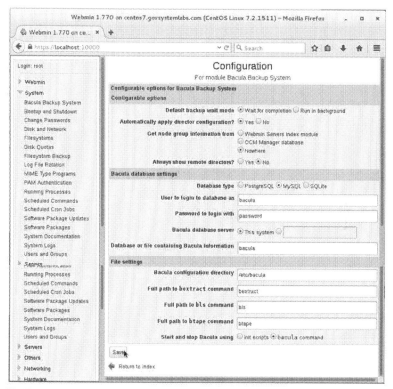

Fig. 62

10. You should now be presented with the Fig. 63, with the single window page shown in two parts.

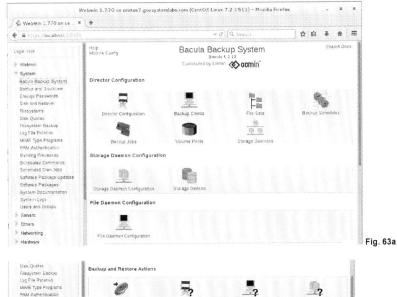

Fig. 63a

Fig. 63b

Note: take your time to move around the Bacula Backup System to get yourself acquainted with the Webmin environment and what kind of task you can accomplish with ease.

11. You're done with this section.

Part 10: Install JBoss (now WidlFly): Open Source J2EE Server and Combined JBoss-Portal on Linux Server on RHEL 7

Step 1: Install JBoss (WildFly)

WildFly formerly known as JBoss AS, or simply JBoss, is an application server authored by JBoss, now developed by Red Hat. WildFly is the next-generation JBoss AS server, written in Java. WildFly is free and open source application server. It's agile and lightweight and a very powerful beast that can run extremely fast with a full J2EE stack including Java EE7. This new Java release provides rich enterprise capabilities in frameworks that reduce technical burden and eliminate boiler plate. WildFly also supports the latest standards for REST based data access, including JAX-RS 2, and JSON-P. It also runs on multiple platforms. WildFly is free and open-source software, subject to the requirements of the GNU Lesser General Public License (LGPL), version 2.1.

1.1 Download WildFly Software on RHEL7

Download WildFly AS "wildfly-9.0.2.Final.zip " from here (This is platform independent software so you can install this software on windows, Linux, Solaris or any other operating system). Here it's assumed that you have installed Java JDK8.

1. You can also use the wget command to download it, type:

```
wget http://download.jboss.org/wildfly/9.0.2.Final/wildfly-9.0.2.Final.zip
```

2. Save file "wildfly-9.0.2.Final.zip" to Linux box directory of choice, in our case, and copy it /usr/ directory:

```
# cp wildfly-9.0.2.Final.zip /usr
```

3. Unzip "wildfly-9.0.2.Final.zip". This will create directory like "wildfly-9.0.2.Final.zip"

```
# cd /usr
# unzip wildfly-9.0.2.Final.zip
```

4. The following command creates a symbolic link to the JBoss directory.

```
# ln -s /usr/wildfly-9.0.2.Final.zip /usr/wildfly9
```

5. Add JBoss to the profile file /etc/profile, so that it now look like:

```
export JAVA_HOME=/usr/java/jdk1.8.0_65
export JBOSS_HOME=/usr/wildfly9
export PATH=$JAVA_HOME/bin:$JBOSS_HOME/bin:$PATH

CLASSPATH=$CLASSPATH:.
```

6. Before we begin, we will need to ensure that $"JBOSS\_HOME"$ is correctly set. To do this, we open a terminal and type the following:

```
# echo $JBOSS_HOME
/usr/wildfly9
```

7. When done with startup, just point your browser to

1.2: Start/Stop WildFly (JBOSS)

8. First we may need to make the server executable, type:

```
# chmod +x $JBOSS_HOME/bin/standalone.sh
```

9. If everything is fine, you can start WildFly9 server with the following command.

```
# $JBOSS_HOME/bin/standalone.sh
```

```
13:31:39,445 INFO  [org.wildfly.extension.undertow] (MSC service thread 1-4) WFL
YUT0006: Undertow HTTP listener default listening on /127.0.0.1:8080 ◄━━━━━
13:31:39,858 INFO  [org.jboss.as.server.deployment.scanner] (MSC service thread
1-4) WFLYDS0013: Started FileSystemDeploymentService for directory /usr/wildfly-
9.0.2.Final/standalone/deployments
13:31:39,928 INFO  [org.jboss.as.connector.subsystems.datasources] (MSC service
thread 1-2) WFLYJCA0001: Bound data source [java:jboss/datasources/ExampleDS]
13:31:40,557 INFO  [org.jboss.ws.common.management] (MSC service thread 1-3) JBW
S022052: Starting JBoss Web Services - Stack CXF Server 5.0.0.Final
13:31:40,998 INFO  [org.jboss.as] (Controller Boot Thread) WFLYSRV0060: Http man
agement interface listening on http://127.0.0.1:9990/management ◄━━━━━
13:31:40,999 INFO  [org.jboss.as] (Controller Boot Thread) WFLYSRV0051: Admin co
nsole listening on http://127.0.0.1:9990
13:31:40,999 INFO  [org.jboss.as] (Controller Boot Thread) WFLYSRV0025: WildFly
Full 9.0.2.Final (WildFly Core 1.0.2.Final) started in 10662ms - Started 203 of
379 services (210 services are lazy, passive or on-demand)
```

Fig. 64

Note: just relax as the server goes through the start-up process.

10. You're done with this section.

1.3: Accessing WildFly Server

11. Open browser and your URL to: http://localhost:8080 or http://mydomain.com:8080

Fig. 65

12. Now, click on the Administration Console link, to access the login page. which will present an error page requiring to add a new user execute the "add-user.sh" that would be able to access the admin console, see Fig. 66:

Fig. 66

```
[root@rhel7 bin]# ./add-user.sh

What type of user do you wish to add?
 a) Management User (mgmt-users.properties)
 b) Application User (application-users.properties)
(a):

Enter the details of the new user to add.
Using realm 'ManagementRealm' as discovered from the existing property
files.
Username : jbuser
Password recommendations are listed below. To modify these
restrictions edit the add-user.properties configuration file.
 - The password should be different from the username
 - The password should not be one of the following restricted values
{root, admin, administrator}
 - The password should contain at least 8 characters, 1 alphabetic
character(s), 1 digit(s), 1 non-alphanumeric symbol(s)
Password :
Re-enter Password :
What groups do you want this user to belong to? (Please enter a comma
separated list, or leave blank for none)[ ]:
About to add user 'jbuser' for realm 'ManagementRealm'
Is this correct yes/no? yes
Added user 'jbuser' to file '/usr/wildfly-
9.0.2.Final/standalone/configuration/mgmt-users.properties'
Added user 'jbuser' to file '/usr/wildfly-
9.0.2.Final/domain/configuration/mgmt-users.properties'
Added user 'jbuser' with groups  to file '/usr/wildfly-
9.0.2.Final/standalone/configuration/mgmt-groups.properties'
Added user 'jbuser' with groups  to file '/usr/wildfly-
9.0.2.Final/domain/configuration/mgmt-groups.properties'
Is this new user going to be used for one AS process to connect to
another AS process?
e.g. for a slave host controller connecting to the master or for a
Remoting connection for server to server EJB calls.
yes/no? yes
To represent the user add the following to the server-identities
definition <secret value="a3ZyMTg1OCUl" />
[root@rhel7 bin]#
```

Note: repeat the same for the Application user.

13. When done, click on the Try Again link at the bottom of Fig.66 above, and you should now be presented with a login screen, see Fig. 67. The default admin credentials Username **"jbuser"** and password **"xxxxx"**, and then click on the **Login** button, see Fig. 67.

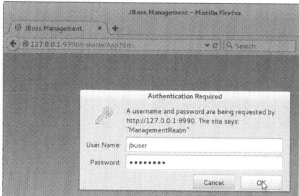

Fig. 67

14. You should be taken to the **WildFly 9.0.2.Final Admin Console**, shown in Fig. 68.

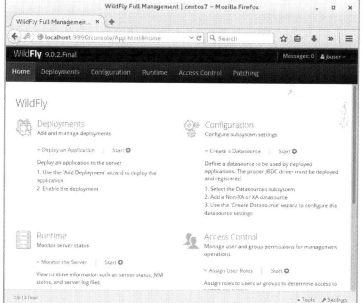

Fig. 68

15. Spent some time to get yourself familiarized with the JBoss AS layout, when done click on the `Logout` link, to logout of the Admin Console.

16. Hit Control C (^C) to stop WildFly AS.

To start the application server using the default configuration in "`domain`" mode, type:

```
# $JBOSS_HOME/bin/domain.sh
```

17. You're done with this section.

18. In the next section, I'll show you how to install JBoss-Portal Bundle.

Step 2: Install JBoss-Portal

This section covers installation of JBOSS (Open Source J2EE Application Server) on RHEL-7 / CentOS 7. Here you're going to learn how to install the bundled JBoss-Portal as Application Server that you can use to develop and setup Single-Sign-On (SSO) Identity Management access control using LDAP (OpenLDAP). You can also use JBoss-Portal to manage network users.

JBoss AS is a J2EE 1.4-certified, open source Java application server. It is the most widely used application server on the market. The highly flexible and easy-to-use server architecture has made JBoss AS the ideal choice for users just starting out with J2EE, as well as senior architects looking for a customizable middleware platform. The ready availability of the source code allows you to debug the server, learn its inner workings and create customized versions for your personal or business use. This guide will show you how to install JBoss AS 7. You will learn how to start and stop your JBoss instance, and you will also learn about the directory structure and understand what the key services and configuration files are.

1.1. Download and Install JBoss-Portal Bundle on RHEL 7 / CentOS 7 Server

1. Download "jboss-portal-2.7.2 -bundled.zip" from:
   http://www.jboss.org/jbossportal/download.html

   Note: you can also use `wget` to download it:

   `wget` http://downloads.sourceforge.net/jboss/jboss-portal-2.7.2-bundled.zip

2. Create a `jportal` directory in `/usr/` directory as follows:

```
# mkdir /usr/jportal
```

3. Move the downloaded package to the `/usr/jportal` directory and then `unzip` it:

```
# cp jboss-portal-2.7.2-bundled.zip /usr/jportal
# cd /usr/jportal
# unzip jboss-portal-2.7.2-bundled.zip
```

19. Add JBoss-Portal to the profile file `"/etc/profile"`, modify it so that it now looks like:

```
export JAVA_HOME=/usr/java/jdk1.8.0_65
export ANT_HOME=/usr/ant
export CATALINA_HOME=/usr/tomcat
export JBOSS_HOME=/usr/jportal/jboss-portal-2.7.2
export
PATH=$JAVA_HOME/bin:$CATALINA_HOME/bin:$ANT_HOME/bin:$JBOSS_HOME/bin:$PATH
CLASSPATH=$CLASSPATH:.
```

20. Now issue the `source` command to update our `"/etc/profile"`, type:

```
# source /etc/profile
```

21. Before we continue, we will need to ensure that `"$JBOSS_HOME"` is correctly set. To do this, we open a terminal and type the following:

```
]# echo $JBOSS_HOME
/usr/jportal/jboss-portal-2.7.2
```

22. To start JBoss-portal, run:

```
# chmod +x $JBOSS_HOME/bin/run.sh
# $JBOSS_HOME/bin/run.sh
```

```
11:59:31,086 INFO  [TomcatDeployer] deploy, ctxPath=/jmx-console, warUrl=.../dep
loy/jmx-console.war/
11:59:31,447 INFO  [Http11Protocol] Starting Coyote HTTP/1.1 on http-127.0.0.1-8
080
11:59:31,521 INFO  [AjpProtocol] Starting Coyote AJP/1.3 on ajp-127.0.0.1-8009
11:59:31,580 INFO  [Server] JBoss (MX MicroKernel) [4.2.3.GA (build: SVNTag=JBos
s_4_2_3_GA date=200807181417)] Started in 1m:25s:266ms
```
Fig. 69

23. To stop JBoss-portal, run:

```
# cd $JBOSS_HOME/bin              \\ change to bin directory
# sh ./shutdown.sh -S             \\ stop server or hit "Ctrl C"
```

24. To access JBoss AS, point your browser to: http://localhost:8080/, note the difference in front page color, as shown in Fig. 70.

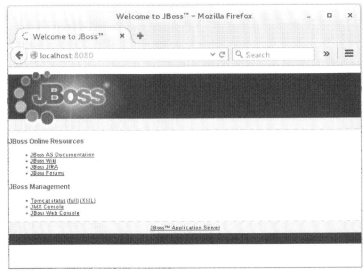

Fig. 70

25. Now to access JBoss-Portal server, point your browser to: http://localhost:8080/portal

Note: click on the Login link, to access the login window, and login with the default admin credentials Username "admin" and password "admin", and then click on the **Login** button. It's recommended that you change admin user login credential from the default one.

Note: this is a Community Release version. You can always get the Enterprise version from Red Hat.

Fig. 71

Fig. 72

26. To add a new user, click on the `Admin` link at the top right-hand corner → **Members** tab.

Fig. 73

27. Under **User Management**, click `Create a new user account`, and complete the required fields, a shown in Fig. 74.

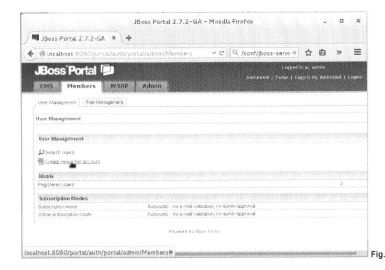

Fig. 74

28. When done click on the **Submit** button, as shown in Fig. 75. Add the new user to Administrator role, and click on the **Submit** button complete user addition.

Fig. 75

29. Logout and try to login with new user account, as shown in Fig. 76.

Fig. 76

30. You're done with this section.

31. Enjoy JBoss-Portal!

Part 11: Install and Configure NFS on RHEL 7

To use NFS successfully, you have to configure the server and the client. In this section, the server is "10.0.2.15" and the client is "10.0.2.16". The folder to be shared is "/nfs-public", and is to be mounted to "/mnt" on the client side.

NSF Server: 192.168.6.15   rhel7.govsystemhost.com
NSF Client: 192.168.6.16   f23.govsystemhost.com

Note: before starting to setup NFS, please do ensure that you can ping both machines, e.g., from server to client machine and vise versa.

Step 1: Install NFS packages On both Server Side and Client Side

1. On the both server RHEL 7 and on client machine running F23 ensure that nfs package is installed, if not then issue the following command:

```
# yum install nfs* -y
```

2. You're done with this section.

Step 2: On the Server Side

A server exports a file system to the specified hosts and allows them to mount it.

1. Make directory that you want to use.

```
# mkdir /nfs-public
```

2. Using you favorite Text editor, edit "/etc/exports", insert the client machine's IP address:

```
# vi /etc/exports
```

and add this line:

```
/nfs-shared rhel7.govsystemhost.com(rw,no_root_squash,sync)
```

3. Save the file.

4. Next, edit "/etc/hosts.allow"

```
# vi /etc/hosts.allow
```

and add this line:

```
ALL:ALL
ALL: 192.168.6.0/255.255.255.0
```

5. Save the file and exit.

6. Finally, start nfs and rpcbind services:

```
# systemctl start rpcbind nfs-server
# systemctl enable rpcbind nfs-server
```

Note: under RHEL7 portmap service has been replaced by rpcbind service

7. Verify that "`exportfs -v`" command that it got exported correctly:

```
[root@rhel7 ~]# exportfs -v
/nfs-public
    rhel7.govsystemhost.com(rw,wdelay,root_squash,no_subtree_check)
[root@rhel7 ~]#
```

8. Now verify using "`showmount -e`" command:

```
[root@rhel7 ~]# showmount -e rhel7
Export list for rhel7.govsystemhost.com:
/nfs-public rhel7.govsystemhost.com
[root@rhel7 ~]#
```

9. You're done with this section.

Step 3: On the client Side – Fedora 23

3. First and foremost make sure that you have connectivity to the NFS server from the NFS client and vise versa. For example, from client side, you can test this using `ping` command, as follows:

```
# ping rhel7.govsystemhost.com
```

4. Similarly from the server side repeat the same:

```
# ping f23.govsystemhost.com
```

10. Finally, start `nfs` and `rpcbind` services:

```
# /etc/init.d/nfs start
# /etc/init.d/rpcbind start
```

Note: under `rhel7 portmap` service has been replaced by `rpcbind` service

5. Make mount-point directory:

```
# mkdir /mnt/nfs-public
```

6. Mount the `nfs` folder

```
# mount -t nfs4 rhel7:/nfs-public /mnt/nfs-public
```

Note: remember to use `nfs4` instead of just `nfs` in the above command-line; otherwise you'll end-up with

7. Check "`/var/log/messages`" for any error that might occur

```
# tailf /var/log/messages
```

8. Use `mount` command to check if the folder is mounted properly:

```
[root@f23 ~]# mount
```

9. Edit "`/etc/fstab`" to mount the shared folder on boot:

```
# vi /etc/fstab
```

and add this line:

```
192.168.6.16:/nfs-public /mnt/nfs-public nfs rw,hard,intr 0 0
```

10. Save the file

11. You can use 'man exports' to see the options available for "`/etc/exports`".

12. You're done with this section

Part 14: Install and Configure Samba Share on RHEL 7

In this section you'll learn how to install and configure Samba server on separate RHEL 7 / CentOS 7 box and create a Samba share store. To do this, you'll need to perform the following procedure:

Step 1: Install SAMBA an Configure SAMBA Share

1. The first step is to install samba (if not already installed), type:

```
# yum install samba -y
```

2. Once installed, overwrite the default "`/etc/samba/smb.conf`" file with the following:

```
[global]
workgroup = WORKGROUP
server string = %h server
encrypt passwords = true
```

```
passdb backend = tdbsam
obey pam restrictions = yes

[FILES]
comment = File Library
path = /store/files/
browseable = yes
public = yes
read only = yes

[ISO]
comment = ISO Library
path = /store/iso/
browseable = yes
public = yes
read only = yes

[MUSIC]
comment = Music Library
path = /store/music/
browseable = yes
public = yes
read only = yes

[SOFTWARE]
comment = Software Library
path = /store/software/
browseable = yes
public = yes
read only = yes

[SWDEV]
comment = Software Development Library
path = /store/swdev/
browseable = yes
public = yes
read only = yes
```

Warning! You should only create a completely open share like the one here if you trust the people who have access to your Samba PDC server; open FTP servers, for example, have been compromised in the past and abused as drop boxes for pirated software.

3. After you've added these shares to your "smb.conf" configuration file, remember to either restart Samba or tell it to reload its configuration files, however, before doing that run the : "testparm" command.

4. Save your changes and run "testparm" command to test your samba configuration:

```
# testparm
```

if all is ok, a sample output should look like:

```
[root@rhel7]# testparm
Load smb config files from /etc/samba/smb.conf
rlimit_max: increasing rlimit_max (1024) to minimum Windows limit
(16384)
Processing section "[FILES]"
Processing section "[ISO]"
Processing section "[MUSIC]"
Processing section "[SOFTWARE]"
Processing section "[SWDEV]"
Loaded services file OK.
Server role: ROLE_STANDALONE

Press enter to see a dump of your service definitions

# Global parameters
[global]
    server string = %h server
    obey pam restrictions = Yes
    idmap config * : backend = tdb


[FILES]
    comment = File Library
    path = /store/files/
    guest ok = Yes


[ISO]
    comment = ISO Library
    path = /store/iso/
    guest ok = Yes


[MUSIC]
    comment = Music Library
    path = /store/music/
    guest ok = Yes


[SOFTWARE]
    comment = Software Library
    path = /store/software/
```

```
guest ok = Yes

[SWDEV]
    comment = Software Development Library
    path = /store/swdev/
    guest ok = Yes
[root@rhel7 samba]#
```

Note: this checks "`smb.conf`" for syntax errors. Any errors must be corrected before moving on. Once all is OK, you can start-up and enable Samba to start automatically on boot, as follows:

```
# systemctl enable smb.service
# systemctl start smb.service
```

5. Set `firewall-cmd` to allow samba service, type:

```
firewall-cmd --permanent --add-service=samba
firewall-cmd --permanent --add-service=samba-client
firewall-cmd --reload
```

6. You're done with this section.

Step 2: Create Shared Folders and Add SAMBA users

The next step is to create the appropriate users and folders. To do this, perform the following steps:

7. Create our directories, type

```
sudo mkdir -p /store/files/
sudo mkdir -p /store/iso/
sudo mkdir -p /store/music/
sudo mkdir -p /store/software/
sudo mkdir -p /store/swdev/
```

8. Add SAMBA user for `iso`, `music`, and `swdev`, type:

```
sudo useradd cadmin
sudo smbpasswd -a cadmin
New SMB Password:
Retype new SMB Password:
Added user cadmin.
```

9. Restart Samba services:

```
# systemctl restart smb.service
```

10. Once you restart samba, you should be able to access the share via "\\<ip address>\iso\.". and other directories. However, before you can do this you need to verify that you can access your SAMBA share. You can use the ping command to test connectivity.

11. The next test is to see if we can access our **iso** share etc, by using smbclient command.

Step 3: Connecting to a Samba Machine in Linux

12. To connect to a Samba machine (Windows or Linux running Samba) from the command line, execute the command (replace MACHINENAME and sharename with the appropriate values):

```
# smbclient //MACHINENAME/sharename
```

Note 1: If you want to pass a different username to the Samba Server, execute the command (replace username with your username):

```
# smbclient //MACHINENAME/sharename -U username
```

Note 2: if a password is associated with the username, you will be prompted for it. Once you are authorized by the SMB protocol, you will be at a "smb: \>" prompt. This is similar to an ftp session where get, put, pwd, ls, etc. can be used to navigate.

Note 3: Type "help" for a list of commands available.

13. Now to access our shared **iso** store using user iso with appropriate password form a remote machine, see Fig. 77:

```
# smbclient //192.168.6.15/iso -U cadmin

[root@rhel7 ~]#  smbclient //192.168.6.15/software -U nadmin
Enter nadmin's password:
Domain=[WORKGROUP] OS=[Windows 6.1] Server=[Samba 4.2.3]
smb: \>
smb: \> ls
                               D        0  Tue Jan  5 17:02:58 2016
  . .                          D        0  Tue Jan  5 16:49:00 2016
  jboss-portal-2.7.2-bundled.zip  N 163797150  Wed Mar 11 14:46:21 2009

              49746196 blocks of size 1024. 43400620 blocks available
smb: \> exit
[root@rhel7 ~]#
```
_____ Fig. 77

85

14. Type `exit` command to exit `smbclient`.

15. You're done with this section.

Step 4: Accessing Samba Shares from Windows Desktop

4.1 Use \\<ip-adress>\sharename

16. First we need to ensure that we can connect from the Windows machine to our Linux machine using `ping` command, as shown in Fig. 78.

```
C:\>ping 192.168.6.15

Pinging 192.168.6.15 with 32 bytes of data:
Reply from 192.168.6.15: bytes=32 time<1ms TTL=64
Reply from 192.168.6.15: bytes=32 time<1ms TTL=64
Reply from 192.168.6.15: bytes=32 time<1ms TTL=64
Reply from 192.168.6.15: bytes=32 time<1ms TTL=64

Ping statistics for 192.168.6.15:
    Packets: Sent = 4, Received = 4, Lost = 0 (0% loss),
Approximate round trip times in milli-seconds:
    Minimum = 0ms, Maximum = 0ms, Average = 0ms

C:\>
```
Fig. 78

17. Start your **Start → Accessories → Windows Explorer,** and under the Address bar type "\\<ip-adress>" or server name "\\servername"

    - When prompted for user name and password, enter appropriate credentials and then click OK, see Fig. 79 (**Note:** ignore the warning and click **OK** button).

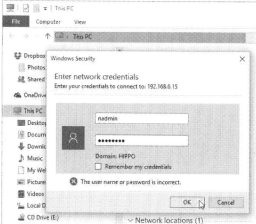
Fig. 79

86

1. You should be logged into the shared folders/directories, as shown in Fig. 80.

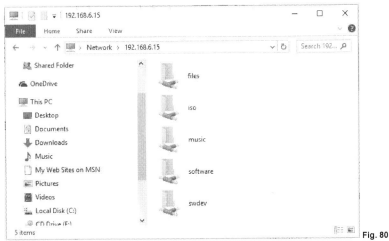

Fig. 80

2. You can also browse the ISO share to view its content, as shown in Fig. 81.

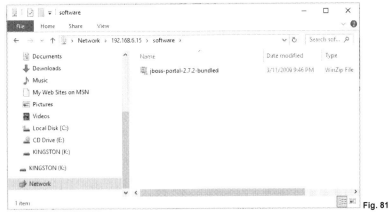

Fig. 81

3. You're done with this section and also the hands-on labs for RHEL 7 server.

Part 6: Install Identity Management with IPA Directory Services on RHEL 7

The IPA (now simply called Identity Management) is an acronym for Identity, Policy, and Auditing. I found that Wikipedia provides a better definition to IPA then what I could do. They refer to it as freeIPA but will just refer to it IPA for short in most of the time. The recent release of Red Hat Enterprise Linux 7 boasts being a great OS to run your identity management infrastructure. It's very easy to get started with one, or two, FreeIPA server(s), and not much trouble after that to enable multi-master replication. This setup should also be applicable to CentOS 7 server.

"As of 2014 FreeIPA uses 389 Directory Server for its LDAP implementation, MIT's Kerberos 5 for authentication and single sign-on, the Apache HTTP Server and Python for the management framework and Web UI, and (optionally) DogTag for the integrated CA, and BIND with a custom plugin for the integrated DNS. Since version 3.0.0, FreeIPA also uses Samba to integrate with Microsoft's Active Directory by way of Cross Forest Trusts (source Wikipedia)". FreeIPA aims to provide support not just for Linux- and Unix-based computers, but ultimately for Microsoft Windows and Apple OS X computers."

Step 1: Modify "/etc/hosts" and "/etc/resolv.conf" files

1. Edit "/etc/hosts" file to reflect the correct hostname, as shown in Fig. 82.

```
127.0.0.1    localhost localhost.localdomain localhost4 localhost4.localdomain4
10.0.2.15    rhel7.govsystemhost.com rhel7 www ftp mail
::1          localhost localhost.localdomain localhost6 localhost6.localdomain6
```

Fig. 82

2. Now to set static IP on eth0, run command:

```
# vi /etc/sysconfig/network-scripts/ifcfg-enp0s3
```

and set the values as shown in Fig. 83, and then save it to update setting.

```
                    ifcfg-enpOs3

TYPE="Ethernet"
HWADDR=08:00:27:49:98:a7
BOOTPROTO="none"
NAME="enp0s3"
DEVICE="enp0s3"
ONBOOT="yes"
IPADDR=10.0.2.5
BROADCAST=10.0.2.255
NETWORK=10.0.2.0
NETMASK=255.255.255.0
GATEWAY=10.0.2.2
DNS1=8.8.8.8
DNS2=10.0.2.5
IPV4_FAILURE_FATAL="no"
USERCTL=no
IPV6INIT=no
```

Fig. 83

3. Next, edit "`/etc/resolv.conf`" file to reflect the correct `namesearch`, domain and search, as shown below.

```
# Generated by NetworkManager
search govsystemhost.com
nameserver  10.0.2.5
```

4. To apply changes, we need to bring the network interface down and back up, issue "`ifdown eth0`" and "`ifup enp0s3`" commands:

```
[root@rhel7 ~]# ifdown enp0s3
Device 'enp0s3' successfully disconnected.
[root@rhel7 ~]#
[root@rhel7 ~]# ifup enp0s3
Connection successfully activated (D-Bus active path: /org/freedesktop/NetworkMa
nager/ActiveConnection/4)
[root@rhel7 ~]#
```
Fig. 84

5. Now use `ifconfig` command, to check and verify your settings.

```
[root@rhel7 ~]# ifconfig
enp0s3: flags=4163<UP,BROADCAST,RUNNING,MULTICAST>  mtu 1500
        inet 10.0.2.5  netmask 255.255.255.0  broadcast 10.0.2.255
        inet6 fe80::a00:27ff:fe49:98a7  prefixlen 64  scopeid 0x20<link>
        ether 08:00:27:49:98:a7  txqueuelen 1000  (Ethernet)
        RX packets 136  bytes 14375 (14.0 KiB)
        RX errors 0  dropped 0  overruns 0  frame 0
        TX packets 193  bytes 19748 (19.2 KiB)
        TX errors 0  dropped 0 overruns 0  carrier 0  collisions 0

lo: flags=73<UP,LOOPBACK,RUNNING>  mtu 65536
        inet 127.0.0.1  netmask 255.0.0.0
        inet6 ::1  prefixlen 128  scopeid 0x10<host>
        loop  txqueuelen 0  (Local Loopback)
        RX packets 685  bytes 217633 (212.5 KiB)
        RX errors 0  dropped 0  overruns 0  frame 0
        TX packets 685  bytes 217633 (212.5 KiB)
        TX errors 0  dropped 0 overruns 0  carrier 0  collisions 0

virbr0: flags=4099<UP,BROADCAST,MULTICAST>  mtu 1500
        inet 192.168.122.1  netmask 255.255.255.0  broadcast 192.168.122.255
        ether 52:54:00:70:55:9e  txqueuelen 0  (Ethernet)
        RX packets 0  bytes 0 (0.0 B)
        RX errors 0  dropped 0  overruns 0  frame 0
        TX packets 0  bytes 0 (0.0 B)
        TX errors 0  dropped 0 overruns 0  carrier 0  collisions 0

[root@rhel7 ~]#
```
Fig. 85

6. Now edit your "/etc/hosts" file to reflect the correct IP address, as shown in Fig. 48.

```
127.0.0.1    localhost localhost.localdomain localhost4
localhost4.localdomain4
10.0.2.5    rhel7.govsystemhost.com rhel7 www ftp mail
::1          localhost localhost.localdomain localhost6
localhost6.localdomain6
```

Fig. 86

7. Now edit your "/etc/resolv.conf" file to reflect the changes, as shown in Fig. 48.

```
# Generated by NetworkManager
search govsystemhost.com
nameserver 8.8.8.8
nameserver 10.0.2.5
```

Fig. 87

8. Check that you're still able to reach the Internet, as shown in Fig. 88.

Fig. 88

9. We're done with this section

Step 2: Install and Configure First IPA Server Directory Services

1. First we need to install the prerequisites, type:

```
yum -y install ipa-server bind-dyndb-ldap firefox xorg-x11-xauth
```

Note 1: we're now ready to begin the setup of IPA. You'll be presented with a couple of questions, the non default answers for this tutorial are highlighted in red font.

Note 2: you may need to temporarily stop the firewalld service due to many ports required IPA to run!

2. Now we need to install the server, run the command "ipa-server-install":

```
[root@rhel7 ~]# ipa-server-install

The log file for this installation can be found in /var/log/ipaserver-
install.log
==============================================================================
==========
This program will set up the IPA Server.

This includes:
  * Configure a stand-alone CA (dogtag) for certificate management
  * Configure the Network Time Daemon (ntpd)
  * Create and configure an instance of Directory Server
```

```
* Create and configure a Kerberos Key Distribution Center (KDC)
* Configure Apache (httpd)

To accept the default shown in brackets, press the Enter key.

WARNING: conflicting time&date synchronization service 'chronyd' will
be disabled
in favor of ntpd

Do you want to configure integrated DNS (BIND)? [no]: yes

Enter the fully qualified domain name of the computer
on which you're setting up server software. Using the form
<hostname>.<domainname>
Example: master.example.com.


Server host name [rhel7.govsystemhost.com]:

Warning: skipping DNS resolution of host rhel7.govsystemhost.com
The domain name has been determined based on the host name.

Please confirm the domain name [govsystemhost.com]:

The kerberos protocol requires a Realm name to be defined.
This is typically the domain name converted to uppercase.

Please provide a realm name [GOVSYSTEMHOST.COM]:
Certain directory server operations require an administrative user.
This user is referred to as the Directory Manager and has full access
to the Directory for system management tasks and will be added to the
instance of directory server created for IPA.
The password must be at least 8 characters long.

Directory Manager password:
Password (confirm):

The IPA server requires an administrative user, named 'admin'.
This user is a regular system account used for IPA server
administration.

IPA admin password:
Password (confirm):
```

```
Existing BIND configuration detected, overwrite? [no]: yes
Do you want to configure DNS forwarders? [yes]:
Enter an IP address for a DNS forwarder, or press Enter to skip:
No DNS forwarders configured
Do you want to configure the reverse zone? [yes]:
Please specify the reverse zone name [6.168.192.in-addr.arpa.]:
Using reverse zone(s) 6.168.192.in-addr.arpa.

The IPA Master Server will be configured with:
Hostname:       rhel7.govsystemhost.com
IP address(es): 192.168.6.15
Domain name:    govsystemhost.com
Realm name:     GOVSYSTEMHOST.COM

BIND DNS server will be configured to serve IPA domain with:
Forwarders:    No forwarders
Reverse zone(s):  6.168.192.in-addr.arpa.

Continue to configure the system with these values? [no]: yes

The following operations may take some minutes to complete.
Please wait until the prompt is returned.

Configuring NTP daemon (ntpd)
  [1/4]: stopping ntpd
  [2/4]: writing configuration
  [3/4]: configuring ntpd to start on boot
  [4/4]: starting ntpd
Done configuring NTP daemon (ntpd).
Configuring directory server (dirsrv). Estimated time: 1 minute
  [1/42]: creating directory server user
  [2/42]: creating directory server instance
  [3/42]: adding default schema
  [4/42]: enabling memberof plugin
  [5/42]: enabling winsync plugin
  [6/42]: configuring replication version plugin
  [7/42]: enabling IPA enrollment plugin
  [8/42]: enabling ldapi
  [9/42]: configuring uniqueness plugin
  [10/42]: configuring uuid plugin
  [11/42]: configuring modrdn plugin
  [12/42]: configuring DNS plugin
  [13/42]: enabling entryUSN plugin
  [14/42]: configuring lockout plugin
```

```
[15/42]: creating indices
[16/42]: enabling referential integrity plugin
[17/42]: configuring certmap.conf
[18/42]: configure autobind for root
[19/42]: configure new location for managed entries
[20/42]: configure dirsrv ccache
[21/42]: enable SASL mapping fallback
[22/42]: restarting directory server
[23/42]: adding default layout
[24/42]: adding delegation layout
[25/42]: creating container for managed entries
[26/42]: configuring user private groups
[27/42]: configuring netgroups from hostgroups
[28/42]: creating default Sudo bind user
[29/42]: creating default Auto Member layout
[30/42]: adding range check plugin
[31/42]: creating default HBAC rule allow_all
[32/42]: adding entries for topology management
[33/42]: initializing group membership
[34/42]: adding master entry
[35/42]: initializing domain level
[36/42]: configuring Posix uid/gid generation
[37/42]: adding replication acis
[38/42]: enabling compatibility plugin
[39/42]: activating sidgen plugin
[40/42]: activating extdom plugin
[41/42]: tuning directory server
[42/42]: configuring directory to start on boot
Done configuring directory server (dirsrv).
Configuring certificate server (pki-tomcatd). Estimated time: 3
minutes 30 seconds
  [1/27]: creating certificate server user
  [2/27]: configuring certificate server instance
  [3/27]: stopping certificate server instance to update CS.cfg
  [4/27]: backing up CS.cfg
  [5/27]: disabling nonces
  [6/27]: set up CRL publishing
  [7/27]: enable PKIX certificate path discovery and validation
  [8/27]: starting certificate server instance
  [9/27]: creating RA agent certificate database
  [10/27]: importing CA chain to RA certificate database
  [11/27]: fixing RA database permissions
  [12/27]: setting up signing cert profile
  [13/27]: setting audit signing renewal to 2 years
```

```
    [14/27]: restarting certificate server
    [15/27]: requesting RA certificate from CA
    [16/27]: issuing RA agent certificate
    [17/27]: adding RA agent as a trusted user
    [18/27]: authorizing RA to modify profiles
    [19/27]: configure certmonger for renewals
    [20/27]: configure certificate renewals
    [21/27]: configure RA certificate renewal
    [22/27]: configure Server-Cert certificate renewal
    [23/27]: Configure HTTP to proxy connections
    [24/27]: restarting certificate server
    [25/27]: migrating certificate profiles to LDAP
    [26/27]: importing IPA certificate profiles
    [27/27]: adding default CA ACL
Done configuring certificate server (pki-tomcatd).
Configuring directory server (dirsrv). Estimated time: 10 seconds
    [1/3]: configuring ssl for ds instance
    [2/3]: restarting directory server
    [3/3]: adding CA certificate entry
Done configuring directory server (dirsrv).
Configuring Kerberos KDC (krb5kdc). Estimated time: 30 seconds
    [1/10]: adding sasl mappings to the directory
    [2/10]: adding kerberos container to the directory
    [3/10]: configuring KDC
    [4/10]: initialize kerberos container
WARNING: Your system is running out of entropy, you may experience
long delays
    [5/10]: adding default ACIs
    [6/10]: creating a keytab for the directory
    [7/10]: creating a keytab for the machine
    [8/10]: adding the password extension to the directory
    [9/10]: starting the KDC
    [10/10]: configuring KDC to start on boot
Done configuring Kerberos KDC (krb5kdc).
Configuring kadmin
    [1/2]: starting kadmin
    [2/2]: configuring kadmin to start on boot
Done configuring kadmin.
Configuring ipa_memcached
    [1/2]: starting ipa_memcached
    [2/2]: configuring ipa_memcached to start on boot
Done configuring ipa_memcached.
Configuring ipa-otpd
    [1/2]: starting ipa-otpd
```

```
   [2/2]: configuring ipa-otpd to start on boot
Done configuring ipa-otpd.
Configuring the web interface (httpd). Estimated time: 1 minute
   [1/19]: setting mod_nss port to 443
   [2/19]: setting mod_nss protocol list to TLSv1.0 - TLSv1.2
   [3/19]: setting mod_nss password file
   [4/19]: enabling mod_nss renegotiate
   [5/19]: adding URL rewriting rules
   [6/19]: configuring httpd
   [7/19]: configure certmonger for renewals
   [8/19]: setting up ssl
   [9/19]: importing CA certificates from LDAP
   [10/19]: setting up browser autoconfig
   [11/19]: publish CA cert
   [12/19]: creating a keytab for httpd
   [13/19]: clean up any existing httpd ccache
   [14/19]: configuring SELinux for httpd
   [15/19]: create KDC proxy user
   [16/19]: create KDC proxy config
   [17/19]: enable KDC proxy
   [18/19]: restarting httpd
   [19/19]: configuring httpd to start on boot
Done configuring the web interface (httpd).
Applying LDAP updates
Upgrading IPA:
   [1/9]: stopping directory server
   [2/9]: saving configuration
   [3/9]: disabling listeners
   [4/9]: enabling DS global lock
   [5/9]: starting directory server
   [6/9]: upgrading server
   [7/9]: stopping directory server
   [8/9]: restoring configuration
   [9/9]: starting directory server
Done.
Restarting the directory server
Restarting the KDC
Configuring DNS (named)
   [1/12]: generating rndc key file
WARNING: Your system is running out of entropy, you may experience
long delays
   [2/12]: adding DNS container
   [3/12]: setting up our zone
   [4/12]: setting up reverse zone
```

```
    [5/12]: setting up our own record
    [6/12]: setting up records for other masters
    [7/12]: adding NS record to the zones
    [8/12]: setting up CA record
    [9/12]: setting up kerberos principal
    [10/12]: setting up named.conf
    [11/12]: configuring named to start on boot
    [12/12]: changing resolv.conf to point to ourselves
Done configuring DNS (named).
Configuring DNS key synchronization service (ipa-dnskeysyncd)
    [1/7]: checking status
    [2/7]: setting up bind-dyndb-ldap working directory
    [3/7]: setting up kerberos principal
    [4/7]: setting up SoftHSM
    [5/7]: adding DNSSEC containers
    [6/7]: creating replica keys
    [7/7]: configuring ipa-dnskeysyncd to start on boot
Done configuring DNS key synchronization service (ipa-dnskeysyncd).
Restarting ipa-dnskeysyncd
Restarting named
Restarting the web server
================================================================================

=========
Setup complete

Next steps:
    1. You must make sure these network ports are open:
        TCP Ports:
          * 80, 443: HTTP/HTTPS
          * 389, 636: LDAP/LDAPS
          * 88, 464: kerberos
          * 53: bind
        UDP Ports:
          * 88, 464: kerberos
          * 53: bind
          * 123: ntp

    2. You can now obtain a kerberos ticket using the command: 'kinit
admin'
       This ticket will allow you to use the IPA tools (e.g., ipa user-
add)
       and the web user interface.

Be sure to back up the CA certificates stored in /root/cacert.p12
```

These files are required to create replicas. The password for these
files is the Directory Manager password
[root@rhel7 ~]#

3. You can now issue the `ipactl status` command to check IPA server, type:

```
[root@rhel7 ~]# ipactl status
Directory Service: RUNNING
krb5kdc Service: RUNNING
kadmin Service: RUNNING
named Service: RUNNING
ipa_memcached Service: RUNNING
httpd Service: RUNNING
pki-tomcatd Service: RUNNING
ipa-otpd Service: RUNNING
ipa-dnskeysyncd Service: RUNNING
ipa: INFO: The ipactl command was successful
[root@rhel7 ~]#
```

4. You're done with this section.

Step 3: Configure Firewall for IPA Ports

5. At this point let's open the ports that allow IPA to communicate, as follows:

```
firewall-cmd --permanent --add-service=ntp

firewall-cmd --permanent --add-service=http

firewall-cmd --permanent --add-service=https

firewall-cmd --permanent --add-service=ldap

firewall-cmd --permanent --add-service=ldaps

firewall-cmd --permanent --add-service=kerberos

firewall-cmd --permanent --add-service=kpasswd

firewall-cmd --reload
```

6. You're done with section.

Step 4: Check Administrator Access

7. First step is to verify that you don't yet have any Kerberos tickets, type;

```
# klist
```

Note: unless you previously had Kerberos setup and logged in, you list of tickets should be empty.

8. Now let's login as the Directory Manager, using "kinit admin" command, you'll be requested to supply the password enter during IPA installation.:

```
[root@rhel7 ~]# kinit admin
Password for admin@GOVSYSTEMHOST.COM:
```

9. Again, let's check your "klist" now,

```
[root@rhel7 ~]# klist
Ticket cache: KEYRING:persistent:0:0
Default principal: admin@GOVSYSTEMHOST.COM

Valid starting       Expires            Service principal
01/04/2016 15:44:26  01/05/2016 15:44:03  krbtgt/GOVSYSTEMHOST.COM@GOVSYSTEMHOST.COM
[root@rhel7 ~]#
```
Fig. 89

Note: as can be seen, you now should have a TGT (ticket granting ticket, which allows you to access other Kerberized services) for the admin@YOUR.REALM.TLD principal.

10. Next, let's check you can administer your shiny new IPA server by getting a listing of all users, type.

```
# ipa user-find
```

this should return your only user, the Directory Manager.

```
[root@rhel7 ~]# ipa user-find
--------------------
1 user matched
--------------------
  User login: admin
  Last name: Administrator
  Home directory: /home/admin
  Login shell: /bin/bash
  UID: 610600000
  GID: 610600000
  Account disabled: False
  Password: True
  Kerberos keys available: True
----------------------------
Number of entries returned 1
```

11. Next, let's again check your "klist" you'll have another ticket.

```
# klist
[root@rhel7 ~]# klist
Ticket cache: KEYRING:persistent:0:0
Default principal: admin@GOVSYSTEMHOST.COM

Valid starting       Expires              Service principal
01/04/2016 15:46:40  01/05/2016 15:44:03  HTTP/rhel7.govsystemhost.com@GOVSYSTEMHOST.COM
01/04/2016 15:44:26  01/05/2016 15:44:03  krbtgt/GOVSYSTEMHOST.COM@GOVSYSTEMHOST.COM
[root@rhel7 ~]#
```
Fig. 90

Note: this time a special "HTTP/ipa-01.your.realm.tld@YOUR.REALM.TLD" ticket shows you have access to administer your IPA server. This was automatically granted when you ran the ipa command.

12. We're now basically done with setting the up the Linux-native Directory Services. Joining to the domain is now a brisk with "ipa-join" command on the client, which we'll do later.

13. You're done with section and thus we'll stop now and go on to configure clients and populate our domain, or go ahead and setup replication. You can also enable replication later with no consequences.

Step 5: Accessing the IPA Server using the Web Interface

You really need to have DNS worked out before you are able to call out https://SERVER.DOMAIN.NAME in your web browser. As long as DHCP is handing clients the IP of you IPA server for DNS, then everything will be fine.

1. Open your browser and pint it https://SERVER.DOMAIN.NAME, ad should be presented with the **RED HAT IDENTITY MANAGEMENT** login screen, as shown in Fig. 91.

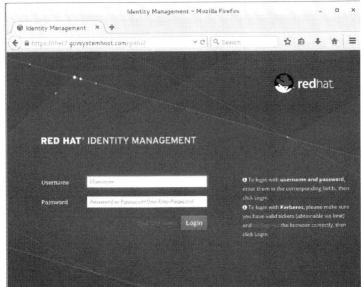
Fig. 91

Note: the login credentials: username `admin` and password is the one you set during the initial installation.

Fig. 92

2. You should be login to Red Hat Identity Management console as shown in Fig. 93.

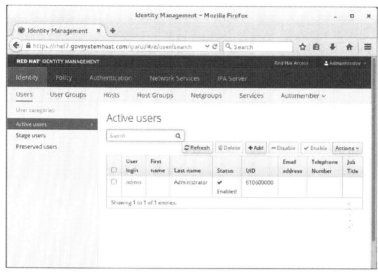

Fig. 93

14. To **start/restart/enable/stop** the IPA server, type:

```
# ipactl start
# ipactl  restart
# ipactl enable
# ipactl stop
```

15. Let's stop the IPA server, type:

```
# ipactl stop
```

```
[root@rhel7 ~]# ipactl stop
Stopping ipa-dnskeysyncd Service
Stopping ipa-otpd Service
Stopping pki-tomcatd Service
Stopping httpd Service
Stopping ipa_memcached Service
Stopping named Service
Stopping kadmin Service
Stopping krb5kdc Service
Stopping Directory Service
ipa: INFO: The ipactl command was successful
```

```
[root@rhel7 ~]#
```

16. You're done with this section.

Step 6: Check and Verify DNS Server Setup

Here will use the `dig` and `nslookup` commands to verify that the DNS is correctly setup and configured

1. Now issue the `dig` command, type:

```
# dig rhel7.systemhost.com
```

```
[root@rhel7 ~]# dig rhel7.govsystemhost.com

; <<>> DiG 9.9.4-RedHat-9.9.4-29.el7_2.1 <<>> rhel7.govsystemhost.com
;; global options: +cmd
;; Got answer:
;; ->>HEADER<<- opcode: QUERY, status: NOERROR, id: 29942
;; flags: qr aa rd ra; QUERY: 1, ANSWER: 1, AUTHORITY: 1, ADDITIONAL: 1

;; OPT PSEUDOSECTION:
; EDNS: version: 0, flags:; udp: 4096
;; QUESTION SECTION:
;rhel7.govsystemhost.com.          IN      A

;; ANSWER SECTION:
rhel7.govsystemhost.com. 1200      IN      A        192.168.6.15

;; AUTHORITY SECTION:
govsystemhost.com.        86400    IN      NS       rhel7.govsystemhost.com.

;; Query time: 0 msec
;; SERVER: 192.168.6.15#53(192.168.6.15)
;; WHEN: Sun Jan 10 05:33:56 EST 2016
;; MSG SIZE  rcvd: 82

[root@rhel7 ~]#
```
—— **Fig. 94**

Note: as can be observed everything is working beautifully.

2. Next, run the `nslookup` command, type:

```
[root@rhel7 ~]# nslookup rhel7.govsystemhost.com
Server:        192.168.6.15
Address:       192.168.6.15#53

Name:   rhel7.govsystemhost.com
Address: 192.168.6.15

[root@rhel7 ~]#
```
Fig. 94

Note: again as can be observed everything is working beautifully.

3. You're done with section.

Part 14: Troubleshooting FTP Client Connection Failure

1. If you try to ftp into your ftp server using "ftp localhost" and you're confronted with error "**500 OOPS: cannot change directory: /home/user1**", as shown in Fig. 69, the check that your firewall or SELinux is not blocking the connection. For testing purposes, you may go ahead and disable firewall and SELinux, and all should be OK.

```
[netadmin@rhel6 ~]$ ftp localhost
Connected to localhost (127.0.0.1).
220 (vsFTPd 2.2.2)
Name (localhost:netadmin): szulu
331 Please specify the password.
Password:
500 OOPS: cannot change directory:/home/szulu
Login failed.
ftp> quit
```
Fig. 69

2. You're done with this section.

Part 15: Troubleshooting SELinux

You have the option to set SELinux into three options: **Permissive, Enforcing** and **Disabled** depending on your requirements. For more info, check: http://www.crypt.gen.nz/selinux/disable_selinux.html

Step 1: Fully Disabling SELinux

Fully disabling SELinux goes one step further than just switching into permissive mode. Disabling will completely disable all SELinux functions including file and process labeling.

3. In Fedora Core, CentOS and RedHat Enterprise, using your favorite Text editor, edit the default "/etc/selinux/config" file and change the SELINUX line to "SELINUX=disabled":

```
# This file controls the state of SELinux on the system.
# SELINUX= can take one of these three values:
# enforcing - SELinux security policy is enforced.
# permissive - SELinux prints warnings instead of enforcing.
# disabled - No SELinux policy is loaded.
SELINUX=disabled
# SELINUXTYPE= can take one of these two values:
# targeted - Only targeted network daemons are protected.
# strict - Full SELinux protection.
SELINUXTYPE=targeted
```

4. Save and then reboot the system.

1. Start/Stop/Reload Firewall-cmd

1. To start/stop/reload/enable and add port and services, do as follows:

```
systemctl stop firewalld
systemctl status firewalld
systemctl disable firewalld
systemctl disable firewalld
```

2. Add port and service to access certain service, e.g.:

```
firewall-cmd --permanent --add-service=ftp
firewall-cmd --reload
```

Note: alternatively, you can also use port number to allow port 21 through instead as follows:

```
firewall-cmd --permanent --add-port=21/tcp
firewall-cmd --reload
```

3. You're done with this section.

Part 16: Hands-on Lab Assignments

1. Install and configure RHEL7 and configure Webmin admin tool
2. Install & Configure Apache, PHP, PostgreSQL & MySQL on Linux. Add FTP and NFS servers.
3. Install and configure DHCP server. Plan Design Implement & Deploy DNS Master and Slave Servers for redundancy Add multiple virtual domains etc.
4. Install and configure Postfix messaging server with SquirrelMail webmail.

5. Install and configure JBoss and JBoss + Portal Bundle
6. Install and configure Liferay Portal
7. Install and configure Samba PDC
8. Install and configure Astaro SG firewall/router for your network.
9. Install & Configure Oscar Cluster with three clients' nodes

Part 17: Need More Training on RHEL-7

Are you having trouble understanding or comprehending the working of Linux RHEL-7, if so, then check out some of our introductory courses on Linux servers at: Global Open Versity, Vancouver Canada.

Mastering RHEL 7 / CentOS 7 Server Administration and System Integration Training - ICT405

You can now register and take our superb Mastering RHEL 7 / CentOS 7 Server Administration. This Training cover compete server installation, administration and system integration from simple task to cloud computing with ownCloud, Seafile Secure Cloud Storage and IPA (Identity Management).

- ICT405 – Mastering RHEL-7 & CentOS-7 Server Installation and Adminstration

Contact us today: **Email:** info@globalopenversity.org   **URL:** www.globalopenversity.org

Other Related Articles:

1. Deploy Secure Messaging Solutions using Sendmail & Dovecot Servers with ClamAV on Linux
2. Install Guide Secure Postfix Messaging Server with Dovecot and ClamAV on Linux v1.2
3. Integration of JBoss Portal with OpenDS LDAP Server v1.2
4. Integrate MS Outlook 2007 Addressbook with SugarCRM Contacts on Windows
5. Step-by-step Install Guide for Moodle with Dimdim Web Meeting
6. Step-By-Step Install Guide Alfresco Community 3.3g on RHEL5 Server v1.0
7. Step-By-Step Install Guide Joomla CMS on Ubuntu 10.04 LTS Server v1.0
8. Build your own ISP Hosting using EHCP on Ubuntu 10.04 LTS Server
9. Deploy Secure Messaging Solutions using USendUmail & Dovecot Servers with ClamAV on Linux
10. Install Guide IPCop Firewall for Network Security with Spam and Virus Protection

Chapter III

Step-By-Step Guide CentOS-7 Infrastructure
Server Installation and Administration

Introduction

CentOS is a community-supported, free and open source operating system based on Red Hat Enterprise Linux. It exists to provide a free enterprise class computing platform and strives to maintain 100% binary compatibility with its upstream distribution .CentOS stands for "Community ENTerprise Operating System". CentOS is the perfect server for people who need an enterprise class operating system stability without the cost of certification and support and pocket burning baggage that comes with proprietary software. And the beauty is CentOS is free.

CentOS-7.0 is based on the upstream release of Red Hat EL 7.0 and includes packages from all variants. All upstream repositories have been combined into one, to make it easier for end users to work with. It exists to provide a free enterprise class computing platform and strives to maintain 100% binary compatibility with its upstream distribution, in this case RHEL 7. To-date, CentOS simply remains the unrivaled champion of rock solid, and with excellent and modern capabilities, good performance and ultra-long support.

CentOS 7 is the first version to be released after the nominally independent CentOS and Red Hat brokered a deal to work together more closely, in away for CentOS to become a staging ground for future features for RHEL, akin to Fedora Project's former status. This could be a plus for Red Hat to reach out more directly to CentOS's vast customer base - the enterprises, service providers, ISPs, and other outfits using CentOS to keep cost low gain on ROI.

Hands-on Lab Session

In this Hands-on lab session, you will learn how to install CentOS-7 with two NICs. You'll also learn how to perform post-installation configuration e.g., upgrade the system with new patches and bug fixes, configure static IP address from dynamic one, change the computer hostname, modify hosts file, perform ping test among others. I'll also show you how to install and administer LAMP stack, setup NFS server, vsftpd server, FileZilla, Apache Tomcat & Apache Ant, JDK 8, JBoss-Portal server, Samba share server. You'll also learn to use virtualization technology by deploying your private cloud using ownCloud and also installing VirtualBox with phpVirtualBox for deploying virtual machines. For backup, you'll learn how to deploy Bacula backup server. Finally, Administering Linux and Unix-based servers does not need to be the scourge of your work day. With a handy tool called Webmin as part of your arsenal, you can regain full control of your servers' setup and configuration via the Web browser. Upon completion of this Hands-on training you should have gained enough skill to deploy, maintain and administer CentOS-7 server with ability to extend it to deploy mainstream applications like webhosting etc.

Part 1: Installing and Updating CentOS-7 Server

Step 1: Install CentOS-7 Server

26. Point your browser to <u>CentOS-7</u> and download DVD ISO Server

27. Once you have downloaded the CentOS-7 ISO specific to your distribution, you have the option burning it into CD or just by using the ISO package to install it from your virtual machine, in our case VMware.

28. Fire-up a new virtual machine and perform the initial configuration and setup to use ISO package.

29. Start the virtual machine, and you should be able to see the first CentOS-7 installation screen.

30. From Fig. 1, and hit **Enter** key to start installation.

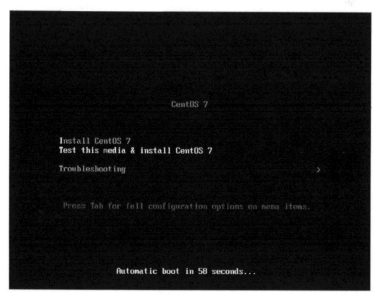

Fig. 1: Hit the <ENETER> key to start loading & installing CentOS-7.

Fig. 1

31. From Fig. 2, **WELCOME TO CETNTOS 7** screen, accept the default selection, or change as desired and then click **Continue** button.

Fig. 2

32. From Fig. 3, **INSTALLATION SUMMARY** screen, here you can customize your installation by using other **Installation Sources** than your local DVD/USB media, such as a network locations using **HTTP, HTTPS, FTP** or **NFS** protocols and even add some additional repositories, but use this methods only if you know what you're doing. So leave the default **Auto-detected installation media** and hit on **Done** to continue

Fig. 3

33. From Fig. 4, **INSTALLATION SUMMARY** screen, click on the SOFTWARE to take you to the **INSTALLATION SOURCE** screen, accept the default selection "Auto-detected instillation media" or change as desired, click on **Done** to continue. (Note: you can also click on the **Verify** button to check on media status)

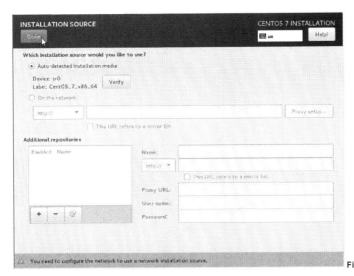

Fig. 4

34. From Fig. 5, **INSTALLATION SUMMARY** screen, click on the INSTALLATION DESTINATION to take you to the **INSTALLATION DESTINATION** screen, accept the default selection "Auto-configure partitioning" or change as desired, click on **Done** to continue.

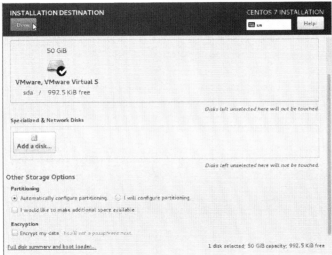

Fig. 5

35. From Fig. 6, **INSTALLATION SUMMARY** screen, click on the INSTALLATION DESTINATION to take you to the **NETWORK & HOST NAME** screen, type hostname, in our case "`centos7.govhostinglabs.com`" change as desired, click on **Done** to continue.

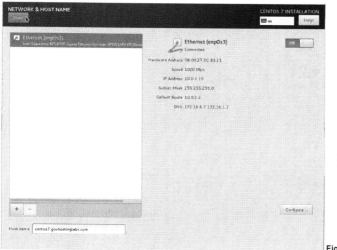

Fig. 6

36. From Fig. 7, **INSTALLATION SUMMARY** screen, you're now ready to begin installation once you're satisfied with your settings, click on **Continue** to continue.

Fig. 7

37. From Fig. 8, **CONFIGURATION** screen, here we're required to set the root password and also add the user as shown, you can set them now by clicking each icon, or set them when done with installation you can set them up.

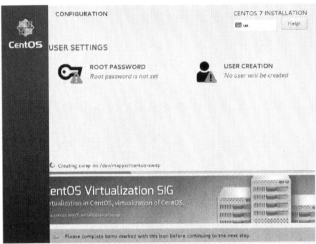

Fig. 8

38. From Fig. 8, **CONFIGURATION** screen, Click on the **ROOT PAASWORD** to set it as shown in Fig. 9, click Done to continue.

Fig. 9

39. Similarly from Fig. 10, **CREATE USER** screen, add the desired user as shown, click Done to continue.

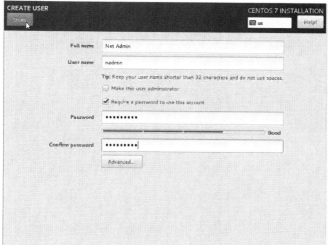

Fig. 10

40. From Fig. 11, **CONFIGURATION** screen, wait for the system to configure root user password and the adding of user.

Fig. 11

41. From Fig. 12, **CONFIGURATION** screen, when done click on **Finish Configuration** to continue.

Fig. 12

42. From Fig. 13, **CONFIGURATION** screen, wait for the systems to complete the task, when done click on **Reboot** button to continue. (**Note**: the license agreement notification)

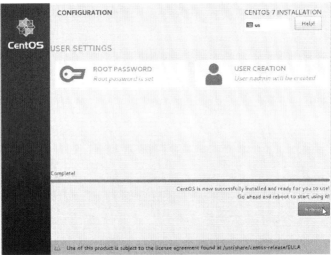

Fig. 13

43. From Fig. 14, the system will go through rebooting as shown, just relax for it to take you to the login screen.

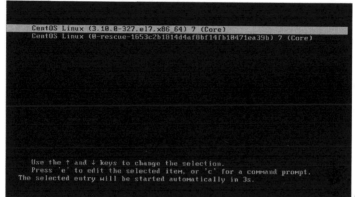

Fig. 14

44. The system will go through a rebooting process, as shown in Fig. 15. Wait for it to complete the process.

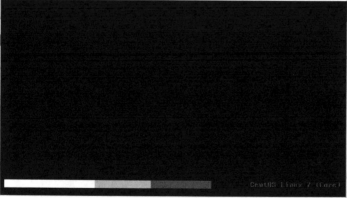

Fig. 15

45. From Fig. 16. the License accepting procedure, Select 1, followed by hitting 2 to accept the license agreement, and then hit c twice to continue

```
=========================================================================
=========================================================================
Initial setup of CentOS Linux 7 (Core)

 1) [!] License information
        (License not accepted)
 Please make your choice from [ '1' to enter the License information spoke | 'q
' to quit |
   'c' to continue | 'r' to refresh]: 1
=========================================================================
=========================================================================
License information

   1) Read the License Agreement

[ ] 2) I accept the license agreement.

 Please make your choice from above ['q' to quit | 'c' to continue |
   'r' to refresh]: 2_
```
Fig. 16a

```
=========================================================================
=========================================================================
License information

   1) Read the License Agreement

[x] 2) I accept the license agreement.

 Please make your choice from above ['q' to quit | 'c' to continue |
   'r' to refresh]: c_
```
Fig. 16b

46. From Fig. 17, you should be presented with the login screen. Click the **Net Admin** user or change as desired.

Fig. 17

47. From Fig. 18, enter the password you set for the user during the initial installation, and then click **Sign In** button.

Fig. 18

48. You should now be on the Net Admin user Desktop (or Home), as shown in Fig. 19.

Fig. 19

49. You're done with CentOS-7 server installation. In the next sections, we're going to perform other post-installation work like system upgrade etc.

Part 2: Post Installation Configurations.

Step 1: Perform System Upgrade

For best practices in IT, it's important to always perform systems upgrade after initial installation is completed. To do this, perform the following procedures:

3. Click **Application -> Favorites** and the select **Terminal**, as shown in Fig. 20.

Fig. 20

4. From **Terminal** window, issue the command "iconfig as shown in Fig. 21, to view the network interface settings.

```
[nadmin@centos7 ~]$ ifconfig
enp0s3: flags=4163<UP,BROADCAST,RUNNING,MULTICAST>  mtu 1500
        ether 08:00:27:5c:83:21  txqueuelen 1000  (Ethernet)
        RX packets 0  bytes 0 (0.0 B)
        RX errors 0  dropped 0  overruns 0  frame 0
        TX packets 0  bytes 0 (0.0 B)
        TX errors 0  dropped 0 overruns 0  carrier 0  collisions 0

lo: flags=73<UP,LOOPBACK,RUNNING>  mtu 65536
        inet 127.0.0.1  netmask 255.0.0.0
        inet6 ::1  prefixlen 128  scopeid 0x10<host>
        loop  txqueuelen 0  (Local Loopback)
        RX packets 6  bytes 436 (436.0 B)
        RX errors 0  dropped 0  overruns 0  frame 0
        TX packets 6  bytes 436 (436.0 B)
        TX errors 0  dropped 0 overruns 0  carrier 0  collisions 0

virbr0: flags=4099<UP,BROADCAST,MULTICAST>  mtu 1500
        inet 192.168.122.1  netmask 255.255.255.0  broadcast 192.168.122.255
        ether 00:00:00:00:00:00  txqueuelen 0  (Ethernet)
        RX packets 0  bytes 0 (0.0 B)
        RX errors 0  dropped 0  overruns 0  frame 0
        TX packets 0  bytes 0 (0.0 B)
        TX errors 0  dropped 0 overruns 0  carrier 0  collisions 0

[nadmin@centos7 ~]$ ▮
```
_____ Fig. 21

5. Next "su -" to sign in as route and then issue the command "ifup eth0" here under
   VirtUalBox it is "ifup eth0" as shown in Fig. 22: This enables the NIC to be activated.

```
[nadmin@centos7 ~]$ su -
Password:
[root@centos7 ~]# ifup enp0s3        ⌶
Connection successfully activated (D-Bus active path: /org/freedesktop/NetworkMa
nager/ActiveConnection/2)
[root@centos7 ~]#
```
                                                  Fig. 22

6. Next, issue the command "ifconfig 3np0s3" to view your interface IP address, as shown in
   Fig. 23:

```
[root@centos7 ~]# ifconfig enp0s3
enp0s3: flags=4163<UP,BROADCAST,RUNNING,MULTICAST>  mtu 1500
        inet 10.0.2.15  netmask 255.255.255.0  broadcast 10.0.2.255
        inet6 fe80::a00:27ff:fe5c:8321  prefixlen 64  scopeid 0x20<link>
        ether 08:00:27:5c:83:21  txqueuelen 1000  (Ethernet)
        RX packets 26323  bytes 24027354 (22.9 MiB)
        RX errors 0  dropped 0  overruns 0  frame 0
        TX packets 10916  bytes 663579 (648.0 KiB)
        TX errors 0  dropped 0 overruns 0  carrier 0  collisions 0

[root@centos7 ~]#
```
_____ Fig. 23

7. From **Terminal** window, issue the command "yum update -y" and issue the command: This
   enables the system to get the latest patches and bug fixes.

```
# yum update -y
```

8. You're now done with system update. In the next section we're going to learn how to change NIC adapter configuration from dynamic IP address to static IP address.

Step 3: Check Computer Hostname

Note 1: The old way of changing hostname by modifying the "/etc/sysconfig/network"; no longer works and if you do so, it will not take an effect of the modification. That is, even to do so, after you reboot the server, the hostname will still remains "localhost.localdomain". The procedure to change the hostname in CentOS 7 is now totally different from the previous version, this section will help you to setup the hostname on both the CentOS.

Note 2: CentOS 7 Supports three class of Hostnames

4. **Static** - The static hostname is the traditional host which can chosen by the user and is stored in "/etc/hostname" file

5. **Transient** - The transient hostname is maintained by the kernel and can be changed by DHCP and mDNS.

6. **Pretty** - It is a free UTF-8 hostname for the presentation to the user.

Note 3: Hostname can be
- 64 character in length
- Recommend to have FQDN
- Consists of: a-z, A-Z, 0-9, "-", and "." only.

1. How to Change Hostname on CentOS 7

In this section we're going to change the computer hostname. But first let's check the current hostname.

8. To check the hostname issue "hostname" command, as shown in Fig. 24. which in our case should show the current hostname as: "centos7.govsystemhost.com"

```
[root@centos7 ~]# hostname
centos7.govhostinglabs.com
[root@centos7 ~]#
```
Fig. 24

9. You're done with this section.

2. Using nmtui tool to Change Hostname on CentOS 7

10. The NetworkManager tool is used to set the static hostname in "/etc/hostname". From the Terminal window issue the command "nmtui" to ass the NetworkManager dialogue box as

shown in Fig. 32. From here you can do three things: Edit a connection; Activate a connection, and Set system hostname. Move to `Set system hostname` and hit **Enter** key or OK.

Fig. 25

11. Now in case, for example, you're interested in changing the hostname to, say: "`server01.mydomain.org`". Now you can modify your hostname as desired and then hit Enter key.

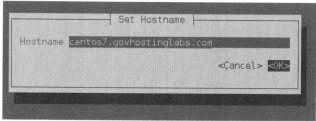

Fig. 26

12. In case you any modification to the hostname, then you'll need to restart the hostname to force the "`hostnamectl`" to notice the change in static hostname.

```
[root@centos7 ~]# systemctl restart systemd-hostname
```

13. You can verify the change in the hostname as shown in Fig. 27:

```
[root@centos7 sysconfig]# cat /etc/hostname
centos7.govhostinglabs.com
[root@centos7 sysconfig]#
[root@centos7 sysconfig]# cat /etc/sysconfig/network
```
Fig. 27

3. Using `hostnamedctl` command to Change Hostname on CentOS 7 / RHEL 7

`Hostnamectl` is used to change the hostname. With this tool we can change all three classes of hostname, however, here we are only interested with the static hostname.

5. First, and as usual, we need to check the current hostname, as shown in Fig. 30:

```
[root@centos7 ~]# hostnamectl status
```

```
[root@centos7 sysconfig]# hostnamectl status
   Static hostname: centos7.govhostinglabs.com
         Icon name: computer-vm
           Chassis: vm
         Machine ID: e4c96e3ea08243e9a8c77c3a6d91d0b9
           Boot ID: 453d62a78601457988ddd51cc18d0960
     Virtualization: oracle
  Operating System: CentOS Linux 7 (Core)
        CPE OS Name: cpe:/o:centos:centos:7
            Kernel: Linux 3.10.0-327.el7.x86_64
       Architecture: x86-64
[root@centos7 sysconfig]#
```
Fig. 30

6. Next, if desired, you can change the hostname, as follows:

```
[root@centos7 ~]# hostnamectl set-hostname centos7.govsystemlabs.com
```

7. Next, check to verify that hostname has been changed, see Fig. 31.

```
[root@centos7 sysconfig]# hostnamectl status
   Static hostname: centos7.govsystemlabs.com
         Icon name: computer-vm
           Chassis: vm
         Machine ID: e4c96e3ea08243e9a8c77c3a6d91d0b9
           Boot ID: 453d62a78601457988ddd51cc18d0960
     Virtualization: oracle
  Operating System: CentOS Linux 7 (Core)
        CPE OS Name: cpe:/o:centos:centos:7
            Kernel: Linux 3.10.0-327.el7.x86_64
       Architecture: x86-64
[root@centos7 sysconfig]#
```
Fig. 31

8. You can also use the hostnamectl command on its own.

```
[root@centos7 ~]# hostnamectl
```

3. Using `nmcli` tool to Change Hostname on CentOS 7

The `nmcli` tool can be used to query and setup the static hostname in "/etc/hostname" file.

5. To check the hostname:

```
[root@centos7 ~]# nmcli general hostname
```

6. To change the hostname:

```
[root@centos7 ~]# nmcli general hostname server01.mydomain.com
```

7. To restart the hostname to force hostnamectl to notice the change in static hostname

```
[root@centos7 ~]# nmcli restart system-hostnamed
```

4. Edit "/etc/hostname" to Change Hostname on CentOS 7 / RHEL 7

Note: this is the simplest but requires a reboot of the server to in order to take effect

You are done with this section.

Part 3: Installing Linux, Apache, Mariadb (MySQL), PHP (LAMP) Stack on CentOS 7 Server

The LAMP stack forms the basic core components for a dynamic, database-driven web site. We'll use "yum" to handle all the required packages. LAMP stack is nothing but software bundle or a platform consisting of Linux operating system, Apache web-server, MySQL (now MariaDB) database server and PHP (or Perl/Python) scripting language. The LAMP stack is used for building heavy duty dynamic websites entirely out of free and open-source software. In this section of the Hands-on guide, we are going to go through on how to install and run LAMP stack. This same guide can be used on RHEL 7.

This section will present us the opportunity to install Apache2 (`httpd`), PHP, MySQL (server and client), and the component that allows PHP to talk to MySQL database.

Step 1: Install Apache on CentOS 7 Server

1. From the Terminal window, run the following `yum` command to install Apache web-server:

```
sudo yum install httpd -y
```

Note: Troubleshooting: In case you encounter dependencies problem, then you can perform `yum` command with "`—skip-broken`" option, as follows:

11. Next, we now need to enable the `httpd` service to start automatically at the boot time, type:

```
sudo systemctl enable httpd.service
```

Note: to disable the `httpd` service at boot time, issue:

```
sudo systemctl disable httpd.service
```

12. Now, we need to start the `httpd` service, type:

```
sudo systemctl start httpd.service
```

13. Finally, test your `httpd` functionality, go to http://localhost or http://your-domain or http://ip-address, and if all works well, it should display **Testing 123...**, as shown in Fig. 32.

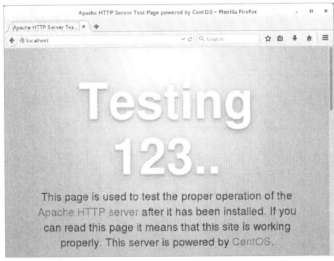

Fig. 32

Note: to stop `httpd` service, run:

```
sudo systemctl stop httpd.service
```

14. To restart `httpd` service, run:

```
sudo systemctl restart httpd.service
```

15. To verify the httpd service status, enter:

```
sudo systemctl is-active httpd.service
```

16. To gracefully restart httpd service status, enter:

```
sudo apachectl graceful
```

17. To test httpd configuration file for errors, enter:

```
sudo apachectl configtest
```

Sample output:

```
Syntax OK
```

18. You're done with Apache2 server setup and testing.

19. You're with this section.

1. The httpd service default configuration
   a. Default config file: /etc/httpd/conf/httpd.conf
   b. Configuration files which load modules: "/etc/httpd/conf.modules.d/" directory (e.g., PHP).
   c. Slect MPMs (Processing Model) as loadable modules [worker, prefolk (default)] and event
      "/etc/httpd/conf.module.d/00-mpm.conf
   d. Default ports: 80 and 443 (SSL)
   e. Default log files: "/var/log/httpd/{access_log, error_log}"

Step 2: Installing MariaDB (MySQL) Database Server

MariaDB is an enhanced, drop-in replacement for MySQL server. RHEL/CentOS 7.x has shift from MySQL to MariaDB for its database management systems needs.

1. Installing MariaDB
6. To install MariaDB run the yum command as follows:

```
sudo yum install mariadb-server maraidb -y
```

7. Start Mariadb (`mariadb`) daemon service, if you haven't done so, run:

```
sudo systemctl start mariadb.service
```

8. To make sure Mariadb (`mariadb`) daemon service start automatically at boot time, type:

```
sudo systemctl enable mariadb.service
```

9. To stop/start and disable mariadb service use the following commands:

```
sudo systemctl stop mariadb.service          # Stop mariadb server
sudo systemctl restart mariadb.service       # Restart mariadb server
sudo systemctl disable mariadb.service       # Disable mariadb server
sudo systemctl is-active mariadb.service      # Is mariadb server
running
```

10. You're with this section.

2. Securing MariaDB

IMPORTANT! Set up the MySQL database root password. Without a password, ANY user on the box can login to mysql as database root. The mysql root account is a separate password from the machine root account.

Now that our MySQL (Mariadb) database is running, we want to run a simple security script that will remove some of the dangerous defaults and also allow us to lock down access to our database a little bit. To do this, from the Terminal window type:

```
sudo mysql_secure_installation
```

The prompt will ask you for your current root password. However, since we have just installed MySQL, you most likely won't have one, so leave it blank by pressing enter. On the next prompt you will be asked if you want to set a root password. Go ahead and enter Y, and follow the instructions as below:

```
Enter current password for root (enter for none):
OK, successfully used password, moving on...

Setting the root password ensures that nobody can log into the MariaDB
root user without the proper authorization.
```

```
New password: password
Re-enter new password: password
Password updated successfully!
Reloading privilege tables..
 ... Success!
```

Note: for the rest of the questions, you should simply hit **"ENTER"** key through each prompt to accept default values, or change as desired. This will remove some of the sample users and databases, disable remote root logins, and load these rules, so that MySQL immediately respects the changes we have made. However, since this is a non production server, which are only using for training, we have left some of the settings as is. (**Note:** for production server please do ensure that the server full locked-down).

11. We can now login into our database as follows (enter the password set above):

```
$ mysql -u root -p
```

```
[nadmin@centos7 ~]$ mysql -u root -p
Enter password:
Welcome to the MariaDB monitor.  Commands end with ; or \g.
Your MariaDB connection id is 9
Server version: 5.5.44-MariaDB MariaDB Server

Copyright (c) 2000, 2015, Oracle, MariaDB Corporation Ab and others.

Type 'help;' or '\h' for help. Type '\c' to clear the current input statement.

MariaDB [(none)]> 
```

Fig. 33

12. You're with this section.

3: Creating Database on MariaDB on CentOS-7

17. Now we need to create a sample database and database user for a sample application. You will use this database and username in your database connection string. The "GRANT" statement actually creates a new MYSQL user account.

```
MariaDB> GREATE DATABASE webdb;
MariaDB> GRANT ALL PRIVILEGES ON webdb.* TO 'webuser'@'localhost'
IDENTIFIED BY 'webpass';
MariaDB> FLUSH PRIVILEGES;
MariaDB>exit
```

128

```
MariaDB [(none)]> CREATE DATABASE webdb;
Query OK, 1 row affected (0.00 sec)

MariaDB [(none)]> GRANT ALL PRIVILEGES ON webdb.* TO 'webuser'@'localhost' IDENT
IFIED BY 'webpass';
Query OK, 0 rows affected (0.03 sec)

MariaDB [(none)]> FLUSH PRIVILEGES;
Query OK, 0 rows affected (0.41 sec)

MariaDB [(none)]>
```

Fig. 34

18. You can check if your "webdb" database has been successfully created, using "show databases" command.

```
MariaDB [(none)]> SHOW DATABASES;
+--------------------+
| Database           |
+--------------------+
| information_schema |
| mysql              |
| performance_schema |
| webdb              |
+--------------------+
4 rows in set (0.12 sec)

MariaDB [(none)]>
```

Fig. 35

19. You're done with MySQL setup, configuration and testing.

20. You're done with this section

Step 3: Installing PostgreSQL on CentOS-7

Here you'll learn how to install the PostgreSQL database server and the component required to write PHP scripts that communicate with postgresql. Do this if you didn't initially install it. We use yum to handle dependencies and gather all of the required packages. For more information on PostgreSQL, see http://www.postgresql.org

1. Installing & Configuring Postgresql on CentOS 7

1. To install PostgreSQL and the component that allows PHP to talk to it, run:

```
# yum -y install postgresql postgresql-server php-pgsql postgresql-
contrib
```

2. We now need to initialize PostgreSQL database, Run:

129

```
sudo service postgresql initdb
```

```
[nadmin@centos7 ~]$ sudo service postgresql initdb
[sudo] password for nadmin:
Hint: the preferred way to do this is now "postgresql-setup initdb"
Initializing database ... OK

[nadmin@centos7 ~]$ █
```
——— Fig. 36

Note 1: the now preferred way is:

```
sudo service postgresql-setup initdb
```

Note 2: when you start postgresql for the first time, it'll initialize the database

3. To start postgresql service, type:

```
sudo systemctl start postgresql
```

4. Configure the new service to start automatically on boot:

```
sudo systemctl enable postgresql
```

5. You're done with this section

2. Creating your first database with Postgresql on CentOS 7
6. Start the postgresql interactive shell and create your first user and database.

```
# su - postgres                                    \\the dash "-" is important!
```

4. Next, issue the command, "psql template1", to enter the default postgresql database

```
-bash-4.2$ psql template1
```

The whole sequence is as shown in Fig. 37.

```
[root@centos7 ~]# su - postgres
-bash-4.2$ psql template1
psql (9.2.13)
Type "help" for help.     I

template1=# █
```
—————————————————————————— Fig. 37

130

Note: "template1"is the database that is included by default with PostgreSQL.

7. Check the version of your postgresql database:

```
template1=# select version();
                                         version
-----------------------------------------------------------------------------

------------------------------
 PostgreSQL 9.2.13 on x86_64-redhat-linux-gnu, compiled by gcc (GCC) 4.8.3 20140
911 (Red Hat 4.8.3-9), 64-bit
(1 row)

template1=#
```
Fig. 38

8. Now create dbase user "webadmin" and make him a superuser:

```
-bash-4.2$ createuser -P webadmin
Enter password for new role:
Enter it again:
Shall the new role be a superuser? (y/n) y
-bash-4.2$
```

9. Next create the database "webdb"

```
-bash-4.2$
-bash-4.2$ createdb -O webadmin webdb
-bash-4.2$
```

13. Now connect into your newly created database:

```
-bash-4.2$ psql webdb
Psql (9.2.13)
Type "help" for help.

web_db=#
```

14. Logout of your dbase:

```
webdb=# \q
-bash-4.1$ logout
[root@centos7 ~]#
```

15. Edit the **postgres** host based access "pg_hba" configuration file:

```
# vi /var/lib/pgsql/data/pg_hba.conf
```

131

16. Modify the local line to use "md5" based authentication rather than "peer". Please review the PostgreSQL documentation before making this change and take the security

```
local          all          all                 md5
```

17. Restart the postgresql database service.

```
# systemctl reload postgresql          \\ restarts postgresql
```

18. Log back into the server

```
# su - postgres
```

19. Test your connection.

```
# psql -U webadmin webdb          \\ or psql webdb
```

```
[root@centos7 ~]# su - postgres
Last login: Wed Dec 23 13:40:30 EST 2015 on pts/1
-bash-4.2$ psql -U webadmin webdb
Password for user webadmin:
psql (9.2.13)
Type "help" for help.

webdb=> \q
-bash-4.2$ logout
[root@centos7 ~]#
```
Fig. 39

20. You're now done with section on installing and configuring PostgreSQL database.

Step 4: Install & Test PHP Installation on CentOS 7

21. To install PHP and modules such as gd/myql type the following yum command:

```
sudo yum install php php-mysql php-pgsql php-gd php-peer -y
```

22. Next you must restart the httpd (Apache) service, type:

```
sudo systemctl restart httpd.service
```

23. Now we need to search all other PHP modules, enter:

```
sudo yum search php-
```

132

See sample below:

```
[root@centos7 ~]# yum search php-
Loaded plugins: fastestmirror, langpacks
Loading mirror speeds from cached hostfile
 * base: mirror.liquidtelecom.com
 * extras: mirror.liquidtelecom.com
 * updates: mirror.liquidtelecom.com
============================ N/S matched: php- ================================
php-bcmath.x86_64 : A module for PHP applications for using the bcmath library
php-cli.x86_64 : Command-line interface for PHP
php-common.x86_64 : Common files for PHP
php-dba.x86_64 : A database abstraction layer module for PHP applications
php-devel.x86_64 : Files needed for building PHP extensions
php-embedded.x86_64 : PHP library for embedding in applications
php-enchant.x86_64 : Enchant spelling extension for PHP applications
php-fpm.x86_64 : PHP FastCGI Process Manager
php-gd.x86_64 : A module for PHP applications for using the gd graphics library
php-intl.x86_64 : Internationalization extension for PHP applications
php-ldap.x86_64 : A module for PHP applications that use LDAP
php-mbstring.x86_64 : A module for PHP applications which need multi-byte string
                    : handling
php-mysql.x86_64 : A module for PHP applications that use MySQL databases
php-mysqlnd.x86_64 : A module for PHP applications that use MySQL databases
php-odbc.x86_64 : A module for PHP applications that use ODBC databases
php-pdo.x86_64 : A database access abstraction module for PHP applications
php-pear.noarch : PHP Extension and Application Repository framework
```

Fig. 40

24. Following the above steps for Apaache2 setup, the document root for Apache is "/var/www/hmtl/"

25. Create a test PHP script file called "/var/www/html/test.php" and place it in the documents root. A useful test script sample:

```
sudo vi /var/www/html/test.php
```

and appended the following code:

```
<?php
    phpinfo(INFO_GENERAL);
?>
```

26. Now fire-up your browser and point it to: http://localhost/test.php and you should the browser rendered as shown in Fig. 41.

133

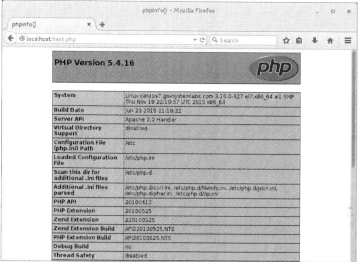

Fig. 41

27. You're done with PHP5 setup and testing.

28. Hooray! – Enjoy working with LAMP server.

Part 4: Installing and Configuring Webmin on CentOS 7

Administering Linux and Unix-based servers does not need to be the scourge of your work day. With a handy tool called **Webmin** as part of your arsenal, you can regain full control of your servers' setup and configuration via the Web browser.

Webmin is the most powerful administration tool in its nature. You can use it, for example, to setup DNS Server, but I will not go over it in detail because you will learn more about it in the coming modules. It is not difficult to use Webmin because it is web based, in any event, you should also know that you can use it remotely to administrate your network servers.

Step 1: Install Webmin

Now we need to install **Webmin** to ease your server administration pain!

1. To Install Webmin and get started, drop by www.webmin.com and download the latest release. You can use RPMs for RHE/CentOS and related systems that support binary installations or

you can build Webmin from source. Webmin also supports a large number of UNIX variants, including Mac OS X.

2. Now download the latest Webmin using the following command or from here. Or use the "wget" command download from the terminal. (Note: at the time of the writing: "webmin-1.770-1.noarch.rpm") file:

```
wget http://prdownloads.sourceforge.net/webadmin/webmin-1.770-1.noarch.rpm
```

3. To install the **rpm**, simply open a terminal session, change to the download directory, and type in: "rpm -ivh webmin*", i.e.,:

```
# rpm -ivh webmin*
```

- When done, open you Web browser and go to: http://localhost:10000 or in our case http://mydomain.com:10000

4. Your browser will be promise you with "**Error –Bad Request**", as shown in Fig. 42. Click on the link to proceed and accept the Untrusted certificate.

Fig. 42

5. From Fig. 43, login with root user credentials and click on Login.

Fig. 43

135

6. Login with root user name and you should be able to access the Webmin admin page as shown in Fig. 44. You may be prompted to update Webmin! Take your time to hand around to acquaint yourself with the tool. Noticed some of the Servers installed from the left hand pane.

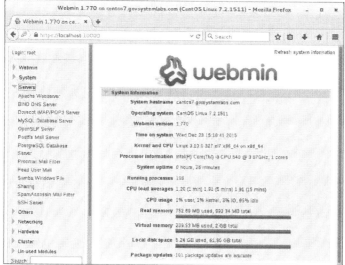

Fig. 44

7. Click **Logout** to exit Webmin

8. You're done with this section.

Part 5: Install and Configure vsFTPD Server on CentOS 7

The Very Secure FTP Daemon (vsftpd) is designed from the ground up to be fast, stable, and, most importantly, secure. Its ability to handle large numbers of connections efficiently and securely is why vsftpd is the only stand-alone FTP distributed with Red Hat Enterprise Linux.

Step 1: Install and Configure vsFTPD Server

1. First, let's verify if vsftpd is installed on your system:

```
# yum list installed | grep ftp
```

```
[root@centos7 ~]# yum list installed | grep ftp
vsftpd.x86_64                         3.0.2-10.el7                    @anaconda
[root@centos7 ~]# █
```

Fig. 45

Note: if nothing shown, then standard CentOS packages seem not have `vsftp` and `proftp`, then you can install these with very easily (via `yum` or `rpm` utility to install)

2. To install `vsftpd` using YUM, run:

```
# yum install vsftpd ftp -y
```

Note: you can also use "`rpm -iUVh vsftpd*.rpm`" (in your CentOS-7 DVD ISO under Centos folder). You can also grab it from DVD.

3. You can now edit "`vsftpd.conf`" file which is the main configuration file for vsFTP and make the necessary changes.

4. But, for best practices, first we need to take backup copy before making any changes to it.

```
# cp /etc/vsftpd/vsftpd.conf /etc/vsftpd/vsftpd.conf.Bkup
```

5. To start `vsftpd` service, type:

```
sudo systemctl start vsftpd.service
```

6. Let's enable `vsftpd` to auto start at boot-time, issue the command:

```
sudo systemctl enable vsftpd.service
```

7. Now check if `ftp` client is running, using either one of these:

```
# netstat -nap | grep 21
```

or:

```
# ps -ef | grep -i ftp
```

```
[root@centos7 ~]# ps -ef | grep -i ftp
root      4169     1  0 05:15 ?        00:00:00 /usr/sbin/vsftpd /etc/vsftpd/vsf
tpd.conf
root      4249  3972  0 05:18 pts/0    00:00:00 grep --color=auto -i ftp
[root@centos7 ~]# █
```

Fig. 46

8. You're done with this section.

Step 2: Securing vsFTPD Server

Before we can make our vsFTP server fully functional, we first need to do some house keeping to make it secure against hacking etc.

9. Now using the favorite text editor, let's open the config file to make some changes:

```
# nano /etc/vsftpd/vsftpd.conf
```

Note: find the "anonymous_enable=YES" and change the value to "NO" to disable anonymous FTP access.

```
anonymous_enable=NO
```

10. Next, uncomment the below line (Line no: 100) to restrict users to only their home directory. Local user will be **'chroot jailed'** and thus denied access to any other parts of the server.

```
chroot_local_user=YES
```

Others:

```
## Uncomment ##
ascii_upload_enable=YES
ascii_download_enable=YES
## Uncomment - Enter your Welcome message - This is optional ##
ftpd_banner=Welcome to GOVSYSTEMLABS FTP Service
```

11. Allow local user to be able to login by changing the "local_enable" setting to "YES"

```
local_enable=YES
```

12. Next, if you want local user to be able to write to a directory, then change the "write_enable" setting to "YES":

```
write_enable=YES
```

13. Finally, add lines below at the end of the file to enable passive mode and allow chroot writable

```
allow_writeable_chroot=YES
user_localtime=YES
pasv_enable=Yes
pasv_min_port=40000
```

138

```
pasv_max_port=40100
```

14. Save and exit the file.

15. Restart `vsftpd` service:

```
sudo systemctl restart vsftpd.service
```

16. Next, you should that ensure your firewall is not blocking (you might temporary disable firewall to diagnose first). Alternatively, you can open `port 21` on the firewall.

```
firewall-cmd --permanent --add-service=ftp
firewall-cmd --reload
```

```
[root@centos7 ~]# firewall-cmd --permanent --add-service=ftp
success
[root@centos7 ~]# firewall-cmd --reload
success
[root@centos7 ~]#
```
Fig. 47

Note: alternatively, you can also use port number to allow port 21 through instead as follows:

```
firewall-cmd --permanent --add-port=21/tcp
firewall-cmd --reload
```

17. Let's now login with **Net Admin** credentials that set during initial installation, changes desired.

```
# ftp localhost
```

```
[nadmin@centos7 ~]$ ftp localhost
Trying ::1...
Connected to localhost (::1).
220 (vsFTPd 3.0.2)
Name (localhost:nadmin):
331 Please specify the password.
Password:
230 Login successful.
Remote system type is UNIX.
Using binary mode to transfer files.
ftp> ls
229 Entering Extended Passive Mode (|||52011|).
150 Here comes the directory listing.
drwxr-xr-x    2 1000     1000             6 Dec 23 02:19 Desktop
drwxr-xr-x    3 1000     1000            27 Dec 23 17:45 Documents
drwxr-xr-x    2 1000     1000             6 Dec 23 02:19 Downloads
drwxr-xr-x    2 1000     1000             6 Dec 23 02:19 Music
drwxr-xr-x    2 1000     1000             6 Dec 23 02:19 Pictures
drwxr-xr-x    2 1000     1000             6 Dec 23 02:19 Public
drwxr-xr-x    2 1000     1000             6 Dec 23 02:19 Templates
drwxr-xr-x    2 1000     1000             6 Dec 23 02:19 Videos
226 Directory send OK.
ftp> exit
221 Goodbye.
[nadmin@centos7 ~]$
```
Fig. 48

Note: you'll be required to login with appropriate username credentials. In case you get login failure , then check troubleshooting notes at the end of this training manual.

18. You can also test `vsftpd` from your browser: ftp://localhost or http:/domain-name or http://ip-address, and browse to the desired folder.

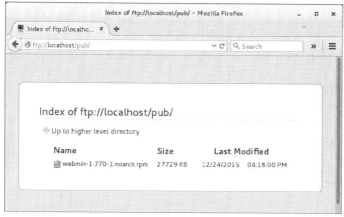

Fig. 49

Note: the `pub` folder is located under "`/var/ftp`" directory, and as you can see I have one file listed in it.

19. The `condrestart` (conditional restart) option only starts `vsftpd` if it is currently running. This option is useful for scripts, because it does not start the daemon if it is not running.
To conditionally restart the server, as root type:

```
sudo condrestart vsftpd.service
```

20. You should be able to upload and download files as we had allowed earlier.

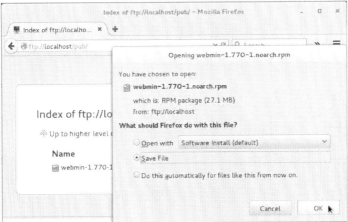

Fig. 50

21. To stop `vsftpd` service:

```
sudo systemctl stop vsftpd.service
```

22. You're done with this section.

1 Login to FTP as a Particular User

3. If you wish to login to FTP using a particular user, then fire-up browser and then navigate to "`ftp://username@FTP-Server-IP-address`". You be asked to enter the password of user, and then you be logged in, as shown in Fig. 51.

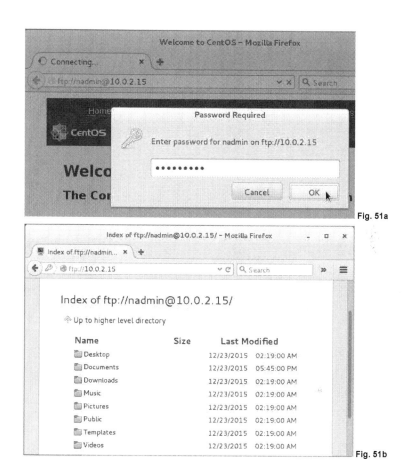

Fig. 51a

Fig. 51b

4. You're done with this section.

Step 3: Secure FTP Server

In order to support secure remote connections to your server, you will need to install the OpenSSH package. This package will come in handy in the future to support administrative tasks on the system. Secure File Transfer Protocol (SFTP) is used to encrypt connections between clients and the FTP server. It's highly recommended to use SFTP because data is transferred over encrypted connection using SSH-tunnel on port 22. By default this package is already installed in the CentOS 7 server option.

1. Install and Configure openSSH-Server

Basically openSSH-server package to enable SFTP to work.

7. To install OpenSSH, issue the following command (skip if you have installed it!):

```
sudo yum install openssh-server -y
```

8. Start and enable sshd service, type:

```
sudo systemctl start sshd
```

```
sudo systemctl enable sshd
```

9. Your SFTP server is configure and ready at your service.

10. To log into a remote computer that is running OpenSSH, you use the ssh username@hostname command, replacing username with a valid user name on the computer you are trying to log into, and replacing hostname with either the fully qualified host name (e.g. example.com) of your server, or it's IP address (e.g., 10.0.2.15).

11. For example, let's login remotely to server via SSH as user nadmin with password xxxxx and IP address 10.0.2.15, run:

```
ssh nadmin@10.0.2.15
```

Note: you'll be asked to respond to yes/no and also enter root's password. And as you can observe we have successfully remotely logged in as user root. Now you can use your usual Linux commands to remotely manage your Linux server.

```
[root@centos7 ~]# ssh nadmin@10.0.2.15
The authenticity of host '10.0.2.15 (10.0.2.15)' can't be established.
ECDSA key fingerprint is 7b:95:bc:b6:82:b7:d8:52:f1:29:01:89:fa:05:94:34.
Are you sure you want to continue connecting (yes/no)? yes
Warning: Permanently added '10.0.2.15' (ECDSA) to the list of known hosts.
nadmin@10.0.2.15's password:
Last login: Thu Dec 24 11:09:56 2015
[nadmin@centos7 ~]$ logout
Connection to 10.0.2.15 closed.
[root@centos7 ~]#
```
Fig. 52

12. You're done with this section

2. FTP User Creation

8. Create user `mjones` (Mary Jones) with "`/sbin/nologin`" shell and also add `ftpaccess` group

```
# groupadd ftpaccess

# useradd -m mjones -s /sbin/nologin -g ftpaccess

# passwd mjones
```

9. Assign root ownership for the home for chroot access and modify permission as follows:

```
# chown root /home/mjones
# chmod 750 /home/mjones
```

10. Next, create a directory www inside `mjones` home directory for writing and modify ownership:

```
# mkdir /home/mjones/www
# chown mjones:ftpaccess /home/mjones/www
```

11. Finally, `mjones` should now be able to use both `ftp` and `sftp`. He can also upload files in www directory.

12. You're done with this section.

3. Adding existing users to ftpaccesss

13. To add the existing users to our ftpaccess group, perform the following actions:

```
# usermod nadmin -g ftpaccess
# chown root /home/szulu
# chmod 750 /home/szulu
# mkdir /home/szulu/www
# chown szulu:ftpaccess /home/szulu/www
```

```
[root@centos7 ~]# ssh szulu@10.0.2.15
szulu@10.0.2.15's password:
[szulu@centos7 ~]$ ls
www
[szulu@centos7 ~]$ logout
Connection to 10.0.2.15 closed.
```

Fig. 53

Note: for those using Windows based systems, they can install PuTTY: a free telnet/ssh client.

144

14. You're done with section.

4. Allowing FTP Access to Files Outside the Home Directory Chroot

Occasionally once we have setup an FTP server software (e.g., proFTP, vsFTP etc.), we might at times be faced with dilemma, i.e., we want to **restrict** the access that ftp users will (in this case limit access to files normally in their home directory), but also we may want to allow them access to **another** directory that is normally in a different location (e.g., in case of a project development files for whatever work they are doing).

6. As you have seen above, if configure the **chroot restriction** for the ftp users, then as expected they will be **locked in the chrooted folder** (e.g., in their home directory or as in the earlier example the www directory we created, and which is shown below). If try to go around this restriction by creating a `symlink` to the other directory that they need access to, it will not allow to change into that directory (i.e., break out of the chroot) and this very normal.

```
[nadmin@centos7 ~]$ ssh szulu@10.0.2.15
szulu@10.0.2.15's password:
Last login: Fri Dec 25 05:43:31 2015 from 10.0.2.15
[szulu@centos7 ~]$ ls
www
[szulu@centos7 ~]$
```
                                                                            Fig. 54

7. Now let's look at an hypothetical situation, and consider a case where we are using **vsftpd** and one user "ftp_user". Further, chroot restriction is enabled on the ftp accounts and his home is in "/home/ftp_user". However, we need to provide the user access to another directory "/var/www/swdev". This concept is also applicable to other ftp server software not just **vsftpd**.

8. As was mentioned earlier the key important point here is to ensure that under **vftpd** configuration file, we have:

```
chroot_local_user=YES
```

Note: alternatively one way to overcome this limitation is to disable chroot and allow the **ftp** users full access to all the system files. However, for best practice, this is not at all recommended. The solution to this problem, is to **mount the needed directory using the -bind parameter**.

To achieve this, from your terminal enter:

```
mkdir /home/ftp_user/www_swdev
mount --bind /var/www/swdev /home/ftp_user/www_swdev
```

145

Note: now the **ftp** users should now be able to see the needed files in home directory and use them in his ftp clients as if they were local files.

9. Finally, in case you need to make this configuration permanent, then you can either add the mount command in some startup script or you can just include a line "/etc/fstab" as follows:

```
/var/www/swdev  /home/ftp_user/www_swdev      none  bind  0      0
```

Note: the vsftpd configuration file can look like:

```
/etc/vsftpd.con
listen=YES
anonymous_enable=NO
Local_enable=NO
write_enable=YES
dirmesaage_enable=YES
xferlog_enable=YES
connect_from_port_20=YES
chroot_local_users=YES
ssecure_chroot_dir=/var/run/vsftpd
pam_service_name=vsftp
rsa_cert_file=/etc/ssl/certs/vsftpd.pem
```

10. You're done with section.

Step 4. Install FileZilla FTP Client on CentOS 7

FileZilla is arguably the most popular FTP client in the world, and the good thing,, it is a free and platform independent i.e., it can be installed on both Linux, Windows and Mac OS. However, FileZilla does not come with the default CentOS repository, so we need to use Fedora EPEL repository instead. Installation is very simple, all we need to do is to first install the EPEL repository and then install FileZilla suing the yum command.

1. Install EPEL Repo on CentOS 7
1. For RHEL based system, you install filezilla using yum command as follows:

```
sudo yum -y install epel-release
```

2. You now simply install filezilla using yum command as follows:

```
sudo yum install filezilla
```

3. Now to open the Filezilla client system click **Applications** → **Internet** → **FileZilla**, as shown in Fig. 55.

Fig. 55

4. From Fig. 56, enter the FTP server hostname address, username, password and port number. Click "**Quickconnect**" to login.

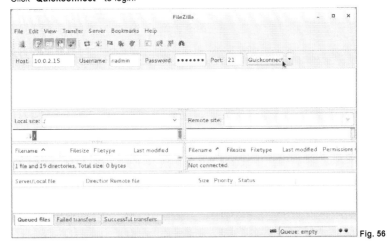

Fig. 56

5. If all is OK, you should now be presented with Fig. 57 showing successful login.

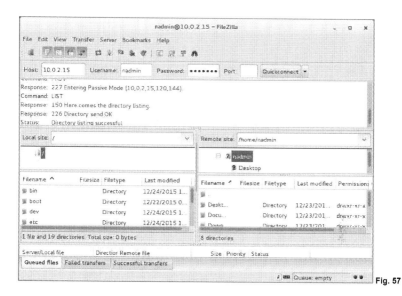
Fig. 57

6. You are done with this section.

Step 5: Users Login

7. Let's login using **ftp** client, as user nadmin with password xxxxxx, as follows:

```
[nadmin@centos7 ~]$ ftp localhost
```

```
[nadmin@centos7 ~]$ ftp localhost
Trying ::1...
Connected to localhost (::1).
220 Welcome to GOVSYSTEMLABS FTP service.
Name (localhost:nadmin):
331 Please specify the password.
Password:
230 Login successful.
Remote system type is UNIX.
Using binary mode to transfer files.
ftp>
```
Fig. 58

8. While still logged in as user Net Admin (nadmin), try to change to "/var/ftp/pub" directory, and you should be able to access all files and folder under this directory.

```
ftp> cd /var/ftp/pub
```

```
ftp> cd /var/ftp/pub/
250 Directory successfully changed.
ftp> ls
229 Entering Extended Passive Mode (|||27509|).
150 Here comes the directory listing.
-rw-r--r--    1 0         0        28393526 Dec 24 16:18 webmin-1.770-1.noarch.rp
m
226 Directory send OK.
ftp>
```

Fig. 59

9. Now let's change to "/home", and although you can see all the other users' home folders, you should **only** be able to access files and folder under only you home directory.

```
ftp> cd /home
```

```
ftp> cd /home/
250 Directory successfully changed.
ftp> ls
229 Entering Extended Passive Mode (|||61903|).
150 Here comes the directory listing.
drwxr-x---    4 0         1001           84 Dec 24 22:58 mjones
drwx------   17 1000      1000         4096 Dec 25 10:09 nadmin
drwxr-x---    4 0         1001           84 Dec 24 23:26 szulu
226 Directory send OK.
ftp>
```

Fig. 59

- Now try to change into user szulu home directory:

```
ftp> cd /home/szulu
550 Failed to change directory.
ftp>
```

- Now try login to your own home directory:

```
ftp> cd /home/nadmin
250 Directory successfully changed.
ftp
```

10. When done, close the ftp connect and exit, as follows:

```
ftp>
ftp> close
221 Goodbye.
ftp> quit
```

149

```
[root@centos7 ~]#
```

11. You're done with this section.

Part 6: Install JDK8 on CentOS 7

CentOS-7 / RHEL 7 now comes pre-installed with OpenJDK, which you can verify by typing:

```
]# java -version
```

```
[root@centos7 ~]# java -version
openjdk version "1.8.0_65"
OpenJDK Runtime Environment (build 1.8.0_65-b17)
OpenJDK 64-Bit Server VM (build 25.65-b01, mixed mode)
[root@centos7 ~]#
```

Fig. 60

However, in case you wish to install the Sun Java, now Oracle, you can perform the following procedure:

3. To download Java SE SDK 8 just go to
   http://www.oracle.com/technetwork/java/javase/downloads/jdk8-downloads-2133151.html
   , and follow the instructions to download a file called: "jdk-8u65-linux-x64-rpm", and save
   it in /opt/java directory. You may have to create the java directory if it's not there.

7. Create directory "/usr/java" directory.

```
sudo mkdir /usr/java
```

8. Copy "jdk-8u65-linux-x64.tar.gz" to "/usr/java" directory and untar it.

```
sudo cp jdk-8u65-linux-x64.tar.gz /usr/java

cd /usr/java

sudo tar -xvzf jdk-8u65-linux-x64.tar.gz
```

9. Insert the following lines inside /etc/profile or /root/.bashrc.

```
export JAVA_HOME=/usr/java/jdk1.80_65
export PATH=$JAVA_HOME/bin:$PATH
```

10. Next, execute the following command to update the changes made without having to reboot the system::

```
source /etc/profile"
```

11. Before we begin, we will need to ensure that JAVA_HOME is correctly set. To do this, open a terminal and type the following:

```
# echo $JAVA_HOME

# java -version
```

```
[root@centos7 ~]# echo $JAVA_HOME
/usr/java/jdk1.8.0_65
[root@centos7 ~]#
[root@centos7 ~]# java -version
java version "1.8.0_65"
Java(TM) SE Runtime Environment (build 1.8.0_65-b17)
Java HotSpot(TM) 64-Bit Server VM (build 25.65-b01, mixed mode)
[root@centos7 ~]#
```
_____ Fig. 61

12. You're done with this section

Part 7: Install Apache Ant Package on CentOS 7

Apache Ant is a Java library and command-line tool whose mission is to drive process described in build files as targets and extension points dependent upon each other. That main known usage of Ant is the build of Java applications. Ant supplies a number of built-in tasks allowing to compile, assemble, test and run Java applications,. Ant can be used effectively to build non Java applications, e.g., C or C++ applications. More generally, Ant can be used to pilot any type of process which can be described in terms of targets and tasks. That is Apache Ant builds a Java project from its source code and libraries by using a similar XML file.

7. To download Apache Ant, just go to http://ant.apache.org/bindownload.cgi, and follow the instructions to download a file called: "apache-ant-1.9.6-bin.tar.gz", and save it in /usr/ directory.

Note: you can also use "wget" command to down it as follows

```
sudo mkdir /usr/ant

wget http://www.eu.apache.org/dist//ant/binaries/apache-ant-1.9.6-bin.tar.gz

sudo tar -xvzf apache-ant-1.9.6-bin.tar.gz

sudo cp -arp * /usr/ant
```

151

8. Add Apache Ant to the profile file `"/etc/profile"`, so that it now look like:

```
export JAVA_HOME=/usr/java/jdk1.8.0_65
export ANT_HOME=/usr/ant
export PATH=$JAVA_HOME/bin:$ANT_HOME/bin:$PATH
```

9. Use the `source` command for the changes to take effect (**Note**: you may need to reboot the system):

```
# source /etc/profile
```

10. Before we begin, we will need to ensure that `"ANT_HOME"` is correctly set. To do this, we open a terminal and type the following:

```
# echo $ANT_HOME
/usr/ant
```

11. Verify that Apache Ant is successfully installed

```
# ant -version
Apache Ant(TM) version 1.9.6 compiled on June 29 2015
```

```
[root@centos7 ~]# echo $ANT_HOME
/usr/ant
[root@centos7 ~]#
[root@centos7 ~]# ant -version
Apache Ant(TM) version 1.9.6 compiled on June 29 2015
[root@centos7 ~]#
```
Fig. 62

12. You're done with this section

Part 8: Install Apache Tomcat 9 Application Server on CentOS 7

11. To download Tomcat 9, just go to http://tomcat.apache.org/, and follow the instructions to download a file called: **apache-tomcat-9.0.0.M1.tar.gz**, and save it in /usr/ directory.

12. Next, we are going to install tomcat in /usr directory, run:

```
# cd /usr
# tar -xvzf apache-tomcat-9.0.0.M1.tar.gz
```

13. While still under `"/usr"` directory, issue the following command to create a symbolic link to the tomcat directory.

152

```
# ln -s apache-tomcat-9.0.0.M1 tomcat
```

14. Add Ant to the profile file /etc/profile, so that it now look like:

```
export JAVA_HOME=/usr/java/jdk1.8.0_65
export ANT_HOME=/usr/ant
export CATALINA_HOME=/usr/tomcat
export PATH=$JAVA_HOME/bin:$CATALINA_HOME/bin:$ANT_HOME/bin:$PATH
CLASSPATH=$CLASSPATH:.
```

15. issue the following command to update "/etc/profile" file:

```
# source /etc/profile
```

16. Before we begin, we will need to ensure that CATALINA_HOME is correctly set. To do this, we open a terminal and run:

```
# echo $CATALINA_HOME
/usr/tomcat
```

17. If everything is fine, you can start Tomcat with the following command.

```
# $CATALINA_HOME/bin/startup.sh
```

```
[root@centos7 usr]# $CATALINA_HOME/bin/startup.sh
Using CATALINA_BASE:   /usr/tomcat
Using CATALINA_HOME:   /usr/tomcat
Using CATALINA_TMPDIR: /usr/tomcat/temp
Using JRE_HOME:        /usr/java/jdk1.8.0_65
Using CLASSPATH:       /usr/tomcat/bin/bootstrap.jar:/usr/tomcat/bin/tomcat-juli
.jar
Tomcat started.
[root@centos7 usr]#
```
Fig. 63

18. Logout and login again for the environment setup to take effect:

19. To verify that the Tomcat installation is complete, open a Web browser, and type in following URL: http://<your-tomcat_IP>:8080, DNS, or you can also simply use http://localhost:8080. If everything is fine, you should be able to see a web page such as one shown in Fig. 64.

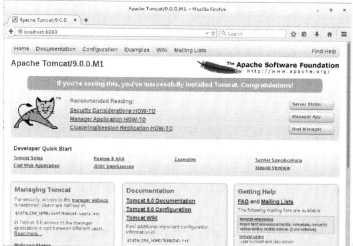

Fig. 64

20. To stop Tomcat, type:

```
# $CATALINA_HOME/bin/shutdown.sh
```

4. You're done with section.

11.1 Accessing Apache Tomcat 9 manager and host-manager webapps

In this section you'll learn how to setup Tomcat 9 manager role in order to access http://localhost:8080/manager/html, which will prompt for a username and password.

To do this, you'll need to modify "/usr/tomcat/conf/tomcat-users.xml" file to add the roles and user as follows:

1. Using your favorite Text editor, open:

```
# vi /usr/tomcat/conf/tomcat-users.xml
```

and you need to add he following text (Note: change as desired!)

```
<tomcat-users>
<role rolename="admin-gui"/>
<role rolename="admin-scrip"/>
<user username="tomcat" password="s3cret1" roles="admin-gui,admin-script"/>
<user username="user1" password="mypassword" roles="standard, managerscript"/>
```

154

```
</tomcat-users>
```

2. Now restarted tomcat service, run:

```
# $CATALINA_HOME/bin/startup.sh
```

3. Using appropriate user credentials you should be able to access
   http://localhost:8080/manager/html, or http://ip-address:8080/manager/html.

11.2 Moving around Apache Tomcat 9 under command-line

5. Open anew Terminal widow and change to /usr/tomcat/ folder which is writeable and run:

```
ls /usr/tomcat/
```

Note: you should see these directories bin, conf, lib, logs, webapps, temp, and work

   c. **webapps** - is where your servlets will go (or at least a xml file that points to them) as a
test download this war file http://simple.souther.us/SimpleServlet.war

   d. Once you have .war file, then you can use the tomcat management page and select
war file to deploy (in the deploy section) to upload this file to your server.

6. Optionally you can download the .war files directly to your the webapps folder

```
cd /usr/tomcat/weapps/
wget http://simple.souther.us/SimpleServlet.war
```

tomcat should recognize the war file and expand it with everything you need

7. Point your browse to http://serverip:8080/SimpleServlet/

Fig. 65

155

8. You're done with this section.

Part 9: How to Install & Configure Backup Server using Bacula and Webmin

In this section you're going to learn how to install and configure a Backup server using Bacula and Webmin on CentOS 7 which also should work on REL 7, Fedora 23 and Scientific Linux distros too. Bacula is an open source, network backup software, used to all Systems Administrators to manage backup, recovery and send the verification of data from any system in any location across network. Thus, its very flexible and robust, which makes it, while slightly cumbersome to configure, suitable for backups in many situations. It's important to note, that a backup system is an important component in most server infrastructures, as recovering from data loss is often a critical part of disaster recovery plans, and a critical component on how an enterprise manages risks to company data.

In this section of the hands-on tutorial, you will learn how to install and configure the server components of Bacula on a CentOS 7 / RHEL 7 server. We will configure Bacula to perform a weekly job that creates a local backup (i.e., a backup of its own host). This, by itself, is not a particularly compelling use of Bacula, but it will provide you with a good starting point for creating backups of your other servers, i.e., the backup clients. Finally, you also learn how to create backups of your other, remote, servers by installing and configuring the Bacula client, and configuring the Bacula server.

1. Prerequisites for Bacula Backup Server
4. One must have a superuser (sudo) access on your CentOS 7 / RHEL 7 server. The server must have adequate disk space for all of the backups that you plan on retaining at given time.

5. It's important that you configure Bacula to use the private FQDN of the server or its IP address. In case you don't have a DNS setup, then instead its recommended to use the appropriate IP addresses. In case you don't private networking enabled, then you can replace all the network connection information given here with network addresses that are reachable by the server in question (e.g., public IP addresses or VPN tunnels).

6. It's also assumed that SELinux is disabled or you are able to troubleshoot SELinux related issues on your own.

2. Overview of Bacula Components
Bacula backup server is compost of several software components, and it follows the server client backup model, with main components, which we concentrate on, being the **backup-server** and the **backup clients**. However, we will mention them here. The Bacula server (or backup server), is made up of the following components:

- **Bacula Director (DIR):** is the software that controls the backup and restore operations, which are performed by File and Storage daemons

156

- **Storage Daemon (SD):** is the software which performs reads and writes on the storage devices used for backups.

- **Catalog:** is the services that maintain a database of files that are backed up. The database is stored in an SQL database e.g., MySQL (MariaDB) or PostgreSQL.

- **Bacula Console:** is a command-line interface that allows the backup administrator to interact with, and control, Bacula Director.

A Bacula backup client, i.e., the server that will be backed up, runs the **File Daemon (FD)** component. The File Daemon is the software that provides the Bacula server (i.e., Director) access to the data that is to be backed up. We will also refer to these servers as (backup clients) or clients. In this hands-on tutorial, we are going to configure the backup server to create a backup of its own filesystem. That is, the backup server will also be a backup client, and will run the File Damon component. Once you acquire the skills you can then go ahead and set the clients backup.

Step 1: Install Bacula Backup Server on CentOS-7

To install a Bacula backup server, we'll be using MySQL (MariaDB) for database, one can also use PostgreSQL database, with server's info shown below (changes as desired):

Backup Server Hostname: centos7.govsystemlabs.com
IP Address: 10.0.2.15

1. Use yum command to install Bacula server, as follows:

    ```
    # yum install bacula-director-mysql bacula-console bacula-client
    bacula-storage-mysql mysql-devel -y
    ```

2. Now we need to run the following sets of commands to create database and necessary tables for Bacula server:

    ```
    # /usr/libexec/bacula/grant_mysql_privileges -u root -p
    # /usr/libexec/bacula/create_mysql_databse -u root -p
    # /usr/libexec/bacula/make_mysql_tables -u root -p
    # /usr/libexec/bacula/grant_bacula_privileges -u root -p
    ```

3. Next set bacula user password on MySQL. To do this, login to MySQL server, enter:

    ```
    # mysql -u root -p
    ```

    and set password, as follows:

    ```
    Welcome to the MariaDB monitor.  Commands end with ; or \g.
    Your MariaDB connection id is 3
    ```

```
Server version: 5.5.44-MariaDB MariaDB Server

Copyright (c) 2000, 2015, Oracle,  MraiDB Corporation Ab and Others.

Type 'help;' or '\h' for help. Type '\c' to clear the current input
statement.

mysql> UPDATE mysql.user SET password=PASSWORD("baculapass") WHERE
user='bacula';
Query OK, 2 rows affected (0.00 sec)
Rows matched: 2  Changed: 2  Warnings: 0

mysql> FLUSH PRIVILEGES;
Query OK, 0 rows affected (0.01 sec)
mysql> exit
Bye
```

4. You're done with this section.

Step 2: Set Bacula to use MySQL Library

By default, Bacula is set to use the PostgreSQL library, and since we are using MySQL (MariaDB),
we need to set it to use the MySQL library instead.

5. To switch from the default PostgreSQL to MySQL database, run:

```
sudo alternatives --cnfig libbaccats.so
```

Note: you should see the following prompt. Enter 1 (MySQL):

```
There are 3 programs which provide 'libbaccats.so'.

  Selection    Command
-----------------------------------------------------------
   1           /usr/lib64/libbaccats-mysql.so
   2           /usr/lib64/libbaccats-sqlite3.so
*+ 3           /usr/lib64/libbaccats-postgresql.so

Enter to keep the current selection[+], or type selection number: 1
```

6. The Bacula server (and client) components are now installed and set to use MySQL. In the next
    step we'll create the backup and restore directory.

7. You're done with this section.
```
```

Step 3: Create Backup and Restore Directories

The Bacula server requires a backup directories, for storing backup archives; and a restore directory, where restored files are placed. In case your system has multiple partitions, then do ensure to create the directories on one that has sufficient disk space.

1. To create the new directories for both purposes, enter:

```
sudo mkdir -p /bacula/backup  /bacula/restore
```

2. Next, we need to change the file permissions so that only bacula process (and a superuser) can access these locations:

```
sudo chown -R bacula:bacula /bacula

sudo chmod -R 700 /bacula
```

3. Now we're ready to configure the Bacula Director

4. You're done with this section.

Step 4: Configure Bacula Components

1: Configure Bacula Director

As earlier mentioned Bacula components now needs to be configured independently in order for it to function correctly. The configuration files are all located in the "/etc/bacula" directory.

First and foremost, we now need to update all Bacula configuration files with the new password and addresses for each Bacula component, each one at a time.

5. To configure Bacula Director, type:

```
# nano /etc/bacula/bacula-dir.conf
```

Note: here we need update Bacula server hostname, bacula mysql user password, Bacula console password, Bacula file daemon password etc. (**Note**: its important that you should use a FQDN name for adding clients or simply use the IP address instead).

```
[...]
Director {                            # define myself
  Name = bacula-dir
  DIRport = 9101                      # where we listen for UA connections
  QueryFile = "/usr/libexec/bacula/query.sql"
  WorkingDirectory = "/var/spool/bacula"
  PidDirectory = "/var/run"
```

```
  Maximum Concurrent Jobs = 1
  Password = "baculapass"              # Console password
  Messages = Daemon
[...]
# Client (File Services) to backup
Client {
  Name = bacula-fd
  Address = 10.0.2.15
  FDPort = 9102
  Catalog = MyCatalog
  Password = "baculapass"              # password for FileDaemon
  File Retention = 30 days             # 30 days
  Job Retention = 6 months             # six months
  AutoPrune = yes                      # Prune expired Jobs/Files
}
[...]
# Definition of file storage device
Storage {
  Name = File
# Do not use "localhost" here
  Address = 10.0.2.15                  # N.B. Use a fully qualified name
here
  SDPort = 9103
  Password = "baculapass"
  Device = FileStorage
  Media Type = File
}
[...]
# Generic catalog service
Catalog {
  Name = MyCatalog
# Uncomment the following line if you want the dbi driver
# dbdriver = "dbi:sqlite3"; dbaddress = 127.0.0.1; dbport =
  dbname = "bacula"; dbuser = "bacula"; dbpassword = "baculapass"
}
[...]
Console {
  Name = bacula-mon
  Password = "baculapss"
  CommandACL = status, .status
}
```

6. You're done with this section.

2. Configure Bacula Console

7. To configure Bacula Console, type:

```
sudo nano /etc/bacula/bconsole.conf
```

change the console password:

```
Director {
  Name = bacula-dir
  DIRport = 9101
  address = localhost
  Password = "baculapass"
}
```

8. You're done with this section.

3. Configure Bacula Storage Daemon

9. To update Storage Daemon, open "/etc/bacula/bacula-sd.conf" using your favorite text editor:

```
sudo nano /etc/bacula/bacula-sd.conf
```

10. Now update the sections marked in red font i.e., the Password and Archive Device, change to suit your settings:

```
[...]
Director {
  Name = bacula-dir
  Password = "baculapass"
}

# Restricted Director, used by tray-monitor to get the
#    status of the storage daemon
#
Director {
  Name = bacula-mon
  Password = "baculapass"
  Monitor = yes
}

[...]

Device {
  Name = FileStorage
  Media Type = File
  Archive Device = /bacula/backup
  LabelMedia = yes;                    # lets Bacula label unlabeled
media
  Random Access = Yes;
  AutomaticMount = yes;                # when device opened, read it
  RemovableMedia = no;
  AlwaysOpen = no;
}
[...]
```

161

11. Save and exit.
12. You're done with this section.

4. Configure File Daemon

13. To update the File Daemon, open "/etc/bacula/bacula-fd.conf" using your favorite text editor:

```
sudo nano /etc/bacula/bacula-fd.conf
```

now update the sections marked in red font i.e., the Password, change to suit your settings:

```
# List Directors who are permitted to contact this File daemon
#
Director {
Name = bacula-dir
Password = "baculapass"
}

# Restricted Director, used by tray-monitor to get the
#    status of the storage daemon
#
Director {
Name = bacula-mon
Password = "baculapass"
Monitor = yes
}
```

14. Finally, when done with updating the respective configuration, we now need to restart all the bacula daemons and make them to automatically start on boot.
15. You're done with this section.

5. Start Bacula Components

12. We need to start the Bacula Director, Storage Daemon, and local File Daemon with the following commands:

```
sudo systemctl start bacula-dir
sudo systemctl start bacula-sd
sudo systemctl start bacula-fd
```

13. Finally, if all is well then lets enable them to start automatically on boot:

```
sudo systemctl enable bacula-dir
sudo systemctl enable bacula-sd
sudo systemctl enable bacula-fd
```

14. Once Bacula has been successfully installed and configured. You can now add clients, jobs and volumes by updating the bacula config files

15. You're done with this section and ready to test that Bacula works by running a backup job.

6. Adjust Firewall/Router

16. Before testing the Bacula server, we first need to open the Webmin port "10000" and Bacula communication ports "9101", "9102", "9103", in order to be able access bacula server remotely, as follows:

```
firewall-cmd --permanent --add-port=9101/tcp
firewall-cmd --permanent --add-port=9102/tcp
firewall-cmd --permanent --add-port=9103/tcp
firewall-cmd --permanent --add-port=10000/tcp
firewall-cmd --reload
```

17. You're done with this section.

7. Manage Bacula with Webmin

You may recall that we had earlier installed Webmin which is extremely useful for system administration for Unix.

18. To access Bacula server via Webmin, point your browser to **"http://server-ip-address:10000"**, and login to access the Webmin admin page.

19. You should now be able to locate the Bacula Backup System in the left pane of the Webmin console i.e., **System → Bacula Backup System**. (**Note**: if not listed, then click on the Refresh Modules link at the bottom of the left-pane to update the Webmin console, followed by clicking on **Module Configuration** link on the right of the "**Bacula Backup System**" page).

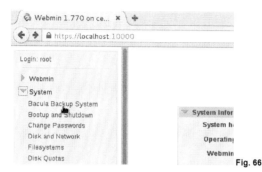

Fig. 66

20. This should bring up the page shown in Fig. 67. Select the database i.e., "MySQL" in this case, and enter `bacula` database user password, as set earlier. Then click on the **Save** button.

Fig. 67

21. You should now be presented with the Fig. 68, with the single window page shown in two parts.

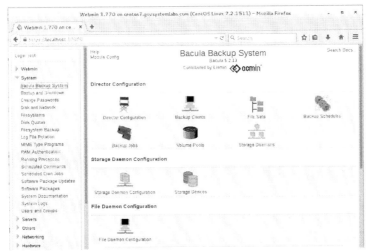

Fig. 68a

Fig. 68b

Note: take your time to move around the Bacula Backup System to get yourself acquainted with the Webmin environment and what kind of task you can accomplish with ease.

22. You're done with this section.

Part 10: Install JBoss: Open Source J2EE Server and Combined JBoss-Portal on Linux Server on CentOS 7 / RHEL 7

Step 1: Install JBoss-Portal

This section covers installation of JBOSS (Open Source J2EE Application Server) on CentOS-7 / RHEL 7. Here you're going to learn how to install the bundled JBoss-Portal as Application Server that you can use to develop and setup Single-Sign-On (SSO) Identity Management access control using LDAP (OpenLDAP). You can also use JPortal to manage network users.

JBoss AS is a J2EE 1.4-certified, open source Java application server. It is the most widely used application server on the market. The highly flexible and easy-to-use server architecture has made JBoss AS the ideal choice for users just starting out with J2EE, as well as senior architects looking for a customizable middleware platform. The ready availability of the source code allows you to debug the server, learn its inner workings and create customized versions for your personal or business use. This guide will show you how to install JBoss AS 6.0. You will learn how to start and stop your JBoss instance, and you will also learn about the directory structure and understand what the key services and configuration files are.

1.1. Download and Install JBoss-Portal Bundle on CentOS-7
1. Download "jboss-portal-2.7.2 -bundled.zip" from:
    http://www.jboss.org/jbossportal/download.html

    Note: you can also use `wget` to download it:

    `wget` http://downloads.sourceforge.net/jboss/jboss-portal-2.7.2-bundled.zip

2. Create a `jportal` directory in `/usr/` directory as follows:

    `# mkdir /usr/jportal`

3. Move the downloaded package to the `/usr/jportal` directory and then `unzip` it:

    ```
    # cp jboss-portal-2.7.2-bundled.zip /usr/jportal
    # cd /usr/jportal
    # unzip jboss-portal-2.7.2-bundled.zip
    ```

4. Add JBoss-Portal to the profile file "`/etc/profile`", modify it so that it now looks like:

    ```
    export JAVA_HOME=/usr/java/jdk1.8.0_65
    export ANT_HOME=/usr/ant
    ```

```
export CATALINA_HOME=/usr/tomcat
export JBOSS_HOME=/usr/jportal/jboss-portal-2.7.2
export
PATH=$JAVA_HOME/bin:$CATALINA_HOME/bin:$ANT_HOME/bin:$JBOSS_HOME/bin:$PATH
CLASSPATH=$CLASSPATH:.
```

5. Now issue the `source` command to update our "`/etc/profile`", type:

```
# source /etc/profile
```

6. Before we continue, we will need to ensure that "`$JBOSS_HOME`" is correctly set. To do this, we open a terminal and type the following:

```
]# echo $JBOSS_HOME
/usr/jportal/jboss-portal-2.7.2
```

7. To start JBoss-portal, run:

```
# chmod +x $JBOSS_HOME/bin/run.sh
# $JBOSS_HOME/bin/run.sh
```

```
11:59:31,086 INFO  [TomcatDeployer] deploy, ctxPath=/jmx-console, warUrl=.../dep
loy/jmx-console.war/
11:59:31,447 INFO  [Http11Protocol] Starting Coyote HTTP/1.1 on http-127.0.0.1-8
080
11:59:31,521 INFO  [AjpProtocol] Starting Coyote AJP/1.3 on ajp-127.0.0.1-8009
11:59:31,586 INFO  [Server] JBoss (MX MicroKernel) [4.2.3.GA (build: SVNTag=JBos
s_4_2_3_GA date=200807181417)] Started in 1m:25s:266ms
```
Fig. 69

8. To stop JBoss-portal, run:

```
# cd $JBOSS_HOME/bin              \\ change to bin directory
# sh ./shutdown.sh -S             \\ stop server or hit "Ctrl C"
```

9. To access JBoss AS, point your browser to: http://localhost:8080/, note the difference in front page color, as shown in Fig. 70.

167

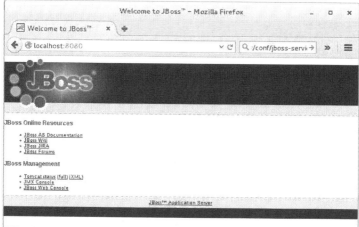
Fig. 70

10. Now to access JBoss-Portal server, point your browser to: http://localhost:8080/portal

Note: click on the Login link, to access the login window, and login with the default admin credentials Username `"admin"` and password `"admin"`, and then click on the **Login** button. It's recommended that you change admin user login credential from the default one.

Note: this is a Community Release version. You can always get the Enterprise version from Red Hat.

Fig. 71

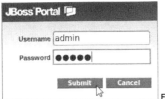

Fig. 72

11. To add a new user, click on the `Admin` link at the top right-hand corner → **Members** tab.

Fig. 73

12. Under **User Management**, click `Create a new user account`, and complete the required fields, a shown in Fig. 74.

Fig. 74

13. When done click on the **Submit** button, as shown in Fig. 75. Add the new user to Administrator role, and click on the **Submit** button complete user addition.

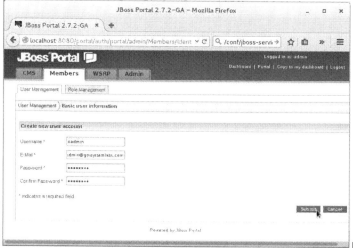

Fig. 75

14. Logout and try to login with new user account, as shown in Fig. 76.

Fig. 76

15. You're done with this section.

16. Enjoy JBoss-Portal!

Part 11: Install and Configure NFS on CenntOS 7

To use NFS successfully, you have to configure the server and the client. In this section, the server is "10.0.2.15" and the client is "10.0.2.16". The folder to be shared is "/nfs-public", and is to be mounted to "/mnt" on the client side.

NSF Server: 10.0.2.15   centos7.govsystemlabs.com
NSF Client: 10.0.2.16   f23.govsystemlabs.com

Note: before starting to setup NFS, please do ensure that you can ping both machines, e.g., from server to client machine and vise versa.

Step 1: Install NFS packages On both Server Side and Client Side

1. On the both server CentOS 7 and on client machine running F23 ensure that nfs package is installed, if not then issue the following command:

```
# yum install nfs* -y
```


Step 2: On the Server Side

A server exports a file system to the specified hosts and allows them to mount it.

2. Make directory that you want to use.

```
# mkdir /nfs-public
```

3. Using you favorite Text editor, edit "/etc/exports", insert the client machine's IP address:

```
# vi /etc/exports
```

and add this line:

```
/nfs-shared centos7.govsystemlabs.com(rw,no_root_squash,sync)
```

4. Save the file.

5. Next, edit "/etc/hosts.allow"

```
# vi /etc/hosts.allow
```

and add this line:

```
ALL:ALL
ALL: 10.0.2.0/255.255.255.0
```

6. Save the file and exit.

7. Finally, start nfs and rpcbind services:

```
# systemctl start rpcbind nfs-server
# systemctl enable rpcbind nfs-server
```

Note: under CentOS-7 portmap service has been replaced by rpcbind service

8. Verify that "exportfs -v" command that it got exported correctly:

```
[root@centos7 ~]# exportfs -v
/nfs-public
    centos7.govsystemlabs.com(rw,wdelay,root_squash,no_subtree_check)
[root@centos6 ~]#
```

9. Now verify using "showmount -e" command:

```
[root@centos7 ~]# showmount -e centos6
Export list for centos7.govsystemlabs.com:
/nfs-public centos7.govsystemlabs.com
[root@centos7 ~]#
```

10. You're done with this section.

Step 3: On the client Side – Fedora 23

11. First and foremost make sure that you have connectivity to the NFS server from the NFS client and vise versa. For example, from client side, you can test this using ping command, as follows:

```
# ping centos7.govsystemlabs.com
```

12. Similarly from the server side repeat the same:

```
# ping f23.govsystemlabs.com
```

13. Finally, start `nfs` and `rpcbind` services:

```
# /etc/init.d/nfs start
# /etc/init.d/rpcbind start
```

Note: under `server01` `portmap` service has been replaced by `rpcbind` service

14. Make mount-point directory:

```
# mkdir /mnt/nfs-public
```

15. Mount the `nfs` folder

```
# mount -t nfs4 centos7:/nfs-public /mnt/nfs-public
```

Note: remember to use `nfs4` instead of just `nfs` in the above command-line; otherwise you'll end-up with

16. Check "`/var/log/messages`" for any error that might occur

```
# tailf /var/log/messages
```

17. Use `mount` command to check if the folder is mounted properly:

```
[root@f23 ~]# mount
```

18. Edit "`/etc/fstab`" to mount the shared folder on boot:

```
# vi /etc/fstab
```

and add this line:

```
10.0.2.16:/nfs-public /mnt/nfs-public nfs rw,hard,intr 0 0
```

19. Save the file

20. You can use 'man exports' to see the options available for "`/etc/exports`".

21. You're done with this section

Part 12: Install ownCloud Storage on CentOS 7

First and foremost, for you to setup your personal cloud storage (**ownCloud**), we must have **LAMP** stack in place. Apart from the LAMP stack you may also need to install **Perl** and **Python** depending our needs and use.

Step 1: Prerequisites Packages

1. First we need to download the release key associated with the **ownCloud** software, to do this type:

```
cd /etc/yum.repos.d/

wget
http://download.opensuse.org/repositories/isv:ownCloud:community/CentO
S_CentOS-7/isv:ownCloud:community.repo
```

2. Next, we need to add `epel` repository too, type:

RHEL/CentOS 7 64-Bit

```
# wget http://dl.fedoraproject.org/pub/epel/7/x86_64/e/epel-release-7-
5.noarch.rpm

# rpm -ivh epel-release-7-5.noarch.rpm
```

Note: you can also simply install it as follows

```
# yum install epel -y
```

3. You're done with this section.

Step 2: Install MySQL (MariaDB) and Create ownCloud Database

4. Install MySQL server, if you hadn't installed before, enter:

```
# yum install httpd mysql-server -y
```

5. Start and enable MariaDB to automatically start on boot.

```
sudo systemctl enable mariadb.service
sudo systemctl start mariadb.service
```

6. Next, start and enable Apache (`httpd`) to automatically start on boot.

```
sudo systemctl enable httpd.service
sudo systemctl start httpd.service
```

7. Next, ensure to make your MySQL database server secure.

```
# mysql_secure_installation
```

Note: enter the correct option as presented to you.

8. Login to the MySQL (now MariaDB), type:

```
# mysql -u root -p
```

Note: enter the MySQL password which you selected before, & create a database for **ownCloud** in MySQL prompt:

9. Now, we need to create a database, e.g., cloud, and grant the privileges to loud user as follows:

```
MariaDB> create database owncloud;
Query OK, 1 row affected (0.00 sec)

MariaDB> grant all on owncloud.* to owncloud@localhost identified by
'password';
Query OK, 0 rows affected (0.14 sec)

MariaDB> flush privileges;
Query OK, 0 rows affected (0.06 sec)

MariaDB>exit
```

10. You're done with this section.

Step 3: Install ownCloud

11. Now to install ownCloud, type:

```
# yum install owncloud  -y
```

12. You're done with this section.

Step 4: Access ownCloud Application

You're now done with the basic requirements and ready to access your personal cloud storage.

13. To access your personal cloud storage, point your browser to:

```
http://localhost/owncloud
```

OR

```
http://your-ip-address/owncloud
```

Note: once you access to ownCloud page, Fig. 77; you'll need to create an admin account and a data folder, where all your files/directories will be stored (you may also leave the default location i.e., "/var/www/html/owncloud/data".

- next you'll need to enter MySQL database username, password and cloud database name, as set earlier

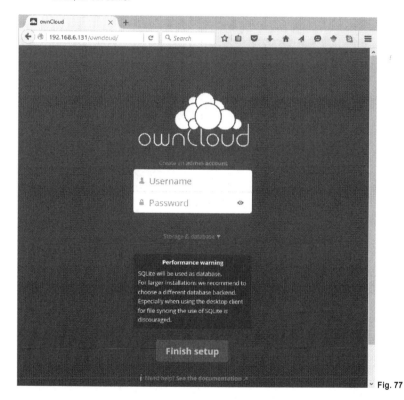

Fig. 77

14. When done with entry as shown in Fig. 2, click **Finish Setup** button, as shown in Fig. 78.

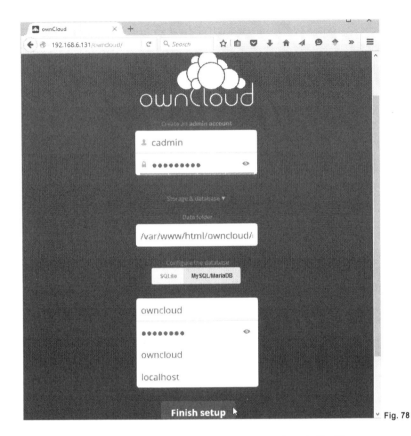

Fig. 78

15. After clicking the **Finish Setup**, you be able to be logged in as shown in Fig. 79.

177

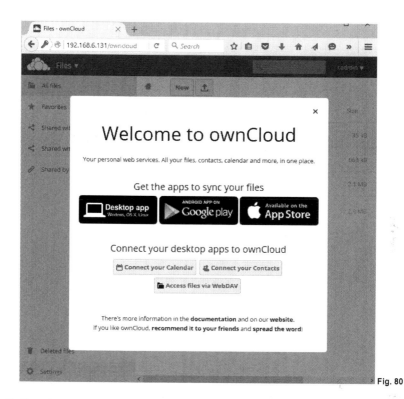

Fig. 80

16. Close the **Welcome to ownCloud** banner to access the ownCloud Console, as shown in Fig. 81.

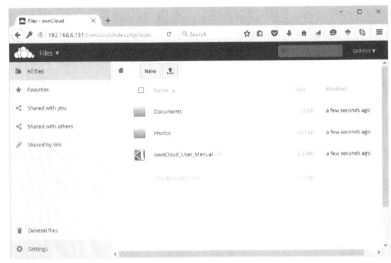

Fig. 81

1. Enjoy your own cloud on your desktop powered by ownCloud technology.

2. You're done with this section.

Part 13: Setup Virtualization with VirtualBox on CentOS 7

In this section we're going to learn how to use virtualization technology by provisioning VirtualBox on CentOS 7. Virtualization is a process for creating virtual OS, Hardware and Network, and toady its one of the most sought after technology for people with this kind of skills. In this section you'll learn how to install and configure virtualization through a step-by-step hands-on.

Oracle VirtualBox is a powerful x86 and AMD64/Intel64 virtualization product for enterprise as well as home use. VirtualBox is a general-purpose full virtualizer for x86 hardware. Targeted at server, desktop and embedded use, it is now the only professional-quality virtualization solution that is also Open Source Software. It supports a large number of guest operating systems, Linux distros, Windows OSes, Solaris, OpenSolaris, and OpenBSD.

Step 1: Preparing the CentOS 7 / RHEL 7 for host Virtual Machines

1. Incase you hadn't installed EPEL, then for RHEL based system, you install filezilla using yum command as follows:

```
sudo yum -y install epel-release
```

1.1 Install VirtualBox Latest Version 5.0 (currently 5.0.12)
2. Install the latest VirtualBox using `yum` command, type:

```
sudo yum install VirtualBox-5.0
```

Note: the command automatically creates virtboxusers group and VirtualBox user who must be a member of that group.

3. Next, we need to rebuild the kernel module, to do this type:

```
# service vboxdrv setup
```

4. You're done with this section.

1.2 Add VirtualBox User(s) to VirtualBox Group
5. Now we need to create a user to manage user `"vbox"` to manage **virtualbox** and add it to group `"vboxusers"`, enter:

```
# usermod -a -G vboxusers vbox
```

6. You're done with this section.

1.3 Start VirtualBox
7. Let's start VirtualBox via command-line, or use launcher from menu:

```
# virtualbox
```

Fig. 82

180

8. Now, you should be presented with the **Oracle VM VirtualBox Manager** page, as shown in Fig. 83.

Fig. 83

9. You're now ready to enjoy virtualization technology at its best using purely open source technology.

10. You're done with this section.

Step 2: Managing your VirtualBox with phpVirtualBox on CentOS 7 / RHEL 7

The phpVirtualBox is a PHP web application where you can manage your virtual machines. it is a great application and similar to the normal desktop GUI for VirtualBox. so if you have installed Oracle VirtualBox on a headless server and you miss the GUI you should definitely install phpvirtualbox.

2.1 Download and Configure phpVirtualBox

1. First let's download the latest phpVirtualBox, type:

```
wget    http://sourceforge.net/projects/phpvirtualbox/files/phpvirtualbox-5.0-
4.zip
```

2. Next, we need to extract the `zip` and copy the extracted folder to HTTP working directory i.e., "/var/www/html", as follows:

```
# cp unzip phpvirtualbox-5.0-4.zip /var/www/htm
# cd /var/www/html
# unzip unzip phpvirtualbox-5.0-4.zip
# mv phpvirtualbox-5.0-4 virtualbox
```

3. Next, change to the directory "/var/www/html/virtualbox/" and rename "config.php-example" to "config.php", as follows:

```
# cd /var/www/html/phpvirtualbox/

# cp config.php-example  config.php
```

4. By default the example `config` file works well. All that is required is to set a username and password for a user which is running the VirtualBox to do this open the new "config.php" and locate and change the following lines to reflect the credentials of your virtualbox user:

```
/* Username / Password for system user that runs VirtualBox */
var $username = 'vboxuser';
var $password = 'password';
```

5. Restart `httpd` (Apache) service, type:

```
# systemctl restart  httpd.service
```

6. Now, start and enable VirtualBox service to automatically start on boot, as follows:

```
# systemctl restart  vboxweb-service.service
# systemctl restart  vboxweb-service.service
```

7. Make sure "firewall-cmd" to allow port 18083, and also ensure that **SELinux** is set to `disabled` during this hands-on tutorial:

```
firewall-cmd --permanent --add-port=18083/tcp
firewall-cmd --reload
```

8. You're done with this section.

2.2 Start VirtualBox Web Server

9. Now lets' start the VirtualBox Web server, to do this, type:

```
[root@cloud ~]# vboxwebsrv -H 127.0.0.1
```

with the output sample shown below:

```
[root@cloud ~]# vboxwebsrv -H 127.0.0.1
Oracle VM VirtualBox web service Version 5.0.12
(C) 2007-2015 Oracle Corporation
All rights reserved.
VirtualBox web service 5.0.12 r104815 linux.amd64 (Dec 18 2015
12:56:49) release log
00:00:00.045247 main     Log opened 2016-01-02T14:09:08.226397000Z
00:00:00.045258 main     Build Type: release
00:00:00.045279 main     OS Product: Linux
00:00:00.045281 main     OS Release: 3.10.0-327.3.1.el7.x86_64
00:00:00.045282 main      OS Version: #1 SMP Wed Dec 9 14:09:15 UTC
2015
00:00:00.045603 main     DMI Product Name: VMware Virtual Platform
00:00:00.045627 main     DMI Product Version: None
00:00:00.045933 main     Host RAM: 1495MB total, 385MB available
00:00:00.045946 main     Executable: /usr/lib/virtualbox/vboxwebsrv
00:00:00.045947 main     Process ID: 16873
00:00:00.045948 main     Package type: LINUX_64BITS_EL_7
00:00:00.710485 SQPmp       Socket connection successful: host =
127.0.0.1, port = 18083, master socket = 8
```

10. Now to access your `phpVirtualBox` web interface, point your browser to:

```
http://localhost/virtualbox/
```

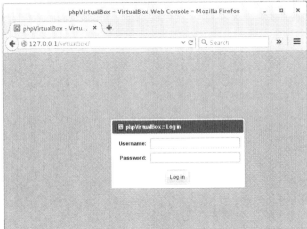

Fig. 84a

183

Note: the default `phpVirtualBox` username and password are:

```
username: admin
password: admin
```

Fig. 84b

11. You should be presented with the phpVirtualBox - Virtual Web Console, as shown in Fig. 85.

Fig. 85

12. You now have the ability to manage your virtual guest machines remotely from anywhere in world if you connected via a public IP address, or with private IP address if located on the LAN.

13. You're done with this section.

Part 14: Install and Configure Samba Share on CentOS 7

In this section you'll learn how to install and configure Samba server on separate CentOS 7 / RHEL 7 box and create a Samba share store. To do this, you'll need to perform the following procedure:

Step 1: Install SAMBA an Configure SAMBA Share

1. The first step is to install samba (if not already installed), type:

```
# yum install samba  -y
```

2. Once installed, overwrite the default "/etc/samba/smb.config" file with the following:

```
[global]
workgroup = WORKGROUP
server string = %h server
encrypt passwords = true
passdb backend = tdbsam
obey pam restrictions = yes

[ISO]
comment = ISO Library
path = /store/iso/
browseable = yes
public = yes
read only = yes

[MUSIC]
comment = Music Library
path = /store/music/
browseable = yes
public = yes
read only = yes

[SOFTWARE]
comment = Software Library
path = /store/software/
browseable = yes
public = yes
read only = yes

[SWDEV]
```

```
comment = Software Development Library
path = /store/swdev/
browseable = yes
public = yes
read only = yes
```

Warning! You should only create a completely open share like the one here if you trust the people who have access to your Samba PDC server; open FTP servers, for example, have been compromised in the past and abused as drop boxes for pirated software.

3. After you've added these shares to your `"smb.conf"` configuration file, remember to either restart Samba or tell it to reload its configuration files, however, before doing that run the : `"testparm"` command.

4. Save your changes and run `"testparm"` command to test your samba configuration:

```
# testparm
```

if all is ok, a sample output should look like:

```
[root@cloud samba]# testparm
Load smb config files from /etc/samba/smb.conf
rlimit_max: increasing rlimit_max (1024) to minimum Windows limit
(16384)
Processing section "[ISO]"
Processing section "[MUSIC]"
Processing section "[SWDEV]"
Loaded services file OK.
Server role: ROLE_STANDALONE

Press enter to see a dump of your service definitions

# Global parameters
[global]
    server string = %h server
    obey pam restrictions = Yes
    idmap config * : backend = tdb

[ISO]
    comment = ISO Library
    path = /store/iso/
    guest ok = Yes
```

```
[MUSIC]
    comment = Music Library
    path = /store/music/
    guest ok = Yes

[SOFTWARE]
    comment = Software Library
    path = /store/software/
    guest ok = Yes

[SWDEV]
    comment = Software Development Library
    path = /store/swdev/
    guest ok = Yes
[root@cloud samba]#
```

Note: this checks `"smb.conf"` for syntax errors. Any errors must be corrected before moving on. Once all is OK, you can start-up and enable Samba to start automatically on boot, as follows:

```
# systemctl enable smb.service
# systemctl start smb.service
```

5. Set `firewall-cmd` to allow samba service, type:

```
firewall-cmd --permanent --add-service=samba
firewall-cmd --permanent --add-service=samba-client
firewall-cmd --reload
```

6. You're done with this section.

Step 2: Create Shared Folders and Add SAMBA users

The next step is to create the appropriate users and folders. To do this, perform the following steps:

7. Create our directories, type

```
sudo mkdir -p /store/iso/
sudo mkdir -p /store/music/
sudo mkdir -p /store/software/
sudo mkdir -p /store/swdev/
```

8. Add SAMBA user for iso, music, and swdev, type:

```
sudo useradd cadmin
sudo smbpasswd -a cadmin
New SMB Password:
Retype new SMB Password:
Added user cadmin.
```

9. Once you restart samba, you should be able to access the share via "\\<ip address>\iso\.". and other directories. However, before you can do this you need to verify that you can access your SAMBA share. You can use the ping command to test connectivity.

10. The next test is to see if we can access our **iso** share etc, by using smbclient command.

Step 3: Connecting to a Samba Machine in Linux

11. To connect to a Samba machine (Windows or Linux running Samba) from the command line, execute the command (replace MACHINENAME and sharename with the appropriate values):

```
# smbclient //MACHINENAME/sharename
```

Note 1: If you want to pass a different username to the Samba Server, execute the command (replace username with your username):

```
# smbclient //MACHINENAME/sharename -U username
```

Note 2: if a password is associated with the username, you will be prompted for it. Once you are authorized by the SMB protocol, you will be at a "smb: \>" prompt. This is similar to an ftp session where get, put, pwd, ls, etc. can be used to navigate.

Note 3: Type "help" for a list of commands available.

12. Now to access our shared **iso** store using user iso with appropriate password form a remote machine, see Fig. 86:

```
# smbclient //192.168.6.131/iso -U cadmin
```

188

```
[root@cloud ~]# smbclient //192.168.6.131/iso -U cadmin
Enter cadmin's password:
Domain=[WORKGROUP] OS=[Windows 6.1] Server=[Samba 4.2.3]
smb: \> ls
                                    D        0  Sun Jan  3 12:17:57 2016
  ..                                D        0  Sun Jan  3 12:45:21 2016
  damnsmall-0.4.10.iso              A 49410048  Sun Jan  3 11:39:21 2016

               49746196 blocks of size 1024. 43793044 blocks available
smb: \> exit
[root@cloud ~]#
```
.... **Fig. 86**

13. Type `exit` command to exit `smbclient`.

14. You're done with this section.

Step 4: Accessing Samba Shares from Windows Desktop

4.1 Use \\<ip-adress>\sharename

15. First we need to ensure that we can connect from the Windows machine to our Linux machine using `ping` command, as shown in Fig. 87.

```
C:\>ping 192.168.6.131

Pinging 192.168.6.131 with 32 bytes of data:
Reply from 192.168.6.131: bytes=32 time<1ms TTL=64
Reply from 192.168.6.131: bytes=32 time<1ms TTL=64
Reply from 192.168.6.131: bytes=32 time<1ms TTL=64
Reply from 192.168.6.131: bytes=32 time<1ms TTL=64

Ping statistics for 192.168.6.131:
    Packets: Sent = 4, Received = 4, Lost = 0 (0% loss),
Approximate round trip times in milli-seconds:
    Minimum = 0ms, Maximum = 0ms, Average = 0ms

C:\>
```
Fig. 87

16. Start your **Start → Accessories → Windows Explorer,** and under the Address bar type "\\<ip-adress>" or server name "\\servername"

- When prompted for user name and password, enter appropriate credentials and then click OK, see Fig. 88 (**Note:** ignore the warning and click **OK** button).

Fig. 88

4. You should be logged into the shared folders/directories, as shown in Fig. 89.

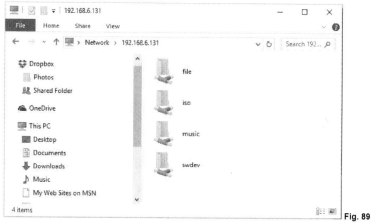
Fig. 89

5. You can also browse the ISO share to view its content, as shown in Fig. 90.

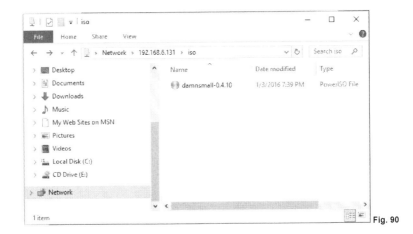

Fig. 90

6. You're done with this section and also the hands-on labs for CentOS 7 server.

Part 15: Troubleshooting JBoos-Portal

1. Troubleshooting JBoss-Portal problem during run time given as follows:

```
Could not create deployment: file:/opt/apps/jboss-
4.2.3.GA/server/default/conf/jboss-service.xml
```

2. To solve the problem was solved by ensuring that the /etc/hosts file is correctly set:, in our case:

```
127.0.0.1    localhost localhost.localdomain localhost4 localhost4.localdomain4
10.0.2.15    centos7.govsystemlabs.com centos7 www mail ftp
::1          localhost localhost.localdomain localhost6 localhost6.localdomain6
```

3. All should be Ok and your JBoss-Portal should run ok.

Part 16: Changing the Interface from the "eno16777736" to the old "eth0"

The VMware 12 Pro, now installs the system with "eno16777736", which will want to change back to the old "eth0".

Step 1: Change Interface from the "eno16777736" to "eth0"

1. The first step is to check the current setting by type "ifconfig" command:

```
[root@centos7 ~]# ifconfig
eno16777736: flags=4163<UP,BROADCAST,RUNNING,MULTICAST>  mtu 1500
        inet 192.168.6.128  netmask 255.255.255.0  broadcast 192.168.6.255
        inet6 fe80::20c:29ff:fe9c:b595  prefixlen 64  scopeid 0x20<link>
        ether 00:0c:29:9c:b5:95  txqueuelen 1000  (Ethernet)
        RX packets 1913  bytes 128626 (125.6 KiB)
        RX errors 0  dropped 0  overruns 0  frame 0
        TX packets 218  bytes 22031 (21.5 KiB)
        TX errors 0  dropped 0 overruns 0  carrier 0  collisions 0

lo: flags=73<UP,LOOPBACK,RUNNING>  mtu 65536
        inet 127.0.0.1  netmask 255.0.0.0
        inet6 ::1  prefixlen 128  scopeid 0x10<host>
        loop  txqueuelen 0  (Local Loopback)
        RX packets 6  bytes 436 (436.0 B)
        RX errors 0  dropped 0  overruns 0  frame 0
        TX packets 6  bytes 436 (436.0 B)
        TX errors 0  dropped 0 overruns 0  carrier 0  collisions 0

virbr0: flags=4099<UP,BROADCAST,MULTICAST>  mtu 1500
        inet 192.168.122.1  netmask 255.255.255.0  broadcast 192.168.122.255
        ether 52:54:00:49:5d:71  txqueuelen 0  (Ethernet)
        RX packets 0  bytes 0 (0.0 B)
        RX errors 0  dropped 0  overruns 0  frame 0
        TX packets 0  bytes 0 (0.0 B)
        TX errors 0  dropped 0 overruns 0  carrier 0  collisions 0
```

Note: you can also check the same using "ip addr show"

2. We now need to edit the "/etc/default/grub" file to update it:

```
[root@centos7 ~]# nano /etc/default/grub

GRUB_TIMEOUT=5
GRUB_DISTRIBUTOR="$(sed 's, release .*$,,g' /etc/system-release)"
GRUB_DEFAULT=saved
GRUB_DISABLE_SUBMENU=true
GRUB_TERMINAL_OUTPUT="console"
GRUB_CMDLINE_LINUX="rd.lvm.lv=rootvg/usrlv rd.lvm.lv=rootvg/swaplv
crashkernel=auto vconsole.keymap=us rd.lvm.lv=rootvg/rootlv
```

vconsole.font=latarcyrheb-sun16 rhgb quiet"
GRUB_DISABLE_RECOVERY="true"

Now look for the line "GRUB_CMDLINE_LINUX" and add the following: "net.ifnames=0 biosdevname=0"

And which should now look like:

GRUB_CMDLINE_LINUX="rd.lvm.lv=rootvg/usrlv rd.lvm.lv=rootvg/swaplv
crashkernel=auto vconsole.keymap=us rd.lvm.lv=rootvg/rootlv
vconsole.font=latarcyrheb-sun16 rhgb quiet net.ifnames=0 biosdevname=0"

3. Next run the following command:

```
[root@centos7 ~]# grub2-mkconfig -o /boot/grub2/grub.cfg
Generating grub configuration file ...
Found linux image: /boot/vmlinuz-3.10.0-327.el7.x86_64
Found initrd image: /boot/initramfs-3.10.0-327.el7.x86_64.img
Found linux image: /boot/vmlinuz-0-rescue-044e020008604b22bcbf5dd4287fbf31
Found         initrd         image:         /boot/initramfs-0-rescue-
044e020008604b22bcbf5dd4287fbf31.img
done
[root@centos7 ~]#
```

Note: if you didn't put any names during the initial installation, you'll need to rename the interface file by renaming the file "/etc/sysconfig/network-scripts/ifcfg*".

```
[root@centos7 ~]# mv /etc/sysconfig/network-scripts/ifcfg-eno16777736
/etc/sysconfig/network-scripts/ifcfg-eth0
```

4. Reboot the system:

```
# shutdown -r now
```

5. After system reboot, run:

```
# ifconfig
```

```
[root@centos7 ~]# ifconfig
eth0: flags=4163<UP,BROADCAST,RUNNING,MULTICAST>  mtu 1500
        inet 192.168.6.128  netmask 255.255.255.0  broadcast 192.168.6.255
        inet6 fe80::20c:29ff:fe9c:b595  prefixlen 64  scopeid 0x20<link>
        ether 00:0c:29:9c:b5:95  txqueuelen 1000  (Ethernet)
        RX packets 282  bytes 22024 (21.5 KiB)
        RX errors 0  dropped 0  overruns 0  frame 0
        TX packets 130  bytes 13472 (13.1 KiB)
        TX errors 0  dropped 0 overruns 0  carrier 0  collisions 0
```

Step 1: Disable Network Manager

6. Disable Network Manager, type:

```
# systemctl disable NetworkManager.service
```

7. You're done with this section.

Part 17: How to Stop and Disable Firewalld on CentOS 7 / RHEL 7

1. Disable Firewalld

1. To disable firewalld, run the following command as root:

```
# systemctl disable firewalld
```

2. Stop Firewalld

2. To stop firewalld, run the following command as root:

```
# systemctl stop firewalld
```

3. Check the Status of Firewalld

3. And finally, to check the status of firewalld, run the following command as root:

```
# systemctl status firewalld
```

4. You're done with this section.

Part 19: Need More Training on CentOS-7

Are you having trouble understanding or comprehending the working of Linux CentOS-7, if so, then check out some of our introductory courses on Linux servers at: Global Open Versity, Vancouver Canada.

Mastering CentOS-7 and RHEL 7 Server Administration and System Integration Training - ICT203

You can now register and take our superb Mastering CentOS-7 and RHEL 7 Server Administration. This Training cover compete server installation, administration and system integration from simple task to cloud computing with Eucalyptus and OpenNebula cloud.

- ICT405 – Mastering RHEL-7 & CentOS-7 Server Installation and Adminstration

Contact us today:

Email: info@globalopenversity.org   **URL:** www.globalopenversity.org

Part 20: Hands-on Labs Assignments

You're required to complete these assignments as part of class assignments and submit the results to your respective instructor. Continue assessment progress marks will be awarded as part of the grading systems:

1. Install Linux CentOS-7 server and ensure it's updated with the latest patches and bug fixes.
2. Install and configure Linux CentOS-7 or Linux distros VM and install DNS Server, Sendmail server with SquirrelMail Webmail on it.
3. Install and configure Linux RHEL-7 or Linux distros VM and install DNS Server, Sendmail server with SquirrelMail Webmail on it.
4. Install and configure Xen Hypervisor virtualization on your CentOS-7.
5. On a second VM, install and configure Linux Ubuntu 14.04 LTS (Lucid Lynx) VM and install Webserver, ftp server on it.
6. On a third VM, install and configure Linux Ubuntu 14.04 LTS (Natty) VM and install EHCP IS Hosting on it.

Other Related Articles:

11. Using Webmin and Bind9 to Setup Enterprise DNS Server on Linux
12. Deploy Secure Messaging Solutions using Sendmail & Dovecot Servers with ClamAV on Linux
13. Install Guide Secure Postfix Messaging Server with Dovecot and ClamAV on Linux v1.2

Chapter IV

Mastering Virtualization with VirtualBox & Cloud Computing on CentOS-7 Infrastructure Server

Introduction

CentOS is a community-supported, free and open source operating system based on Red Hat Enterprise Linux. It exists to provide a free enterprise class computing platform and strives to maintain 100% binary compatibility with its upstream distribution .CentOS stands for "Community ENTerprise Operating System". CentOS is the perfect server for people who need an enterprise class operating system stability without the cost of certification and support and pocket burning baggage that comes with proprietary software. And the beauty is CentOS is free.

Oracle VirtualBox is a powerful x86 and AMD64/Intel64 virtualization product for enterprise as well as home use. VirtualBox is a general-purpose full virtualizer for x86 hardware. Targeted at server, desktop and embedded use, it is now the only professional-quality virtualization solution that is also Open Source Software. It supports a large number of guest operating systems, Linux distros, Windows OSes, Solaris, OpenSolaris, and OpenBSD.

ownCloud is a web application that can store and serve content from a centralized location, much like Dropbox. The difference is that ownCloud 8 allows you to host the serving software on your own machines, taking the trust issues out of putting your personal data someone else's server. The ownCloud also provides access to your data through a web interface or WebDAV while providing a platform to easily view, sync and share across devices—all under your control. ownCloud's open architecture is extensible via a simple but powerful API for applications and plugins and works with any storage.

The Seafile Secure Cloud Storage is an open source cloud platform. In this section you'll lean how to install, configure and Seafile cloud storage which you can use to synchronize your files and data with PC and mobile devices or access via web interface for managing your data files from home, workplace or just anywhere or as ago about your business. Thus, its ideal for small Storage solution mostly for small to medium business purposes, eLearning, joint project management - i.e., a place where you have the flexibility of group sharing and multiple projects, with no need for a public server provision, and has complete security provided by the client-side encryption of the data. You can choose to host your data on the Seafile cloud or provision it through your local Seafile server which you'll have gained expertise to setup after undertaking the Tech Training Series provision using RHEL 7 / CentOS 7 server.

Pydio is an alternative to Dropbox and box.com, for enterprise. You need to access your documents across multiple devices, and regularly share documents (weblinks) and folders with your contacts and teams. Still, using a consumer SaaS box or drive service is neither practical nor safe. And enterprise SaaS box or drive services are expensive and come with Disk Storage that you already have on your servers or private cloud. Pydio file sharing & sync includes applications for web, desktop and mobile assuring that your end users can easily manage their critical documents everywhere. Pydio is hosted exclusively on your private server or cloud so you can rest assured that files are securely managed under company control.

Cloud storage is nothing but an enterprise-level cloud data storage model to store the digital data in logical pools, across the multiple servers. You have the option to deploy your own on-premise private cloud solution or you can use public cloud from hosting company such as Amazon, Google, Rackspace, Dropbox and others for keeping your data available and accessible 24/7/365. You can access data stored on cloud storage via API or desktop/mobile apps or web based systems.

Hands-on Lab Session

This document describes how to install and configure ownCloud 8, Seafile Secure Cloud Storage, and VirtualBox-5 with phpVirtualBox-5 on CentOS 7 infrastructure server. You'll learn how to install VirtualBox with phpVirtualBox and use web interface to install a Linux virtual machine. You will also learn how to connect to the ownCloud Server's data and Seafile shared folders with Linux servers and Windows 10 Desktop. Similarly you'll have a opportunity to build virtual machine remotely using VirtualBox web access powered phpVirtualBox. Install and configure Pydio file sharing & synch cloud server. When done with hands-on tutorial you should have gain enough skill and expertise to enable you to work in skills requiring virtualization and cloud computing technology.

Part 1: Installing and Updating CentOS-7 Server

Assumptions

It's assumed that you have a good understanding of Linux operating system and its working environment. It's also assumed that you know how to install and configure Linux CentOS 7, if not go ahead and pop over to scribd.com and check out a good HowTo entitled "Step-By-Step Guide CentOS 7 Server Installation and Administration" to get you started.

Part 2: Setup Virtualization with VirtualBox on CentOS 7 / RHEL 7

In this section we're going to learn how to use virtualization technology by provisioning VirtualBox on CentOS 7. Virtualization is a process for creating virtual OS, Hardware and Network, and toady its one of the most sought after technology for people this kind of skill. In this section you'll earn how to install configure virtualization through a step-by-step hands-on.

Oracle VirtualBox is a powerful x86 and AMD64/Intel64 virtualization product for enterprise as well as home use. VirtualBox is a general-purpose full virtualizer for x86 hardware. Targeted at server, desktop and embedded use, it is now the only professional-quality virtualization solution that is also Open Source Software. It supports a large number of guest operating systems, Linux distros, Windows OSes, Solaris, OpenSolaris, and OpenBSD.

Step 1: Preparing the CentOS 7 / RHEL 7 for host Virtual Machines

1. Incase you hadn't installed EPEL, the for RHEL based system, you install filezilla using yum command as follows:

```
sudo yum -y install epel-release
```

2. You're done with this section.

1.1 Install VirtualBox Latest Version 5.0 (currently 5.0.12)

2. Install the latest VirtualBox using yum command, type:

```
sudo yum install VirtualBox-5.0
```

Note: the command automatically creates virtboxusers group and VirtualBox user who must be a member of that group.

3. Next, we need to rebuild the kernel module, to do this type:

```
# service vboxdrv setup
```

4. You're done with this section.

1.2 Add VirtualBox User(s) to virtualbox Group

5. Now we need to create a user to manage user "vbox" to manage **virtualbox** and add it to group "vboxusers", enter:

```
# usermod -a -G vboxusers vbox
```

6. You're done with this section.

1.3 Start VirtualBox

7. Let's start VirtualBox via command-line, or launcher from menu:

```
# virtualbox
```

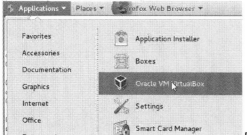

Fig. 1

8. Now, you should be presented with the **Oracle VM VirtualBox Manager** page, as shown in Fig. 2.

Fig. 3

9. You're now ready to enjoy virtualization technology at its best using purely open source technology.

10. You're done with this section.

Step 2: Managing your VirtualBox with phpVirtualBox on CentOS 7 / RHEL 7

The phpVirtualBox is a PHP web application where you can manage your virtual machines. it is a great application and similar to the normal desktop GUI for VirtualBox. so if you have installed Oracle VirtualBox on a headless server and you miss the GUI you should definitely install phpvirtualbox.

2.1 Download and Configure phpVirtualBox

1. First let's download the latest phpvirtualbox, type:

    ```
    wget    http://sourceforge.net/projects/phpvirtualbox/files/phpvirtualbox-5.0-
    4.zip
    ```

2. Next, we need to extract the `zip` and copy the extracted folder to HTTP working directory i.e., "`/var/www/html`", as follows:

    ```
    # cp unzip phpvirtualbox-5.0-4.zip /var/www/htm
    # cd /var/www/html
    # unzip unzip phpvirtualbox-5.0-4.zip
    # mv phpvirtualbox-5.0-4 virtualbox
    ```

3. Next, change to the directory "`/var/www/html/virtualbox/`" and rename "`config.php-example`" to "`config.php`", as follows:

    ```
    # cd /var/www/html/phpvirtualbox/

    # cp config.php-example   config.php
    ```

4. By default the example `config` file works well. All that is required is to set a username and password for a user which is running the virtualbox to do this open the new "`config.php`" and locate and change the following lines to reflect the credentials of your virtualbox user:

    ```
    /* Username / Password for system user that runs VirtualBox */
    var $username = 'vboxuser';
    var $password = 'password';
    ```

5. Restart `httpd` (Apache) service, type:

    ```
    # systemctl restart  httpd.service
    ```

6. Now, start and enable virtualbox service to automatically start on boot, as follows:

    ```
    # systemctl restart  vboxweb-service.service
    # systemctl restart  vboxweb-service.service
    ```

7. Make `firewall-cmd` to allow port `18083`, and also ensure that **SELinux** is set to `disabled` during this hands-on tutorial:

```
firewall-cmd --permanent --add-port=18083/tcp
firewall-cmd --reload
```

8. You're done with this section.

2.2 Start VirtualBox Web Server
9. Now lets' start the VirtualBox Web server, to do this type:

```
[root@cloud ~]# vboxwebsrv -H 127.0.0.1
```

with the output sample shown below:

```
[root@cloud ~]# vboxwebsrv -H 127.0.0.1
Oracle VM VirtualBox web service Version 5.0.12
(C) 2007-2015 Oracle Corporation
All rights reserved.
VirtualBox web service 5.0.12 r104815 linux.amd64 (Dec 18 2015
12:56:49) release log
00:00:00.045247 main     Log opened 2016-01-02T14:09:08.226397000Z
00:00:00.045258 main     Build Type: release
00:00:00.045279 main     OS Product: Linux
00:00:00.045281 main     OS Release: 3.10.0-327.3.1.el7.x86_64
00:00:00.045282 main     OS Version: #1 SMP Wed Dec 9 14:09:15 UTC
2015
00:00:00.045603 main     DMI Product Name: VMware Virtual Platform
00:00:00.045627 main     DMI Product Version: None
00:00:00.045933 main     Host RAM: 1495MB total, 385MB available
00:00:00.045946 main     Executable: /usr/lib/virtualbox/vboxwebsrv
00:00:00.045947 main     Process ID: 16873
00:00:00.045948 main     Package type: LINUX_64BITS_EL_7
00:00:00.710485 SQPmp        Socket connection successful: host =
127.0.0.1, port = 18083, master socket = 8
```

10. Now to access your `phpVirtualBox` web interface, point your browser to:

```
http://localhost/virtualbox/
```

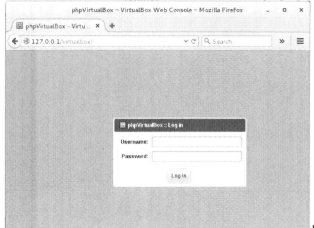

Fig. 4a

Note: the default `phpVirtualBox` username and password are:

```
username: admin
password: admin
```

Fig. 4b

11. You should be presented with the phpVirtualBox - Virtual Web Console, as shown in Fig. 5.

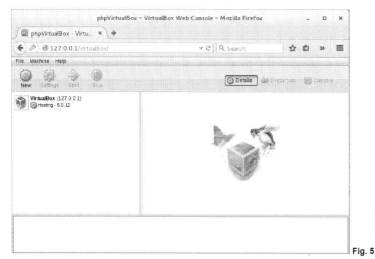

Fig. 5

12. You now have the ability to manage your virtual guest machines remotely from anywhere in world if you connected via a public IP address, or with private IP address if located on the LAN.

13. You're done with this section.

Part 3: Install Kali-Linux-Light using VirtualBox on CentOS 7

Step 1: Download Kali-Linux-Light

1. Point your browser to the Damnsmall Linux download page and download the ISO.

Step 2: Start VirtualBox Web Server

2. Now lets' start the VirtualBox Web server, to do this type:

```
[root@cloud ~]# vboxwebsrv -H 127.0.0.1
```

3. Now to access your phpVirtualBox web interface, point your browser to:

```
http://localhost/virtualbox/
```

4. Login to access the phpVirtualBox - Virtual Web Console, as shown in Fig. 6.

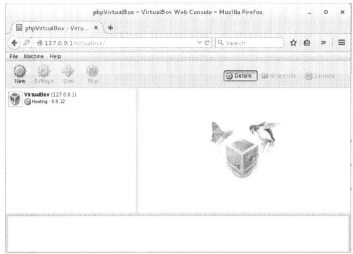

Fig. 6

5. You're done with section.

Step 3: Install Adobe Flash Plugin for Firefox on CentOS 7 / RHEL 7

The default installation of CentOS Linux 7 / RHEL 7 does not come with installation of adobe flash player for Firefox web browser and thus must be installed separately. To begin flash player installation first we need to include Adobe's repository. This can be achieved by the following command:

We'll need Adobe flash to manage our virtual machine installation.

6. Let's grab the latest Adobe Flash package using `wget` command, type:

```
wget http://linuxdownload.adobe.com/adobe-release/adobe-release-x86_64-1.0-1.noarch.rpm
```

7. Next, install it as follows;

```
# rpm -ivh adobe-release-x86_64-1.0-1.noarch.rpm
```

8. Confirm Adobe repository has been include, type:

```
# yum repolist | grep -i adoobe
```

205

```
[root@cloud ~]# yum repolist | grep -i adobe
adobe-linux-x86_64        Adobe Systems Incorporated
[root@cloud ~]#
```

9. At this stage we are ready to install adobe flash player using yum command:

```
# yum install flush-plug-in
```

Note: once the adobe flash plugin installation complete restart your Firefox browser so the new flash plugin may take defect. To check if installed correctly, point your browser to: https://www.adobe.com/software/flash/about/ - and as shown in Fig. 7, its ok.

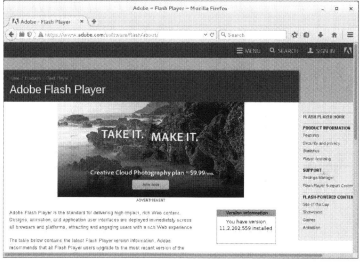

Fig. 7

10. You're done with this section.

Step 4: Install Kali-Linux-Light 64b

11. From Fig. 7 above click on the New button to access Fig. 8 Enter the required info and click **Next**.

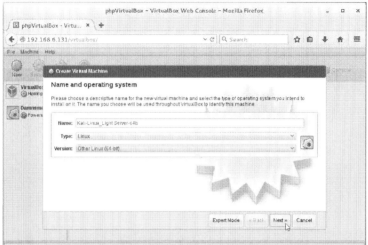

Fig. 8

12. From Fig. 9, **Create Virtual Machine** screen, accept the default **Memory Size** setting or change as desired.

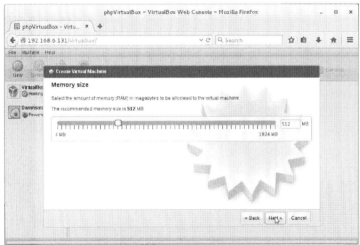

Fig. 9

13. From Fig. 10, **Create Virtual Machine Hard Disk** screen, accept the default **Hard disk** options, or change as desired.

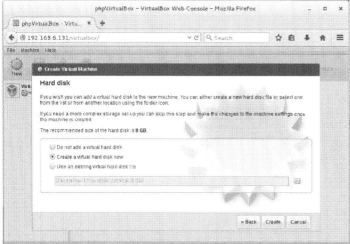

Fig. 10

14. From Fig. 11, **Create Virtual Machine Hard Disk** screen, accept the default **Hard disk file type** options, or change as desired.

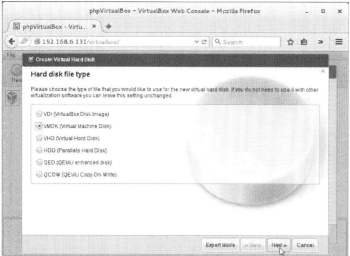

Fig. 11

15. From Fig. 12, **Create Virtual Machine Hard Disk** screen, accept the default **Storage on physical had disk** options, or change as desired.

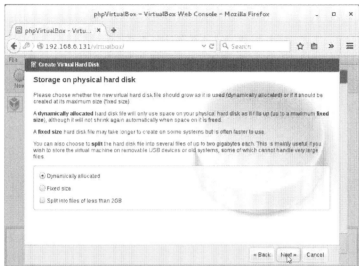

Fig. 12

16. From Fig. 13, **Create Virtual Machine** screen, accept the default **File location and size** options, or change as desired.

Fig. 13

17. Your Kali-Linux-Light 64b is now ready for installation but we need to some house cleaning first. Highlight it and then click on Settings icon, as shown in Fig. 14.

Fig. 14

18. From Fig. 15, click on the **Storage** in the left-pane, then under `Storage` in center-pane under Controller IDE, click on `Empty` followed by clicking CD/DVD to select the ISO file. When done click **OK** to continue

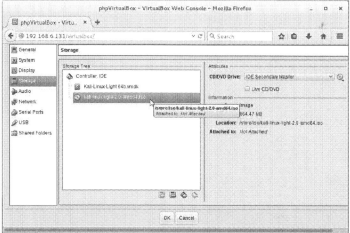

Fig. 15

19. Repeat the same for Network setting, here just accept the default **NAT** selection, see Fig. 16.

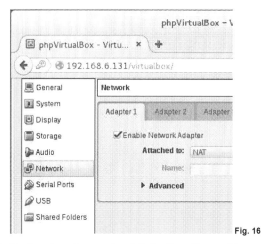

Fig. 16

20. Finally, when done and satisfied with settings, click on the Start button to commence installation, see Fig. 17.

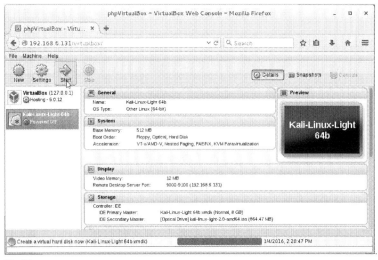

Fig. 17

21. You should now see the Damnsmall VM running under the Preview window, Fig. 19.

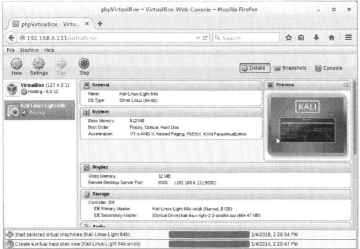
Fig. 19

22. From the right-hand-corner of Fig. 20, click on the Console tab to as shown in Fig. 21, followed by clicking on the Connect to access Fig. 22.

Fig. 20

23. You should be presented with Fig. 21. Select the **Install** option and hit **Enter** key.

Fig. 21

24. We'll continue from the host computer to get a wider space to view our installation process. Now accept the default language selection or change as desired, see Fig. 22, Repeat the same for location and Keyboard selections on consequent pages.

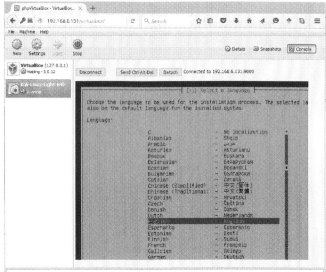

Fig. 22

25. Now set back relax as the system completes the current process, as shown in Fig. 23.

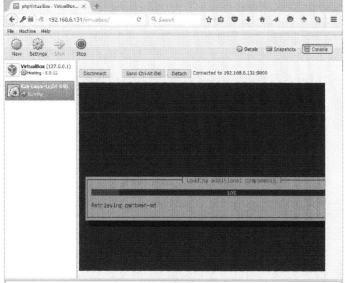

Fig. 23

26. From Fig. 24, accept the default selected hostname of change as desire, and hit the Enter key.

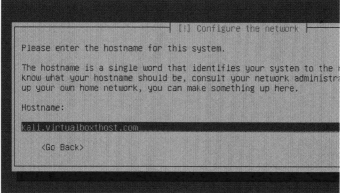

Fig. 24

27. From Fig. 25, enter the root and confirm password and hit **Enter** to continue.

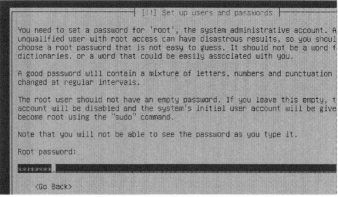

Fig. 25

28. From Fig. 26, just relax as the just system completes the current process..

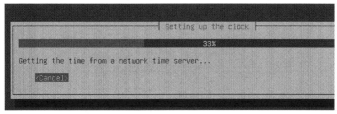

Fig. 26

29. From Fig. 27, accept the default selection or changes as desired and hit enter key.

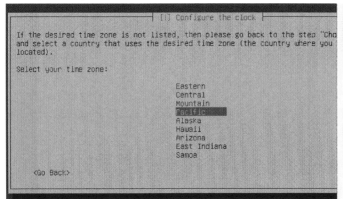

Fig. 27

30. From Fig. 28, accept the default selection or changes as desired and hit enter key.

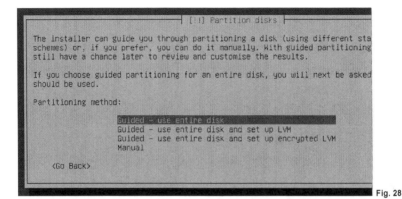

Fig. 28

31. From Fig. 29, just relax as the just system completes the current process..

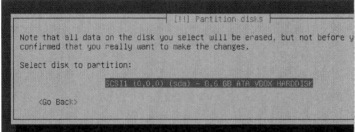

Fig. 29

32. From Fig. 30, accept the default selection or changes as desired and hit enter key.

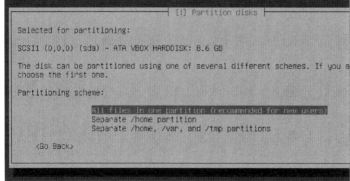

Fig. 30

33. From Fig. 31, accept the default selection or changes as desired and hit enter key.

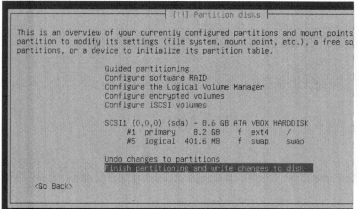

Fig. 31

34. From Fig. 32, read and select Yes and hit enter key to continue.

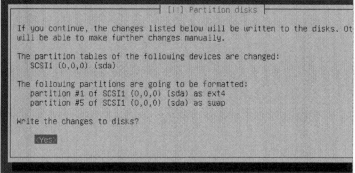

Fig. 32

35. From Fig. 33, just relax as the just system completes the current process..

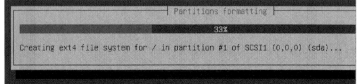

Fig. 33

36. On consequent screens attend to the requested info to continue until you reach the Finish the Installation screen, see Fig. 34. Just relax as the system completes the current task.

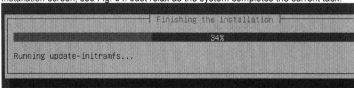

Fig. 34

37. From Fig. 35, you're done with installation, just hit enter key to reboot the system.

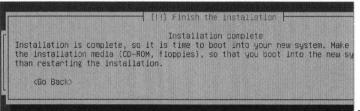

Fig. 35

38. From Fig 36, just relax as the system boots up.

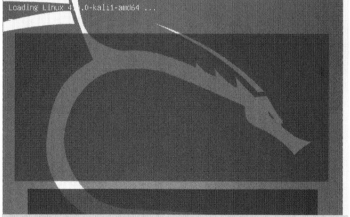

Fig. 36

39. You now be presented with login screen, just login the credentials set during installation, see Fig. 37.

Fig. 37

40. You now be presented with your Desktop screen see Fig. 38.

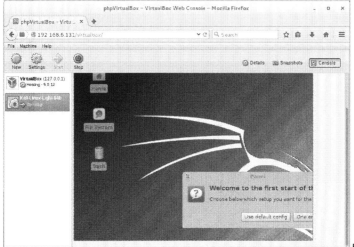

Fig. 38

41. Congrats - you're done with section and virtual machine installation using web access.

42. You can power off the VM when done exploring the capability of Kali Linux.

Part 4: Install Vagrant VirtualBox on CentOS7 / RHEL 7 Server/ Fedora 23

Step 1: Install Vagrant on Fedora 23

Vagrant is computer software that creates and configures virtual development environments. It can be seen as a higher-level wrapper around virtualization software such as VirtualBox, VMware, KVM

219

and Linux Containers (LXC), and around configuration management software such as Ansible, Chef, Salt, and Puppet. Vagrant was originally tied to VirtualBox, but version 1.1 added support for other virtualization software such as VMware and KVM, and for server environments like Amazon EC2. Vagrant is written in Ruby, but can be used in projects written in other programming languages such as PHP, Python, Java, C# and JavaScript. Since version 1.6, Vagrant natively supports Docker containers, which in some cases can serve as a substitute for a fully virtualized operating system. Vagrant plugins also exist, including vagrant-libvirt that adds support for libvirt, vagrant-lxc that adds support for lxc, and vagrant-vsphere that adds support for VMware's ESXi. (Source: Wikipedia)

1. To install vagrant, type:

```
$ sudo dnf install vagrant  -y
```

Point your browser Here to download the latest Vagrant RPM "vagrant_1.8.1_x86_64.rpm" file

You can also use wget command to download

```
wget
https://releases.hashicorp.com/vagrant/1.8.1/vagrant_1.8.1_x86_64.rpm
```

2. Install it using the following command

```
# rpm -ivh vagrant_1.8.1_x86_64.rpm
```

3. Now run "vagrant init" to create a new Vagrant environment.

```
# vagrant init
A `Vagrantfile` has been placed in this directory. You are now
ready to `vagrant up` your first virtual environment! Please read
the comments in the Vagrantfile as well as documentation on
`vagrantup.com` for more information on using Vagrant.
[root@f23 ~]#
```

4. Next, run "vagrant up" to make sure that everything loads properly:

```
# vagrant up
```

5. Checkout Vagrant version, type:

```
# vagrant --version
Vagrant 1.8.1
```

6. You're done with this section.

Step 2: How to add, install and run CentOS 7 Vagrant box to VirtualBox using Vagrant

To add, install and run CentOS 7 Vagrant box to VirtualBox using Vagrant, perform the following procedures:

1. Download CentOS 7 Vagrant box
7. First we need to download CentOS 7 vagrant box from: <u>download the CentOS 7 box</u>. Also you can point you browser **http://www.vagrantbox.es/** to download other distros options.

    Note 1: to use the available boxes just replace {title} and {url} with the information in the table below.

    ```
    $ vagrant box add {title} {url}
    $ vagrant init {title}
    $ vagrant up
    ```

    Note 2: at the time of writing we downloaded "centos-7.0-x86_64.box" file

2. Add a new vagrant user
8. To add a new user named vagrant so that we can use to run vagrant, type:

    ```
    $ useradd vagrant
    ```

9. Create a "/vagrant/centos7" directory, type:

    ```
    $ mkdir -p ~/vagrant/centos7
    ```

10. Change to the directory and copy the downloaded centos7 vagrant box into it

    ```
    $ cp centos-7.0-x86_64.box ~/vagrant/centos7
    $ cd ~/vagrant/centos7
    ```

11. Add the centos7 box by typing the following command:

    ```
    $ vagrant box add centos-7.0-x86_64.box --name centos7
    ```

221

```
[cadmin@cloud centos7]$ vagrant box add centos-7.0-x86_64.box --name centos7
==> box: Box file was not detected as metadata. Adding it directly...
==> box: Adding box 'centos7' (v0) for provider:
    box: Unpacking necessary files from: file:///home/cadmin/vagrant/centos7/cen
tos-7.0-x86_64.box
==> box: Successfully added box 'centos7' (v0) for 'virtualbox'!
[cadmin@cloud centos7]$ ▮
```

Fig. 39

Note 1: replace "centos7" by the box you and the "centos-7.0-x86_64.box" by the name of the box you have downloaded.

Note 2: if the Virtual machine was created on VirtualBox, You should see the message: "The box successfully added biox `centos7` (v0) for `virtualbox`".

12. Finally, run "vagrant init" to create the "Vagrantfile" needed to start the vm, type:

```
$ vagrant init
```

```
[cadmin@cloud centos7]$ vagrant init
A `Vagrantfile` has been placed in this directory. You are now
ready to `vagrant up` your first virtual environment! Please read
the comments in the Vagrantfile as well as documentation on
`vagrantup.com` for more information on using Vagrant.
[cadmin@cloud centos7]$
```

```
[cadmin@cloud centos7]$ ls
centos-7.0-x86_64.box  Vagrantfile
```

13. Now, we need to edit the "Vagrantfile" and replace the name of box inside the file with the name you specified in the "--name" option while creating the vm from the box file. For example, for this hands-on lab, the name is "centos7". Use any editor you like, make changes and save them to the file.

```
$ nano Vagrantfile
```

```
Open ▼   🔂                                                    Save

# -*- mode: ruby -*-
# vi: set ft=ruby :

# All Vagrant configuration is done below. The "2" in Vagrant.configure
# configures the configuration version (we support older styles for
# backwards compatibility). Please don't change it unless you know what
# you're doing.
Vagrant.configure(2) do |config|
  # The most common configuration options are documented and commented below.
  # For a complete reference, please see the online documentation at
  # https://docs.vagrantup.com.

  # Every Vagrant development environment requires a box. You can search for
  # boxes at https://atlas.hashicorp.com/search.
  # config.vm.box = "base"
config.vm.box = "centos7"
  # Disable automatic box update checking. If you disable this, then
  # boxes will only be checked for updates when the user runs
  # `vagrant box outdated`. This is not recommended.
  # config.vm.box_check_update = false
```

Fig. 40

14. Now it's time to start the added box, type:

```
$ vagrant up

[cadmin@cloud centos7]$ vagrant up
Bringing machine 'default' up with 'virtualbox' provider...
==> default: Importing base box 'centos7'...
==> default: Matching MAC address for NAT networking...
==> default: Setting the name of the VM: centos7_default_1452710971923_98926
==> default: Clearing any previously set forwarded ports...
==> default: Clearing any previously set network interfaces...
==> default: Preparing network interfaces based on configuration...
    default: Adapter 1: nat
==> default: Forwarding ports...
    default: 22 (guest) => 2222 (host) (adapter 1)
==> default: Booting VM...
==> default: Waiting for machine to boot. This may take a few minutes...
    default: SSH address: 127.0.0.1:2222
    default: SSH username: vagrant
    default: SSH auth method: private key
    default:
    default: Vagrant insecure key detected. Vagrant will automatically replace
    default: this with a newly generated keypair for better security.
    default:
    default: Inserting generated public key within guest...
    default: Removing insecure key from the guest if it's present...
```

223

```
    default: Key inserted! Disconnecting and reconnecting using new SSH key...
==> default: Machine booted and ready!
==> default: Checking for guest additions in VM...
    default: The guest additions on this VM do not match the installed version
of
    default: VirtualBox! In most cases this is fine, but in rare cases it can
    default: prevent things such as shared folders from working properly. If
you
    default: shared folder errors, please make sure the guest additions within
the
    default: virtual machine match the version of VirtualBox you have
installed on
    default: your host and reload your VM.
    default:
    default: Guest Additions Version: 4.3.28
    default: VirtualBox Version: 5.0
==> default: Mounting shared folders...
    default: /vagrant => /home/cadmin/vagrant/centos7
[cadmin@cloud centos7]$
```

15. Next, login to the CentOS 7 Virtual Machine with the command

```
$ vagrant ssh
```

```
[cadmin@cloud centos7]$ vagrant ssh
Last login: Thu Jul 16 08:48:31 2015 from 10.0.2.2
Welcome to your Vagrant-built virtual machine.
[vagrant@localhost ~]$
```

```
[cadmin@cloud centos7]$ vagrant ssh
Last login: Thu Jul 16 08:48:31 2015 from 10.0.2.2
Welcome to your Vagrant-built virtual machine.
[vagrant@localhost ~]$ ls
base.sh  cleanup.sh  puppet.sh  vagrant.sh  virtualbox.sh  zerodisk.sh
[vagrant@localhost ~]$ exit
logout
Connection to 127.0.0.1 closed.
[cadmin@cloud centos7]$
```

Note: as you can observed, we have managed to successfully login to the `centos7 box` on Virtualbox. You can do system update and upgrade.

Note: next time you want to ssh in to the `centos7 box` added, just change to the directory you created and do i.e., "cd ~/vagrant/centos7", and the type:

```
$ vagrant ssh
```

16. You're done with this section.

Step 2: Managing your `centos7 box` from VirtualBox Web Server

1. Start VirtualBox Web Server

43. Now lets' start the VirtualBox Web server, to do this type:

```
$ vboxwebsrv -H 127.0.0.1
```

44. Now to access your `phpVirtualBox` web interface, point your browser to:

```
http://localhost/virtualbox/
```

45. Login to access the phpVirtualBox - Virtual Web Console, as shown in Fig. 41.

Fig. 41

46. You're done with section.

2. Destroying/Deleting Vagrant Virtualbox

47. After we are finished with the lab, you can delete or destroy your running vagrant virtual box. To do this, run "`vagrant destroy`" command, which will destroy it, type:

```
$ vagrant destroy
```

17. You're done with this section.

Part 5: Why use open source cloud storage software?

Cloud storage is nothing but an enterprise-level cloud data storage model to store the digital data in logical pools, across the multiple servers. You have the option to deploy your own on-premise private cloud solution or you can use public cloud from hosting company such as Amazon, Google, Rackspace, Dropbox and others for keeping your data available and accessible 24/7/365. You can access data stored on cloud storage via API or desktop/mobile apps or web based systems.

Step 1: Why use Open Source Cloud Storage Software?

Deploying an enterprise-level your own public or private cloud open source cloud storage solution build and deployed using open source software gives the freedom to provision and manage your own digital data without fear of risk or loss of privacy and more as follows:

1. Create a cloud on your own server or data center
2. Control and own your data - i.e., know where data is at anytime.
3. Gives your the peace of mind as concerns the privacy protection
4. Provides you ability to manage your CIA (Confidentiality, Integrity and Availability) with encryption providing confidentiality of data - thus avoiding spying on your files on the server
5. Verify source code of bugs and/or backdoors associated risks
6. Legal compliance with HIPAA, SOX etc.
7. Provide good performance, reliability and availability as your data to local storage on the LAN instead of remote data center - thus, you longer depend upon WAN bandwidth or the service provider for network.
8. No critical imposed limits on client connections, storage space etc.
9. Share your files and data with any level of password depending on the level of criticality of the data, share publicly, or privately. No 3rf party corporation own your data.

Part 6: Install ownCloud Storage on CentOS 7 / RHEL 7

First and foremost, for you to setup your personal cloud storage (**ownCloud**), we must have **LAMP** stack in place. Apart from the LAMP stack you may also need to **Perl** and **Python** depending our needs and use.

Step 1: Prerequisites Packages

1. First we need to download the release key associated with the ownCloud software, to do this type:

```
cd /etc/yum.repos.d/
```

```
wget
http://download.opensuse.org/repositories/isv:ownCloud:community/CentO
S_CentOS-7/isv:ownCloud:community.repo
```

2. Next, we need to add `epel` repository too, type:

RHEL/CentOS 7 64-Bit

```
# wget http://dl.fedoraproject.org/pub/epel/7/x86_64/e/epel-release-7-
5.noarch.rpm

# rpm -ivh epel-release-7-5.noarch.rpm
```

3. You're done with this section.

Step 2: Install MySQL (MariaDB) and Create ownCloud Database

4. Install MySQL server, enter:

```
# yum install httpd mysql-server  -y
```

5. Start and enable MariaDB to automatically start on boot.

```
sudo systemctl enable mariadb.service
sudo systemctl start mariadb.service
```

6. Next, start and enable Apached (httpd) to automatically start on boot.

```
sudo systemctl enable httpd.service
sudo systemctl start httpd.service
```

7. Next, ensure to make your MySQL database server secure.

```
# mysql_secure_installation
```

Note: enter the correct option as presented to you.

8. Login to the MySQL (now MariaDB), type:

```
# mysql -u root -p
```

Note: enter the Mysql password which you selected before, & create a database for ownCloud in Mysql prompt:

9. Now, we need to create a database, e.g., cloud, and grant the privileges to loud user as follows:

```
MariaDB> create database owncloud;
Query OK, 1 row affected (0.00 sec)

MariaDB> grant all on owncloud.* to owncloud@localhost identified by
'password';
Query OK, 0 rows affected (0.14 sec)

MariaDB> flush privileges;
Query OK, 0 rows affected (0.06 sec)

MariaDB>exit
```

10. You're done with this section.

Step 3: Install ownCloud

11. Now install ownCloud, type:

```
# yum install owncloud  -y
```

12. You're done with this section.

Step 4: Access ownCloud Application

You're now done with the basic requirements and ready to access your personal cloud storage.

13. To access your personal cloud storage, point your browser to:

```
http://localhost/owncloud
```

OR

```
http://your-ip-address/owncloud
```

Note: once you access to ownCloud page, Fig. 42; you'll need to create an admin account and a data folder, where all your files/directories will be stored (you may also leave the default location i.e., "/var/www/html/owncload/data".

- next you'll need to enter mysql database username, password and cloud database name, as set earlier

- App directory "/var/www/owncloud/apps" not found! Please put the ownCloud apps folder in the ownCloud folder or the folder above. You can also configure the location in the config.php file.

228

Fig. 42

14. When done with entry as shown in Fig. 43, click **Finish Setup** button.

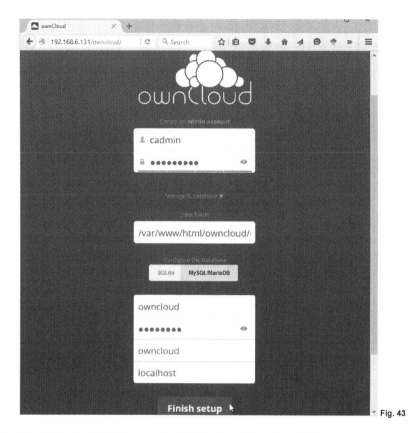

Fig. 43

3. After clicking the Finish Setup, you be able to be logged in as shown in Fig. 44.

230

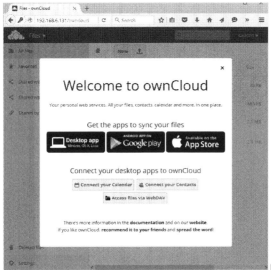

Fig. 44

4. Close the **Welcome to ownCloud** banner to access the ownCloud Console, as shown in Fig. 5.

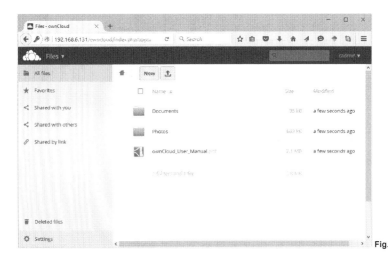

Fig. 45

5. Enjoy your own cloud on your desktop powered by ownCloud technology.

6. You're done with this section.

Part 7: Install, Configure and Secure Seafile Cloud Storage on CentOS 7 / RHEL 7

The Seafile Secure Cloud Storage is an open source cloud platform. In this section you'll lean how to install, configure and Seafile cloud storage which you can use to synchronize your files and data with PC and mobile devices or access via web interface for managing your data files from home, workplace or just anywhere or as ago about your business. Thus, its ideal for small Storage solution mostly for small to medium business purposes, eLearning, joint project management - i.e., a place where you have the flexibility of group sharing and multiple projects, with no need for a public server provision, and has complete security provided by the client-side encryption of the data.

You can choose to host your data on the Seafile cloud or provision it through your local Seafile server which you'll have gained expertise to setup after undertaking the Tech Training Series provision using RHEL 7 / CentOS 7 server.

Step 1: Install Seafile Prerequisites

Seafile Secure Cloud like any application software depends on upon an number of prerequisites to be in place before it can be successfully installed.

1. Systems Update

You'll need to first and foremost update your RHEL 7 / CentOS 7 server. To do this, you'll need a root user credentials, configure FQDN with a static IP address. Here we're using CentOS 7 server, but can easily do the same with RHEL 7.

1. To update your server with latest updates, run following command, type:

```
sudo yum update
```

2. You're done with this section.

2. Install LAMP Stack

It's assumed that you have setup or know how to setup LAMP stack server and ensure that is working successfully. In this Hands-on Tech Training Series, we're using Apache web server (httpd), MariaDB (formerly MySQL) database server.

3. Install Python Packages

Seafile secure storage cloud setup does require a couple of python module to be in place before you can be able to successfully install it, otherwise your install installation setup will be unsuccessful - leading to errors that will require to install missing dependencies.

3. Some of Python packages Seafile requires are not by default provided on CentOS 7 distro, therefore, we'll first need to EPEL option which contain most packages required for enterprise CentOS 7 server applications, to do this run:

```
sudo yum install epel-release
```

4. Now, you can install the required python modules by issuing the following command, type:

```
# yum install MySQL-python python-imaging python-simplejson python-setuptools
-y
```

5. You're done with this section.

Step 2: Download and Install Seafile Server Package

To download Seafile server package, point your browser to official link Here and download the latest file. You'll have option to download the package that fits your operating system from Windows to Linux etc. with an option of 64bit or 32bit architecture. Here, we downloaded the "seafile-server_5.0.3_x86-64.tar.gz" at the time of writing this hands-on training manual.

6. You can also use the wget command to download it, type:

wget https://bintray.com/artifact/download/seafile-org/seafile/seafile-server_5.0.3_x86-64.tar.gz

7. Next, we need to create a new directory in the web document root directory, and extract the Seafile server package into it as follows:

```
# yum install MySQL-python python-imaging python-simplejson python-setuptools
-y
```

8. Now make the directory to setup the Seafile server as follows:

```
sudo mkdir /var/www/storage
sudo tar -xvxf seafile-server_5.0.3_x86-64.tar.gz -C /var/www/storage
```

9. You're done with this section.

1. Setup Seafile Server

10. Now, we are ready to setup the Seafile server. Change to directory where extracted the installation package and execute the following command, as follows:

```
# cd /var/www/storage/seafile-server-5.0.3
# mv seafile-server-5.0.3/ seafile-server
```

next run the setup (Note: the script will first check the dependencies, and then will ask you to Press the Enter key to continue).

```
[root@centos7 seafile-server]# ./setup-seafile-mysql.sh
Checking python on this machine ...
  Checking python module: setuptools ... Done.
  Checking python module: python-imaging ... Done.
  Checking python module: python-mysqldb ... Done.


-----------------------------------------------------------------
This script will guide you to setup your seafile server using MySQL.
Make sure you have read seafile server manual at

        https://github.com/haiwen/seafile/wiki

Press ENTER to continue
-----------------------------------------------------------------


What is the name of the server? It will be displayed on the client.
3 - 15 letters or digits
[ server name ] centos7

What is the ip or domain of the server?
For example: www.mycompany.com, 192.168.1.101
[ This server's ip or domain ] 192.168.6.10

Where do you want to put your seafile data?
Please use a volume with enough free space
[ default "/var/www/storage/seafile-data" ] ⏎

Which port do you want to use for the seafile fileserver?
[ default "8082" ] ⏎


-------------------------------------------------
Please choose a way to initialize seafile databases:
-------------------------------------------------


[1] Create new ccnet/seafile/seahub databases
[2] Use existing ccnet/seafile/seahub databases

[ 1 or 2 ] 1

What is the host of mysql server?
```

```
[ default "localhost" ] ↵

What is the port of mysql server?
[ default "3306" ] ↵

What is the password of the mysql root user?
[ root password ]

verifying password of user root ...  done

Enter the name for mysql user of seafile. It would be created if not
exists.
[ default "root" ] seafile

Enter the password for mysql user "seafile":
[ password for seafile ] ↵

Enter the database name for ccnet-server:
[ default "ccnet-db" ] ↵

Enter the database name for seafile-server:
[ default "seafile-db" ] ↵

Enter the database name for seahub:
[ default "seahub-db" ] ↵

-----------------------------------
This is your configuration
-----------------------------------

    server name:          centos7
    server ip/domain:     192.168.6.10

    seafile data dir:     /var/www/storage/seafile-data
    fileserver port:      8082

    database:             create new
    ccnet database:       ccnet-db
    seafile database:     seafile-db
    seahub database:      seahub-db
    database user:        seafile


-----------------------------------
Press ENTER to continue, or Ctrl-C to abort
-----------------------------------

Generating ccnet configuration ...

done
Successly create configuration dir /var/www/storage/ccnet.
Generating seafile configuration ...
```

```
Done.
done
Generating seahub configuration ...

_____

Now creating seahub database tables ...

_____

creating seafile-server-latest symbolic link ...  done

_____
Your seafile server configuration has been finished successfully.
_____

run seafile server:    ./seafile.sh { start | stop | restart }
run seahub  server:    ./seahub.sh { start <port> | stop | restart
<port> }

_____
If you are behind a firewall, remember to allow input/output of these
tcp ports:
_____

port of seafile fileserver:    8082
port of seahub:                8000

When problems occur, Refer to

        https://github.com/haiwen/seafile/wiki

for information.

[root@centos7 seafile-server]#
```

Note: the symbol ⏎ indicate the place where you hit the **Enter** key, with red font text indicating the option where you type the required info.

2. Staring Seafile Server

11. To start the Seafile server, execute the following script, type:

```
[root@centos7 seafile-server]# ./seafile.sh start

[01/08/16 15:39:40] ../common/session.c(132): using config file
/var/www/storage/conf/ccnet.conf
[01/08/16 15:39:40] ../common/ccnet-db.c(76): max_connections: 100
Starting seafile server, please wait ...
Seafile server started
```

236

```
Done.
[root@centos7 seafile-server]#
```

next, run the seahub.sh script, type:

```
[root@centos7 seafile-server]# ./seahub.sh start

LC_ALL is not set in ENV, set to en_US.UTF-8
Starting seahub at port 8000 ...

-----------------------------------------
It's the first time you start the seafile server. Now let's create the
admin account
-----------------------------------------

What is the email for the admin account?
[ admin email ] nadmin@govsystemlabs.com

What is the password for the admin account?
[ admin password ]

Enter the password again:
[ admin password again ]

-----------------------------------------
Successfully created seafile admin
-----------------------------------------

LC_ALL is not set in ENV, set to en_US.UTF-8
Starting seahub at port 8000 ...

Seahub is started

Done.

[root@centos7 seafile-server]#
```

12. When done with the starting the server, you'll now be asked

3. Login to Seafile Server
We are now ready to access the Seahub dashboard in order to manage and share your libraries
and folders/directories etc.

13. Now fire-up your browser to access the Seahub dashboard console, using your server's IP
    address or FQDN with your configure default ports. Login with your admin email address that
    you created during the Seahub server startup.

    ```
    http://your_server_ip:8000
    ```

237

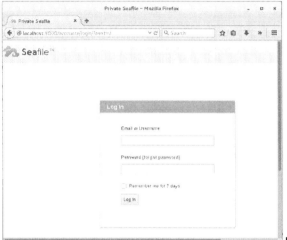

Fig. 46a

Fig. 46b

14. When successfully logged in, you'll be presented with the Welcome to Seafile! alert, close it in order access Seahub management console.

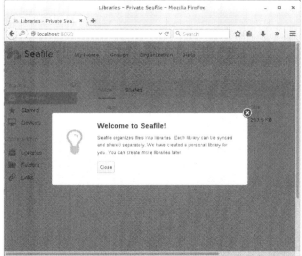
Fig. 47a

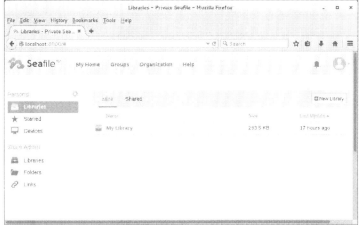
Fig. 47b

Note: Once you have successfully logged in and have access to the Seahub dashboard, you now have the possibility to organize files into libraries and each library can be synched and shared separately. As can be observed there is an already created -personal library, however, you're now free to create more libraries for personal use or for sharing purpose.

15. You're done with this section, take your time explore around to enjoy the power of Seafile Secure Cloud Storage.

Step 3: Creating New Libraries on Seahub console

We're now ready to proceed with creating new libraries for personal use or for sharing with friends, workmates, groups etc.

1. To do this, click on the New Library link as shown in Fig. 48.

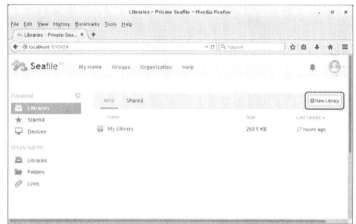

Fig. 48

2. You're done with this section.

Step 4: Uploading your Data to Seahub Server

3. To upload your data, click on the My Library link, from Fig. 45 above, you will be presented the page shown in Fig. 49. From here you can perform a couple of different tasks: upload data e.g., folders, images; create **New Folder**; create **New File** or Share your contents.

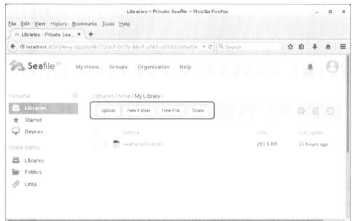
Fig. 49

4. You're done with this section.

1. Uploading file from CentOS 7 machine

5. To upload a file, click on the **Upload** tab from Fig. 49 above, and should be presented with Fig. 50. Select desired file, then click on the Open button.

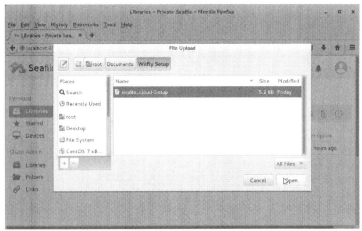
Fig. 50

6. After a while your uploaded file should listed your My Library list, a shown in Fig. 51.

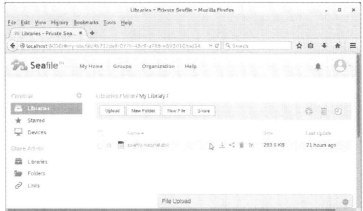

Fig. 51

7. Go ahead perform other tasks as desired.

8. You're done with this section.

Step 5: Install & Configure Seafile Client for Windows

1. Point your browser Here to download the latest Seafile Client for Windows. At the time of writing we downloaded "seafile-5.0.2-en.msi" file.

2. Access the folder where the file is located and double-click it to start the installation process. You should be presented with **Welcome to the Seafile 5.0.2 Setup Wizard**, click **Next** to continue, see Fig. 52.

Fig. 52

3. From Fig. 53, accept the default selected location, and then click on **Next**.

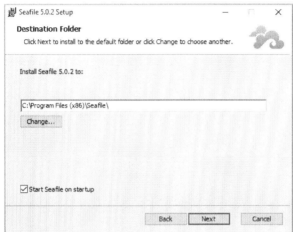

Fig. 53

4. From Fig. 54, **Ready to Install Seafile** screen, click the **Install** button.

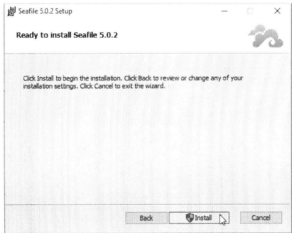

Fig. 54

5. The system will go through the installation process, when done click on the **Finish** button, see Fig. 52.

Fig. 55

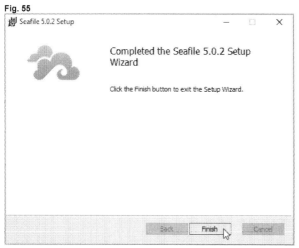

6. Next, you'll required to **Choose Seafile folder**, click on the **Choose..** button to select the desired folder, see Fig. 56.

Fig. 56

7. From Fig. 57, select the folder to share and then click on the **Select Folder** button.

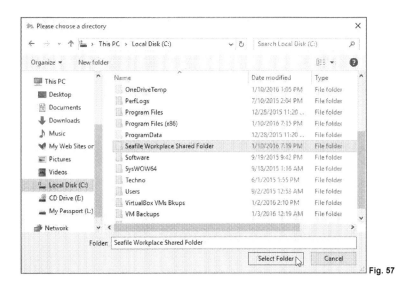
Fig. 57

8. From Fig. 58, when satisfied with the selected folder to share, then click on **Next**.

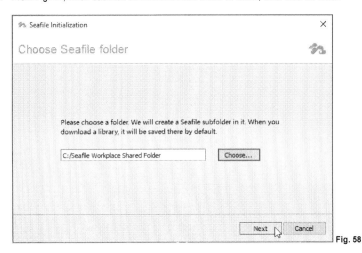
Fig. 58

9. From Fig. 59, **Add an Account** screen, enter the required info and then click on the **Login** button.

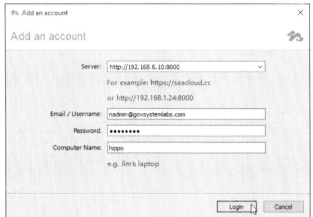

Fig. 59

10. From Fig. 60, you will be presented with two screens: (a) **Download Default Library**, (b) **Seafile** messenger, from (a) click on **Yes** button o accept and continue.

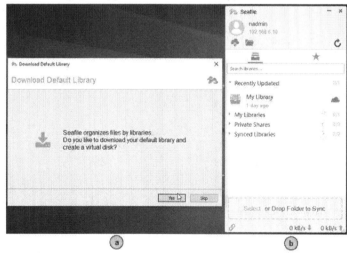

Fig. 60

11. From 61, you have the option to select **Open** to view your selection or select **Finish** to complete the task.

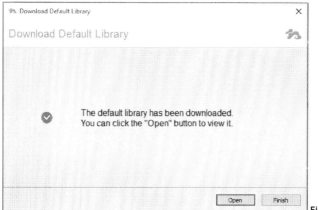

Fig. 61

12. From Fig. 62 above select the **Open** option to view your shared content, and you should be presented with Fig. 63.

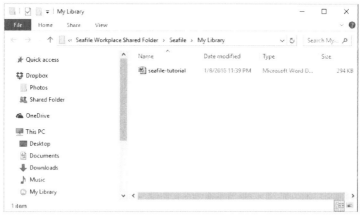

Fig. 63

13. You now have a cool option to **Select or DRAG FOLDER to Sync** your shared library contents on the fly anytime, anywhere anyplace 24/7/365, see Fig. 64.

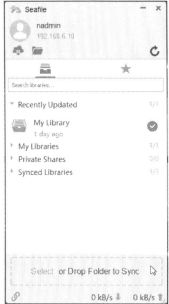

Fig. 64

14. Enjoy the power of accessing your shared data securely with Seafile Secure Cloud Storage on the fly.

15. You're done with ICT skills enhancement hands-on training labs - Good luck!

Part 8: Install, Configure Pydio Self-Hosted Cloud Storage on CentOS 7 / RHEL 7

Pydio is an alternative to Dropbox and box.com, for enterprise. You need to access your documents across multiple devices, and regularly share documents (weblinks) and folders with your contacts and teams. Still, using a consumer SaaS box or drive service is neither practical nor safe. And enterprise SaaS box or drive services are expensive and come with Disk Storage that you already have on your servers or private cloud.

Features:
- Central server with file-revision history
- Web interface with file management and link sharing
- Dropbox-style synchronization with Pydio Sync (in beta)

248

- Multi storage configuration (SFTP, local, samba, POP3/IMAP, MySQL, Amazon S3, WebDAV)
- Loads of plugins and integrations

Step 1: Install Prerequisites for Pydio Server

1. First and foremost we need to ensure that all OS packages are up to date by executing the following command:

```
# yum update -y
```

2. Install all required packages and dependencies:

```
# yum install epel-release -y
# yum -y install php php-gd php-ldap php-pear php-xml php-xmlrpc php-mbstring
curl php-mcrypt* php-mysql
```

3. Install Apache web server:

```
# yum install httpd -y
```

4. Now, start the httpd service and enable it to start on boot (if you didn't install it before!):

```
# systemctl enable httpd.service
# systemctl start httpd.service
```

5. Pydio requires database to store the information, therefore if you hadn't installed MySQL (MariaDB) database, then run following command:

```
# yum install mariadb mariadb-server -y
```

6. Now, start the MariaDB service and enable it to start on boot:

```
# systemctl enable mariadb.service
# systemctl start mariadb.service
```

Note: if its the first time you're installing MariaDB, then we need to secure the MariaDB server and set the MariaDB root password, run the "mysql_secure_installation" script as root.

7. Now, we need to create a new MariaDB database and user:

```
mysql -u root -p
CREATE DATABASE pydio;
CREATE USER 'pydiouser'@'localhost' IDENTIFIED BY 'pydiopass';
```

```
GRANT ALL PRIVILEGES ON pydio.* TO 'pydiouser'@'localhost';
FLUSH PRIVILEGES;
exit
```

Note: here we have added database=pydiodb user=pydiouser and password=pydiopass :

```
[root@cloud ~]# mysql -u pydiouser -p
Enter password:
MariaDB [(none)]> show databases;
+--------------------+
| Database           |
+--------------------+
| information schema |
| pydio              |
+--------------------+
```

8. You're done with this section.

Step 2: Download & Install Pydio

9. Now we need to go to Pydio's official website and download the latest stable release of the software using wget command:

wget http://liquidtelecom.dl.sourceforge.net/project/ajaxplorer/pydio/stable-channel/6.2.1/pydio-core-6.2.1.zip

10. Next, extract the zip archive to the "/var/www/html/" directory on your server:

```
# unzip pydio-core-6.2.1.zip -d /var/www/html/
```

11. Now, rename the "pydio-core-6.2.1" directory to "pydio":

```
mv /var/www/html/pydio-core-6.2.1/ /var/www/html/pydio
```

12. All pydio files have to be readable by the web server, so set the proper ownership:

```
chown -R apache:apache /var/www/html/pydio/
```

13. Next under CentOS 7 and Fedora 22+, we need to create/modify and add the following lines to the Pydio configuration file "pydio.conf" as follows:

```
# vi /etc/httpd/conf.d/pydio.conf

#<Directory "/usr/share/pydio">
```

```
#         Options FollowSymLinks
#         AllowOverride Limit FileInfo
#         Order allow,deny
#         Allow from all
#      php_value error_reporting 2
#</Directory>


<Directory /usr/share/pydio>
    Options FollowSymlinks
    AllowOverride none
    Require all granted
    php_value error_reporting 2
</Directory>
```

14. Next configure "php.ini" to allow max file upload, disable php output buffering and increase "memory_limit" to boost performance of Pydio as shown:

```
# vi /etc/php.ini

post_max_size = 1G
upload_max_filesize = 1G
output_buffering = Off
memory_limit = 1024M
```

15. Now, start the **httpd** service and enable it to start on boot (if you didn't install it before!):

```
# systemctl enable httpd.service
# systemctl start httpd.service
```

7. Now set correct charset encoding in your locale definition in the form: "en_us.UTF-8". First find out current charset lang of system by running following command

```
# echo $LANG

[root@cloud ~]# echo $LANG
en_US.UTF-8
```

Note: if different, then using your favorite text editor open "/etc/pydio/bootstrap_conf.php" file and add the following line.

```
define("AJXP_LOCALE", "en_US.UTF-8");
```

16. Finally, point your browser to the URL http://server1.example.com/pydio or http://ip-address/pydio, you should be presented with checklist page which if all is OK, i.e., without errors, then click Next.

251

17. From Fig. 66, accept the default selection or change as desired, and the click on the Start Wizard to continue.

Fig. 65

18. From Fig. 66, **Main Option** page, accept the default selections and also enter, and the click on the **>>** to continue. (**Note:** create admin user=`cadmin` and password=`adminpass`, change as desired!)

Fig. 66

19. From Fig. 67, **Database Connection** page, accept the default selection or change as desired, and the click on the **>>** to continue. Select storage type as Database system, and put the `Database=pydio user=pydiouser` and `password=pydiopass` or change as per your setup. (**Note:** you may click on **Test Connection** to test database connectivity).

Fig. 67

20. From Fig. 68, **Advanced Options** page, accept the default selection or change as desired, and the click on the **Install Pydio** to continue.

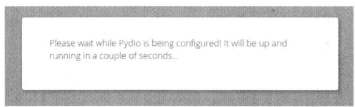

Fig. 68

21. From 69, please relax while the system completes the current tasks.

Please wait while Pydio is being configured! It will be up and running in a couple of seconds...

Fig. 69

22. When done, you should be presented with login page, as shown in Fig. 70. Use the credential we created earlier, i.e.: admin user: `cadmin` and admin password: `adminpass` (change as per your settings.)

Fig. 70a

Fig. 70b

23. You should be presented with Pydio Welcome admin console, as shown in Fig. 71.

Fig. 71

24. From Fig. 71, click on the **Common Files** link, to access Fig. 72.

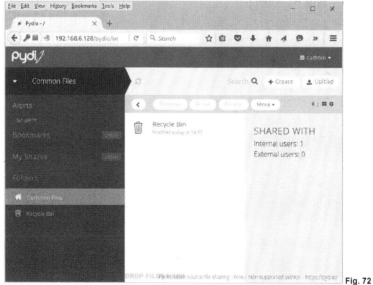

Fig. 72

25. Similarly, from Fig. 71, click on the **My Files** link, to access Fig. 73.

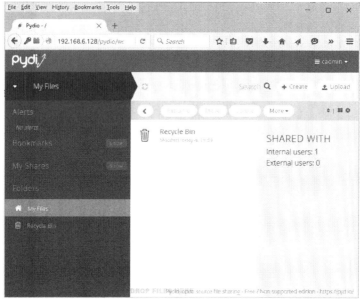

Fig. 73

26. You can access your settings by the clicking the current logged in user icon, as shown in Fig. 74.

Fig. 74

27. You're done with this section.

Step 3: Install and Configure Pydio Client for Windows

1. Point your browser to download page Here. at the time of writing we downloaded "**Pydio-0.8.4-Windows-x86_64-Setup.msi**".

2. Access the download folder and double-click the just downloaded file to commence the installation process. You should be presented with the Setup page as show n in Fig. 75. Click on the Install button to install it.

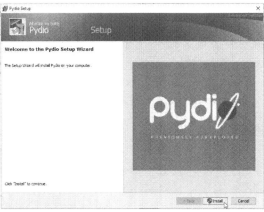

Fig. 75

3. Just relax while system completes the current tasks.

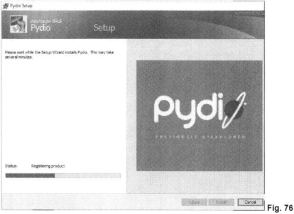

Fig. 76

4. From Fig. 77, click on the Finish button to complete the setup.

Fig. 77

5. You should be presented with Server Connection dialogue box, enter the required entries, follow the instruction select the **Workspace** and **Local Folder** selection.

Fig. 78a

6. Set the desired **Execution Parameters**, as shown in Fig. 78b.

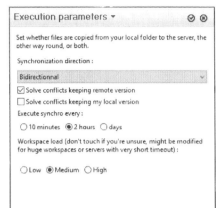

Fig. 78b

7. Now from your notification window select the Pydio client as shown in Fig. 79.

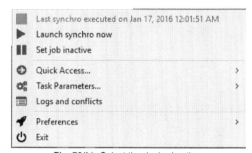

Fig. 79(a): Click on the Pydio client.

Fig. 79(b): Select the desired option.

8. From the **Quick Access** option you can choose to **Open local folder** or **Access remote server**, as shown in Fig. 80

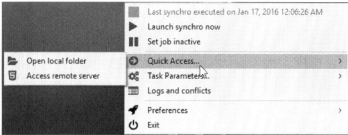

Fig. 80

9. Now lets share shown folders. From the Windows Explorer, locate your Public shared folder and under **Public Music** place shown music folder, **Celtic Love Collection Vol. 1**, which we want to share with others. We had already set this in Fig. 78a.

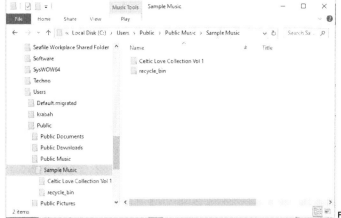

Fig. 81

10. Now open the Pydio server and should see that indeed its shared under **My Files** location as shown in Fig. 82.

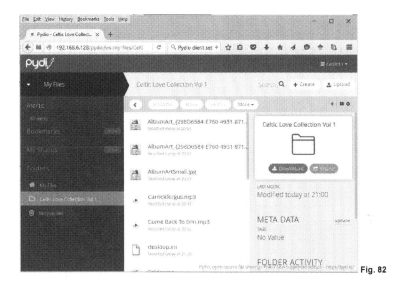
Fig. 82

11. You're done with this section and also the Pydio server installation - Enjoy.

Part 9: Troubleshooting Seafile Cloud Seahub Start LC_ALL Error on RHEL 7 / CentOS 7

```
[root@centos7 seafile-server]# ./seahub.sh start-fastcgi

LC_ALL is not set in ENV, set to en_US.UTF-8
Starting seahub (fastcgi) at 127.0.0.1:8000 ...
Error:Seahub failed to start.
```

Solution:
1. To fix the problem, as root, create the /etc/environment, type:

```
# nano /etc/environment
```

and add the following entries:

```
LANG=en_US.UTF-8
LC_ALL=en_US.UTF-8
```

2. Save and exit.

3. Now you should now be able to run your Sealfile cloud with any problem.

```
[root@cloud seafile-server]# ./seahub.sh start-fastcgi
```

4. You're done with this section.

Part 10: Troubleshooting SELinux

You have the option to set SELinux into three options: **Permissive**, **Enforcing** and **Disabled** depending on your requirements. For more info, check: http://www.crypt.gen.nz/selinux/disable_selinux.html

Step 1: Fully Disabling SELinux

Fully disabling SELinux goes one step further than just switching into permissive mode. Disabling will completely disable all SELinux functions including file and process labeling.

1. In Fedora Core, CentOS and RedHat Enterprise, using your favorite Text editor, edit the default "/etc/selinux/config" file and change the SELINUX line to "SELINUX=disabled":

```
# This file controls the state of SELinux on the system.
# SELINUX= can take one of these three values:
# enforcing - SELinux security policy is enforced.
# permissive - SELinux prints warnings instead of enforcing.
# disabled - No SELinux policy is loaded.
SELINUX=disabled
# SELINUXTYPE= can take one of these two values:
# targeted - Only targeted network daemons are protected.
# strict - Full SELinux protection.
SELINUXTYPE=targeted
```

2. Save and then reboot the system.

3. You're done with section.

Part 11: Need More Training on Mastering ICT Infrastructure Development & Deployment

Are you having trouble understanding or comprehending ICT infrastructure planning, design and deployment projects with Microsoft Windows Server, Linux (CentOS, RHEL etc.), DNS servers provisioning, IPA (Identity Management) provisioning, Application Servers (WildFly, JBoss, GlassFish, Joomla CMS, Moodle LMS), Public, private to personal cloud provisioning with ownCloud, Seafile secure cloud storage, eyesCloud, Eucalyptus cloud, OpenNebula, FastStack etc.), if so, then check out some of our top ICT skills enhancement training courses at: Global Open Versity, Vancouver Canada.

Mastering RHEL 7 / CentOS 7 Server Administration and System Integration Training - ICT405

You can now register and take our superb Mastering RHEL 7 / CentOS 7 Server Administration. This Training cover compete server installation, administration and system integration from simple task to cloud computing with ownCloud and Seafile Secure Cloud Storage and virtualization skills enhancement with VirtualBox integrated with phpVirtualBox web management console.

- ICT405 – Mastering RHEL 7 / CentOS 7 Training

Contact us today: Email: info@globalopenversity.org   **URL:** www.globalopenversity.org

Other Related Articles:
1. Step-By-Step Guide Using Webmin and Bind9 on CentOS-7 Infrastructure Server to Setup Robust DNS Sever
2. Install Guide Secure Postfix Messaging Server with Dovecot and ClamAV on Linux v1.2
3. Build and Deploy Enterprise sipXecs Integration with Openfire
4. Step-By-Step Build & Deploy Citrix XenServer and XenCenter v1.0
5. Step-By-Step Install Guide Xen Hypervisor on Linux Server v1.1
6. Step-By-Step Build & Deploy Citrix XenServer and XenCenter v1.2
7. Step-By-Step Install Guide Alfresco Community 3.3g on RHEL5 Server v1.0
8. Build your own ISP Hosting using EHCP on Ubuntu 10.04 LTS Server
9. Step-By-Step Install Guide DTC on Linux CentOS5 Server v1.0

Other References
https://www.digitalocean.com/community/tutorials/how-to-install-bacula-server-on-centos-7
https://www.digitalocean.com/community/tutorials/how-to-back-up-a-centos-7-server-with-bacula
http://www.unixmen.com/install-and-configure-bacula-server-in-centos-6-4-rhel-6-4/

Chapter V

Step-By-Step Guide Using Webmin and Bind9 on CentOS-7 Server to Setup Robust DNS Sever

Introduction

The Domain Name System, or DNS, is one of the Internet's fundamental building blocks. It is the global, hierarchical, and distributed host information database that's responsible for translating names into addresses and vice versa, routing mail to its proper destination, and many other services.

BIND (Berkeley Internet Name Domain) is an implementation of the DNS protocols and provides an openly redistributable reference implementation of the major components of the Domain Name System, including: Domain Name System (DNS) server; Domain Name System resolver library; including tools for managing and verifying the proper operation of the DNS server. The BIND DNS Server is used on the vast majority of name serving machines on the Internet, providing a robust and stable architecture on top of which an organization's naming architecture can be built. One also needs to setup a slave DNS server to handle redundancy in case the primary DNS server goes down or crashes under any kind of disaster.

A slave DNS is simply a name server that copies zones files from a master server. For network infrastructure planning, designing and implementation and web deploying best practices, it's always recommended that additional DNS servers for redundancy purposes. This is very important to maintaining a 24/7/365 and 999.9 uptime availability of your web servers to your customers.

Once you have planned, designed, implemented and deployed a robust DNS server infrastructure, and it's up and running – you can go ahead and push the boundaries of your network infrastructure to enterprise level e.g., building large data center or large multinational corporation. For those who're interested in moving into ISP biz, or those with large enterprise network infrastructure – you can also use the DNS server to setup and manage virtual web hosting and become an Internet Service Provider (ISP), or those with an eye to start running data centers.

In this guide, we present a step-by-step installation and configuration of DNS server (Bind9) using Webmin on Linux CentOS-7. I'll also show you how to add a virtual domain (virtual hosting) to extend your network infrastructure capability. Also to be learned is how to install & set up a slave DNS to handle your DNS redundancy. You'll also learn how to test if your DNS redundancy can survive a catastrophic failure of one the DNS server, and still be in business. All the lab-work on this install guide was done using Linux CentOS-7 on VMware.

Hands-on Labs:

In this Hands-on Lab session, you'll learn how to setup two virtual machines using VMware (you may also use any other virtual machines like MS VirtualPC, Linux Xen, or Oracle VirtualBo) or a physical server if you have one in place. Next, you will learn how to install and configure Webmin, which we'll use to configure the DNS Master Server, Virtual Hosting site and Slave DNS Server for redundancy. The first Virtual machine will be used to host DNS Master Server on Linux CentOS-7. You'll also learn how to install & configure a second virtual machine with Linux CentOS-7 for hosting the Slave DNS Server. Finally you'll have an opportunity to do the Hands-on Labs assignments to test what you have learned in this lesson. Once you're done with this labs session you should have gained an experience, skills and capability to enable you to plan design implement and deploy a complete enterprise DNS infrastructure, which will allow you to install enterprise business solutions that require DNS in place like Messaging server (e.g., Sendmail), LDAP, and Identity Management and SSO.

Assumptions:
It's assumed that you have a good understanding of Linux operating system and its working environment. It's also assumed that you know how to install and configure Linux CentOS-7, if not go ahead and pop over to scribd.com and check out a good HowTo entitled "Step-By-Step Guide CentOS-7 Infrastructure Server Installation and Administration" to get you started.

Part 1: Installing and Configuring Webmin

1. Administering Linux and Unix-based servers does not need to be the scourge of your work day. With a handy tool called Webmin as part of your arsenal, you can regain full control of your servers' setup and configuration via the Web browser.

2. To Install Webmin and get started, drop by www.webmin.com and download the latest release. You can use RPMs for RHE/CentOS and related systems that support binary installations or you can build Webmin from source. Webmin supports a large number of UNIX variants, including Mac OS X. To install the rpm, simply open a terminal session, and type in:

```
# rpm -ivh webmin*
```

   • as root user in the directory in which Webmin was downloaded

3. Webmin is the most powerful administration tool in its nature. We will use it to set up our DNS, but I will not go over it in detail because its assumed that you already know how to use other administrative tools. In any case, it is not difficult to use because it is web based, i.e., in any event, you should know that you can use it remotely to administer the system. In this hands-on training guide, we're going to use Webmin to setup DNS Server and mail, www and ftp servers on Linux CentOS-7.

4. While here also note our hostname and IP address:

```
rhel7.govsystemlabs.com    192.168.6.10
```

   Other servers are:

```
mail.govsystemlabs.com
www.govsystemlabs.com
ftp.govsystemlabs.com
```

5. I assumed that you know how to install CentOS-7 using static IP address, which is very important for DNS server. Once you're done with the installation then verify that your hosts file is setup correctly.

6. Check out "/etc/hosts" to ensure that you have a correct setup, in our case, it's as follows:

```
127.0.0.1    localhost localhost.localdomain localhost4 localhost4.localdomain4
192.168.6.10    centos7.govsystemlabs.com  centos7 www  ftp  mail
::1          localhost localhost.localdomain localhost6 localhost6.localdomain6
```

Fig. 1

7. To do this, first we need to change to the directory as shown to update the "ifcfg-eth0", to static IP address, type:

```
# cd /etc/sysconfig/network-scripts/
# nano ifcfg-eth0
```

then set the configuration as follows:

```
TYPE="Ethernet"
BOOTPROTO="static"
NM_CONTROLLED="no"
IPADDR=192.168.6.10
BROADCAST=192.168.6.255
NETWORK=192.168.6.0
NETMASK=255.255.255.0
GATEWAY=192.168.6.2
DNS1=192.168.6.10
IPV4_FAILURE_FATAL="no"
IPV6INIT=no
USERCTL=no
NAME="eth0"
UUID="60a16494-752d-4bbc-9cd1-4c83eac0b97b"
DEVICE="eth0"
ONBOOT="yes"
```

8. Reboot the server.

9. Now check to verify that the network is set correctly:

```
# ifconfig eth0
```

```
[root@centos7 ~]# ifconfig
eth0: flags=4163<UP,BROADCAST,RUNNING,MULTICAST>  mtu 1500
        inet 192.168.6.10  netmask 255.255.255.0  broadcast 192.168.6.255
        inet6 fe80::20c:29ff:fe82:bc1a  prefixlen 64  scopeid 0x20<link>
        ether 00:0c:29:82:bc:1a  txqueuelen 1000  (Ethernet)
        RX packets 62  bytes 7407 (7.2 KiB)
        RX errors 0  dropped 0  overruns 0  frame 0
        TX packets 83  bytes 9217 (9.0 KiB)
        TX errors 0  dropped 0 overruns 0  carrier 0  collisions 0
```
Fig. 2

10. Now edit your "/etc/resolv.conf" file to reflect the changes, as shown in Fig. 3.

```
# Generated by NetworkManager
search localdomain govsystemlabs.com
nameserver 192.168.6.10
nameserver 192.168.6.2
```
Fig. 3

11. Make sure that all the required services are running including Webmin.

12. Now open the web browser and type:

    http://localhost:100000 or http://127.0.0.1:10000 **or**
    http://yourdomain:10000

    in our case: http://rhel7.govsystemhost.com:10000

Fig. 4: Adding Webmin as trusted service

13. When you open the web browser and execute the 10000 port you will see an error, describing that the web server is running in SSL mode and gives you a link to try instead. Click on the link, you may see another error describing that the server certificate failed; click on Continue. Another warning pops up.

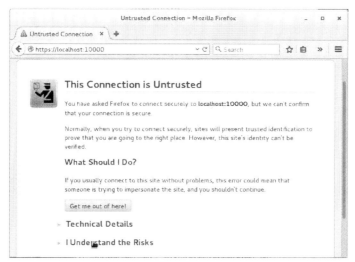

Fig 5: Accepting the certificate

- Click on "I Understand the Risks" link to continue.

14. Next enter the user name and password to authenticate.

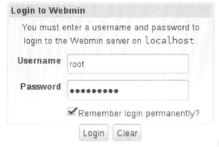

Fig 6

- **Note**: for security best practices in a production environment, never use "Remember login" password.

- Also note that this is run by root, but you can still give permission to other users with limited privilege to run it.

- I suggest that you never give this power to any other user except to you, the administrator.

15. Click on Login to enter Webmin and get started.

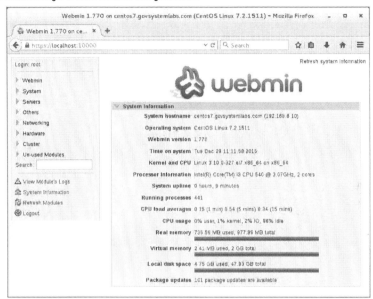

Fig 7: Webmin interface.

16. You're done with this section.

Part 2: Install & Configure Bind9 DNS server

1. Figure 7 above shows Webmin's management console page, a generic most wanted administrative tool. But of course with all the tools, you probably won't rely on Webmin for all admin purposes. Although, Webmin is useful for automating tasks, for teaching purpose, it's always preferable to do things manually via command line so that apprentices can have a better understanding of what actually happens in the background.

   • Feel free to explore and actually try to use the available modules in Webmin. Once you learn how to use it, it will become your favorite remote administrative tool.

2. From Fig. 7 clicking on **Servers** allows you to see all the installed servers, while these may not be all other servers that are available in this panel, and which are installed on this machine.

3. In case Bind9 is not installed, then issue yum command to install BIND **DNS Server (BIND9)**, as follows:

```
#yum install bind* -y
```

4. Let's start and enable named to also start automatically on boot.

```
systemctl start named.service
systemctl enable named.service
```

5. Now, from Fig. 7; scroll down and from the left column click on 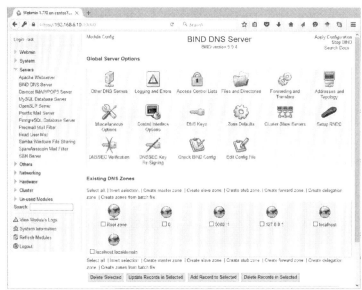 Refresh Modules link to update the Webmin's available modules.

6. Again, from Fig. 8; click on **Bind DNS Server** to start our DNS configuration. For this article we used Bind9, however, do make a point to download the latest Bind server package and ensure that you update your system before proceeding with setup. The network address used here is for LAN, but you can easily replace it with a public IP address if you have a legal domain name and have an IP address issued to you by your ISP or domain hosting company.

7. From Fig. 8, choose the option best suited for your setup. In our case we opted for the second option. Checking the second option and clicking **Create Primary Configuration and Start Nameserver** brings you to the Bind DNS Server panel (this may be already there).

8. When done you should be presented with page as shown in Fig. 8.

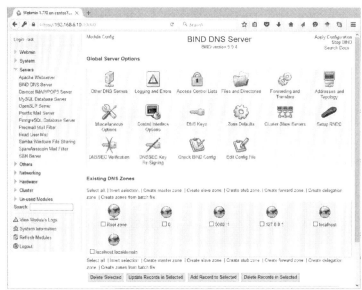

Fig 8

9. Note that Bind DNS Server panel is divided into three different sections:

- Global server options
- Existing DNS zones (which will be our working section, see Fig. 9)
- Client's view designed on the server

Existing DNS Zones

Select all. | Invert selection. | Create master zone | Create slave zone. | Create stub zone | Create forward zone | Create delegation zone. | Create zones from batch file

☐ Root zone   ☐ 0   ☐ 0000::1   ☐ 127.0.0.1   ☐ localhost

☐ localhost.localdomain

Select all. | Invert selection. | Create master zone | Create slave zone. | Create stub zone. | Create forward zone | Create delegation zone. | Create zones from batch file.

| Delete Selected | Update Records in Selected | Add Record to Selected | Delete Records in Selected |

Fig. 9

From **Fig.10**: Our working section, **Existing DNS Zone**: Click Create master zone.

Step 1: Creating the Master Domain Server

Our Domain: govsystemlabs.com
Note the period (.) at the end of the domain name during the configuration, it has to be there – it's not a mistake.

Adding the zone / Forward Zone!

1. Click on "Create master zone" tab
2. Zone type: Forward (forward name to address) select it
3. Domain name /Network: govsystemlabs.com. (domain here)
4. Record file: Automatic
5. Master server: centos7.govsystemlabs.com [/] Check Add NS record for master server?
6. Email address: root@localhost or root@govsystemlabs.com
7. Use zone template: no
8. Leave the rest as default
9. Click on "Create" button

272

Fig. 10

Note: once the zone is created you can proceed to edit its properties, it takes you to this panel automatically.

Step 2: Edit Master Zone

[In govystemlabs.com]

Fig 11

273

*Adding the address:

1. Click on "**Address**" icon
2. Enter name: govsystemlabs.com.
3. Enter address: 192.168.6.10 (note: this is the physical address domain)
4. Time-To Leave: default
5. Update reverse?: yes
6. Click on "**create**" button

Name	TTL	Address
☐ govsystemlabs.com.	Default	192.168.6.10

Fig. 12: Your address record should look like this

7. Click "Return to record types" link

----

8. Again click on "**Address**" icon
9. Enter name: centos7.govsystemlabs.com.
10. Enter address: 192.168.6.10 (note: this is the physical address domain)
11. Time-To Leave: default
12. Update reverse?: yes
13. Click on "**create**" button

Name	TTL	Address
☐ govsystemlabs.com.	Default	192.168.6.10
☐ centos7.govsystemlabs.com.	Default	192.168.6.10

Fig. 13: Your address record should look like this

14. Click "Return to record types" link

Step 3: Add Name Server records (NS)

(**Note**: this section may be already updated)

1. Click "**Name Server**" icon
2. Enter Zone Name: govsystemlabs.com.
3. Time-To-Leave : Default
4. Enter Name server: centos7.govsystemlabs.com. (e.g., host.domain.com)
5. Click on "Create" button

Name	TTL	Name Server
☐ govsystemlabs.com.	Default	centos7.govsystemlabs.com.

Fig. 14: If already updated, it should look like this

6. Click "Return to record types" link

Step 4: Add Name Alias Record (CNAME)

1. Click "Names Alias" icon
2. Name: www
3. Time-To-Leave: Default
4. Real Name: govsystemlabs.com.
5. Click on "Create" button
    ----
6. Name: mail
7. Time-To Leave: Default
8. Real Name: govsystemlabs.com.
9. Click on "Create" button
    ----
10. Name: ftp
11. Time-To-Leave: Default
12. Real Name: govsystemlabs.com.
13. Click on "Create" button

Name	TTL	Real Name
☐ www.govsystemlabs.com.	Default	govsystemlabs.com.
☐ ftp.govsystemlabs.com.	Default	govsystemlabs.com.
☐ mail.govsystemlabs.com.	Default	govsystemlabs.com.

Fig. 15: Your alias should look like this

14. Click "Return to record types" link

Step 5: Mail Exchange Record (MX record)

1. Click "Mail Server" icon
2. Name: govsystemlabs.com.
3. Time-To-Leave: Default
4. Mail Server: mail.govsystemlabs.com.
5. Priority: 10
6. Click on "Create" button

Name	TTL	Priority	Mail Server
☐ govsystemlabs.com.	Default	10	mail.govsystemlabs.com.

Fig. 16

7. Click "Return to record types" link

We just finished creating the forward zone. At the very bottom of this current panel (Edit Master Zone), **click on** "Return to zone list".

From the zone list

* Click on "Apply Configuration" **at the top to modify the changes made.**

Note: your existing DNS Zones should now look like Fig. 18.

Fig. 17

The next step is to create the Reverse Zone for govsystemlabs.com

Step 6: Adding the Reverse Zone

1. Click on "Create master zone"
2. Now the Zone type will be: Reverse
3. Domain name/network: 192.168.6 (The last number is left out which is 10)
4. Records file: Automatic
5. Master server: centos7.govsystemlabs.com [/] Check Add NS record for master server?
6. Email address: root@localhost or root@govsystemlabs.com
7. Use template: no
8. Refresh time: leave as default

9. **Expiry time:** `leave as default`
10. **IP address for template:** `leave blank`
11. **Transfer retry time:** `leave as default`
12. **Default time to leave:** `leave as default`
13. Click on "Create" button

Now Edit the Master Zone properties for the Reverse that we just created.

Step 7: Create Pointer/Reverse Address Record

1. Click on PT "Reverse Address" ◀◀ icon
2. Now add Reverse Address Record
3. **Address:** `192.168.6.10` (type complete IP address here)
4. **Host name:** `govsystemlabs.com.`
5. **Update forward:** `yes`
6. Click on "Create" button

Address	TTL	Hostname
☐ 192.168.6.10	Default	govsystemlabs.com.

Fig. 18: After creating it should look like this

7. Click "Return to record types" link

Step 8: Add Name Server (NS)

(This data may be already updated)

1. Click "Name Server" icon
2. **Zone Name:** `6.168.192`
3. **Name Server:** `centos7.govsystemlabs.com.`
4. **Time to leave:** `Default`
5. Click on "Create" button

Name	TTL	Name Server
☐ 6.168.192.in-addr.arpa.	Default	centos7.govsystemlabs.com.

Fig. 19: If already updated should look like this

6. Click "Return to record types" link

Step 9: Add Name Alias Record (CN)

----

1. Click "Name Alias" icon
2. **Name:** www

3. **Time-To-Leave:** `Default`
4. **Real Name:** `govsystemlabs.com.`
5. Click on **"Create"** button
----
6. **Name:** `mail`
7. **Time-to-Leave:** `Default`
8. **Real Name:** `govsystemlabs.com.`
9. Click on **"Create"** button
----
10. **Name:** `ftp`
11. **Time-to-Leave:** `Default`
12. **Real Name:** `govsystemlabs.com.`
13. Click on **"Create"** button

Name	TTL	Real Name
☐ www.6.168.192.in-addr.arpa.	Default	govsystemlabs.com.
☐ mail.6.168.192.in-addr.arpa.	Default	govsystemlabs.com.
☐ ftp.6.168.192.in-addr.arpa.	Default	govsystemlabs.com.

Fig. 20: After you have entered all the aliases it should look like this

14. Click **"Return to record types"** link
15. Click on **"Return to zone list"** link
16. Click **"Apply Configuration"** link
17. Click **"Stop Bind"** followed by **"Start Bind"** link

Note: our final newly modified zone list should now look like shown in Fig. 21:

Fig. 21: Final Existing DNS Zone

We just completed a robust and fully functional DNS server configuration!
You can now verify the changes in the main configuration file, as follows: `/etc/named.conf`

Note: that a new zone has been added, which can be found at: `/var/named/`, these are:
`govsystemlabs.com.hosts` and `192.168.6.rev`.

```
zone "govsystemlabs.com" {
        type master;
        file "/var/named/govsystemlabs.com.hosts";
        };
zone "6.168.192.in-addr.arpa" {
        type master;
        file "/var/named/192.168.6.rev";
        };
```
Fig. 22

Contents of these files in: `/var/named/`

This is the content of the file: `govsystemhost.com.hosts`

Fig. 23

This is the content of the file: `192.168.6.rev`

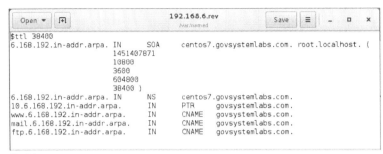

Fig. 24

Note: as you can see, using Webmin is the fastest and surest way to set up a DNS server; or you can sit there all day and type line by line and still get wrong.

Note: now issue the "dig centos7.govsystemlabs.com", however, if you encountered any error like shown in Fig. 25.

```
[root@centos7 ~]# dig centos7.govsystemlabs.com

; <<>> DiG 9.9.4-RedHat-9.9.4-29.el7 <<>> centos7.govsystemlabs.com
;; global options: +cmd
;; connection timed out; no servers could be reached
[root@centos7 ~]#
```

Fig. 25

Note: if you encountered any error, like **"connection timed out no servers could be reached"**, then instead issue the "dig @localhost centos7.govsystemlabs.com",

Note: you can also run, "tail /var/log/messages" to view what's going on!

Note: this could also be the case where your instance of BIND is probably listening on the loopback (127.0.0.1) and won't answer when addressed by an IP address that's associated with a real physical interface (in our case 192.168.6.10)

Solution: Look in your "/etc/named.conf" file for the "listen-on" directive and ensure to change it from 127.0.0.1 either your IP address or "any". You may also need to change "allow-query" from "localhost" to "any", and now you should be able to use "dig" and "nslookup" without any problem.

You're done with this section.

Step 10: Querying the DNS Server

1. Now let's test our DNS server using `dig` and `nslookup` to test and ensure that our master DNS is working as expected. Figure 26 shows the `dig` query and Fig. 27 with `nslookup` query, which confirms that all is working well with our DNS server.

```
[root@centos7 ~]# dig govsystemlabs.com

; <<>> DiG 9.9.4-RedHat-9.9.4-29.el7 <<>> govsystemlabs.com
;; global options: +cmd
;; Got answer:
;; ->>HEADER<<- opcode: QUERY, status: NOERROR, id: 12156
;; flags: qr aa rd ra; QUERY: 1, ANSWER: 1, AUTHORITY: 1, ADDITIONAL: 2

;; OPT PSEUDOSECTION:
; EDNS: version: 0, flags:; udp: 4096
;; QUESTION SECTION:
;govsystemlabs.com.              IN      A

;; ANSWER SECTION:
govsystemlabs.com.      38400   IN      A       192.168.6.10

;; AUTHORITY SECTION:
govsystemlabs.com.      38400   IN      NS      centos7.govsystemlabs.com.

;; ADDITIONAL SECTION:
centos7.govsystemlabs.com. 38400 IN     A       192.168.6.10

;; Query time: 0 msec
;; SERVER: 192.168.6.10#53(192.168.6.10)
;; WHEN: Tue Dec 29 16:02:49 EST 2015
;; MSG SIZE  rcvd: 100

[root@centos7 ~]#
```
Fig. 26

Note: for the mail server run "`dig mx govsystemlab.com`":

```
[root@centos7 ~]# dig mx govsystemlabs.com

; <<>> DiG 9.9.4-RedHat-9.9.4-29.el7 <<>> mx govsystemlabs.com
;; global options: +cmd
;; Got answer:
;; ->>HEADER<<- opcode: QUERY, status: NOERROR, id: 50587
;; flags: qr aa rd ra; QUERY: 1, ANSWER: 1, AUTHORITY: 1, ADDITIONAL: 2

;; OPT PSEUDOSECTION:
; EDNS: version: 0, flags:; udp: 4096
;; QUESTION SECTION:
;govsystemlabs.com.              IN      MX

;; ANSWER SECTION:
govsystemlabs.com.      38400   IN      MX      10 mail.govsystemlabs.com.

;; AUTHORITY SECTION:
govsystemlabs.com.      38400   IN      NS      centos7.govsystemlabs.com.

;; ADDITIONAL SECTION:
centos7.govsystemlabs.com. 38400 IN     A       192.168.6.10

;; Query time: 34 msec
;; SERVER: 192.168.6.10#53(192.168.6.10)
;; WHEN: Tue Dec 29 16:13:14 EST 2015
;; MSG SIZE  rcvd: 105

[root@centos7 ~]#
```
Fig. 27

Do the same to test on the Alias names: www, ftp, and mail, issue the following commands:

```
[root@centos7 ~]# dig www.govsystemlabs.com

; <<>> DiG 9.9.4-RedHat-9.9.4-29.el7 <<>> www.govsystemlabs.com
;; global options: +cmd
;; Got answer:
;; ->>HEADER<<- opcode: QUERY, status: NOERROR, id: 64886
;; flags: qr aa rd ra; QUERY: 1, ANSWER: 2, AUTHORITY: 1, ADDITIONAL: 2

;; OPT PSEUDOSECTION:
; EDNS: version: 0, flags:; udp: 4096
;; QUESTION SECTION:
;www.govsystemlabs.com.          IN      A

;; ANSWER SECTION:
www.govsystemlabs.com.  38400   IN      CNAME   govsystemlabs.com.
govsystemlabs.com.      38400   IN      A       192.168.6.10

;; AUTHORITY SECTION:
govsystemlabs.com.      38400   IN      NS      centos7.govsystemlabs.com.

;; ADDITIONAL SECTION:
centos7.govsystemlabs.com. 38400 IN     A       192.168.6.10

;; Query time: 0 msec
;; SERVER: 192.168.6.10#53(192.168.6.10)
;; WHEN: Tue Dec 29 16:16:55 EST 2015
;; MSG SIZE  rcvd: 118

[root@centos7 ~]#
```
.... **Fig. 28**

Repeat the same with mail. and ftp.

2. Now let's test them with "NSLOOKUP" command:

```
[root@centos7 ~]# nslookup  govsystemlabs.com
Server:         192.168.6.10
Address:        192.168.6.10#53

Name:   govsystemlabs.com
Address: 192.168.6.10

[root@centos7 ~]#
```
_____ **Fig. 29**

3. Now let's test them with "NSLOOKUP" for mail server:

```
[root@centos7 ~]# nslookup  -query=mx govsystemlabs.com
Server:         192.168.6.10
Address:        192.168.6.10#53

govsystemlabs.com       mail exchanger = 10 mail.govsystemlabs.com.

[root@centos7 ~]#
```
.... **Fig. 30**

4. Let's check the DNS of your Alias Records with "NSLOOKUP":

```
[root@centos7 ~]# nslookup  www.govsystemlabs.com
Server:          192.168.6.10
Address:         192.168.6.10#53

www.govsystemlabs.com  canonical name = govsystemlabs.com.
Name:   govsystemlabs.com
Address: 192.168.6.10

[root@centos7 ~]#
```
Fig. 31

Similarly, repeat for ftp.

5. You're done with this section.

Part 3: Deploying your DNS Server on your Network

Step 1: Deploying client to query DNS server

1. Now that the DNS is working properly, let's go ahead and configure any computer in your network. Set it in the same subnet-mask and pick any unused IP address. Note that it can be a windows, Linux or Mac OS machine. For example, for Win XP/Vista/8/10/2k12, browse to the network properties, and configure to include the DNS IP address, as shown in Fig. 32. Once you're done testing, and you have DHCP running on your network, then you use dynamic IP address configuration for your client instead of static configuration.

Fig. 32

2. Before commencing the test, do ensure that your firewall is allowed to trust UDP/TCP port 53 which is the service port for DNS messages and queries. On CentOS7/RHEL7, type:

```
firewall-cmd --permanent --add-port=53/tcp
firewall-cmd --permanent --add-port=53/udp
firewall-cmd --reload
```

Note: also do ensure too that SELinux security is set to `disabled` during testing, which you re-enable appropriately later.

3. From Windows system, ping the DNS server IP address (192.168.6.10), see Fig. 33.

```
C:\>ping 192.168.6.10

Pinging 192.168.6.10 with 32 bytes of data:

Reply from 192.168.6.10: bytes=32 time<1ms TTL=64
Reply from 192.168.6.10: bytes=32 time<1ms TTL=64
Reply from 192.168.6.10: bytes=32 time<1ms TTL=64
Reply from 192.168.6.10: bytes=32 time<1ms TTL=64

Ping statistics for 192.168.6.10:
    Packets: Sent = 4, Received = 4, Lost = 0 (0% loss),
Approximate round trip times in milli-seconds:
    Minimum = 0ms, Maximum = 0ms, Average = 0ms
C:\>
```
Fig. 33

4. From Windows system, perform **NSLOOKUP** query, see Fig. 34.

```
C:\>nslookup govsystemlabs.com
Server:  govsystemlabs.com
Address:  192.168.6.10

Name:    govsystemlabs.com
Address:  192.168.6.10

C:\>
C:\>nslookup -query=mx govsystemlabs.com
Server:  govsystemlabs.com
Address:  192.168.6.10

govsystemlabs.com       MX preference = 10, mail exchanger = mail.govsystemlabs.
com
govsystemlabs.com       nameserver = centos7.govsystemlabs.com
centos7.govsystemlabs.com       internet address = 192.168.6.10
C:\>
```
Fig. 34

5. All looks good, we can safely continue.

6. Now that we have created a perfect master DNS; we can go ahead and use our system for almost anything, e.g., ftp, mail, and www. The same way we created this master DNS you can also create a slave DNS server at a different IP address to provide for redundancy. That is,

by creating a slave DNS, they can replicate each other's data so that if one of the servers goes down, the other one will respond to the queries transparently without affecting the network clients.

Fig. 35: Test Web page running from our DNS server running on Linux CentOS-7.

7. So what is the big picture – i.e., in a simple language – having perfectly functioning redundancy DNS server within your network enables both servers and clients in your network to use different IP addresses and will be resolved by your DNS server.

8. Now you can go ahead install messaging server like Zimbra which require that master DNS is installed and working.

.

Step 2: Final Testing DNS Derver

If you're on a public IP address network, you can use www.dnsreport.com, for further testing of your DNS server. Browse to www.dnsreport.com and enter your domain name, e.g., mycomapny.com. Dnsreport.com will give you detailed results about your domain.

Part 4: ISP Providers

Contact the Domain Registrar

For those who are interested in starting an ISP business – once BIND is setup and running good – you can pass your name server information to the domain registrar.

Part 5: Virtual Hosting

Now that we have our DNS server up and running – we can go ahead and push the boundaries of our network infrastructure to enterprise level e.g., building large data center or large multinational corporation. For those who're interested in moving into ISP biz, or those with large enterprise network infrastructure – can now use the DNS server to do virtual hosting and become an ISP, or those with an eye to start running data centers.

Step 1: Adding and Configuring a Virtual Domain to the DNS Server

In this section we're going to add a new virtual (0host domain to our DNS server. To do this, perform the following procedures.

1. Fire-up your browser and open Webmin to configure the new virtual domain.

2. Click **Servers → Bind DNS Server**, and then scroll to the bottom to the Existing DNS Zone section, see Fig. 36.

Existing DNS Zones

Select all. | Invert selection. | Create master zone. | Create slave zone. | Create stub zone. | Create forward zone. | Create delegation zone. | Create zones from batch file.

Fig. 36: Bind9 DNS Server – **Existing DNS Zones** section

Step 2: Creating the Master Virtual Domain

> **Virtual Domain Name:** crmhostlabs.com
> **IP Address:** 192.168.6.20
>
> (**Note:** This is the IP address of the virtual domain; do ensure that it's not in use)

Adding the zone / Forward Zone!

To add the forward zone, perform the following proceduress:

1. Click on "Create master zone" tab
2. Zone type: Forward (forward name to address) select it
3. Domain name /Network: crmhostlabs.com. (domain here)
4. Record file: Automatic
5. Master server: centos7.govsystemlabs.com [/] Add NS record for Master Server?
6. Email address: root@localhost or root@govsystemlabs.com
7. Use zone template: No
8. **Refresh time:** leave as default
9. **Expiry time:** leave as default
10. **IP address for template records:** leave as blank
11. **Transfer retry time:** leave as default
12. **Default time-to-leave:** leave as default
13. Click on the "Create" button
14. **Return to zone list**
15. Click "Return to zone list" link

Fig. 36

Note: you updated Existing DNS Zones should now look like shown in Fig. 37, note the additional crmhostlabs.com icon.

Select all. | Invert selection. | Create master zone. | Create slave zone. | Create stub zone | Create forward
zone. | Create delegation zone. | Create zones from batch file.

Select all. | Invert selection. | Create master zone. | Create slave zone. | Create stub zone | Create forward
zone. | Create delegation zone. | Create zones from batch file.

| Delete Selected | Update Records in Selected | Add Record to Selected | Delete Records in Selected |

Fig. 37

You're done with this section.

Step 3: Edit Master Zone

```
[In crmhostlabs.com]
```

Fig. 38

Note: Click on the `crmhosthostlabs.com` to edit the Master Zone, see Fig. 38.

*Adding the address:

1. Click on "**Address**" icon
2. Enter name: `crmhostlabs.com`.
3. Enter address: `192.168.6.20` (Note: this is the physical address virtual domain)
4. Time-To Leave: default
5. Update reverse?: yes
6. Click on "**create**" button

Name	TTL	Address
crmhostlabs.com.	Default	192.168.6.20

Fig. 39: Your address record should look like this

288

7. Click "Return to record types" link

Step 4: Add Name Server records (NS)

(**Note**: this section may be already updated)

1. Click "Name Server" icon
2. Enter Zone Name: crmhostlabs.com.
3. Time-To-Leave : Default
4. Enter Name server: centos7.govsystemlabs.com.
5. Click on "Create" button

Name	TTL	Name Server
☐ crmhostlabs.com.	Default	centos7.govsystemlabs.com.

Fig. 41: If already updated, it should look like this

6. Click "Return to record types" link

Step 5: Add Name Alias Record (CNAME)

1. Click "Names Alias" icon
2. Name: www
3. Time-To-Leave: Default
4. Real Name: crmhostlabs.com.
5. Click on "Create" button

----

6. Name: mail
7. Time-To Leave: Default
8. Real Name: crmhostlabs.com.
9. Click on "Create" button

----

10. Name: ftp
11. Time-To-Leave: Default
12. Real Name: crmhostlabs.com.
13. Click on "Create" button

Name	TTL	Real Name
☐ www.crmhostlabs.com.	Default	crmhostlabs.com.
☐ mail.crmhostlabs.com.	Default	crmhostlabs.com.
☐ ftp.crmhostlabs.com.	Default	crmhostlabs.com.

Fig. 41: Your alias should look like this

14. Click "Return to record types" link

Step 6: Mail Exchange Record (MX record)

1. Click "Mail Server" icon
2. Name: crmhosting.com.
3. Time-To-Leave: Default
4. Mail Server: govsystemlabs.com.
5. Priority: 20
6. Click on "Create" button

Name	TTL	Priority	Mail Server
☐ crmhostlabs.com.	Default	20	govsystemlabs.com.

Fig. 42: The mail record should look like this

7. Click "Return to record types" link

We just finished creating the virtual forward zone. At the very bottom of this current panel (Edit Master Zone), **click on** "Return to zone list".

From the zone list:

Click on "Apply Configuration" at the top to modify the changes made.

The next step is the Reverse Zone for our virtual domain crmhostlabs.com

Step 6: Adding the Reverse Zone for our Virtual Zone

1. Click on "Create master zone"
2. Now the Zone type will be: Reverse
3. Domain name/network: 192.168.6.20

4. Records file: `Automatic`
5. Master server: `centos7.govsystemlabs.com` **[/]** Check: Add NS record for Master Server?
6. Email address: `root@localhost` or `root@govsystemlabs.com`
7. Use template: `No`
8. Refresh time: `leave as default`
9. Expiry time: `leave as default`
10. IP address for template: `leave blank`
11. Transfer retry time: `leave as default`
12. Default time to leave: `leave as default`
13. Click on "Create" button
14. Click "Return to record types" link

Now Edit the Master Zone properties for the Reverse that we just created.

Step 7: Create Pointer/Reverse Address Record

1. Click on PT "Reverse Address" icon
2. Now add Reverse Address Record
3. Address: `192.168.6.20` (type complete IP address here)
4. Host name: `crmhostlabs.com.`
5. Update forward: `yes`
6. Click on "Create" button

Address	TTL	Hostname
☐ 192.168.6.20	Default	crmhostlabs.com.

Fig. 43: The virtual host IP Address

7. Click "Return to record types" link

Step 8: Add Name Server (NS)

(**Note:** This data may be already updated)

1. Click "Name Server" icon
2. Zone Name: `crmhosting.com`
3. Name Server: `centos7.govsystemlabs.com.`
4. Time to leave: `Default`
5. Click on "Create" button

Name	TTL	Name Server
☐ 20.6.168.192.in-addr.arpa.	Default	centos7.govsystemlabs.com.

Fig. 44: The virtual host IP Address

291

6. Click "Return to record types" link

Step 9: Add Name Alias Record (CN)

1. Click "Name Alias" icon
2. Name: www
3. Time-To-Leave: Default
4. Real Name: crmhosting.com.
5. Click on "Create" button

----

6. Name: mail
7. Time-to-Leave: Default
8. Real Name: crmhosting.com.
9. Click on "Create" button

----

10. Name: ftp
11. Time-to-Leave: Default
12. Real Name: crmhosting.com.
13. Click on "Create" button

Name	TTL	Real Name
mail.20.6.168.192.in-addr.arpa.	Default	crmhostlabs.com.
ftp.20.6.168.192.in-addr.arpa.	Default	crmhostlabs.com.
www.20.6.168.192.in-addr.arpa.	Default	crmhostlabs.com.

Fig. 45: After you have entered all the virtual domain aliases it should look like this

14. Click "Return to record types" link
15. Click on "Return to zone list" link
16. Click "Apply Configuration" link
17. Click "Stop Bind" followed by "Start Bind" link
18. We're done with the DNS Server setup – Enjoy!

Our newly modified zone list now is as shown in Fig. 46:

Existing DNS Zones

Select all. | Invert selection. | Create master zone. | Create slave zone. | Create stub zone. | Create forward zone. | Create delegation zone. | Create zones from batch file.

☐ Root zone	☐ 0	☐ 0000.:1	☐ 127.0.0.1	☐ 192.168.6
☐ 192.168.6.20	☐ crmhostlabs.com	☐ govsystemlabs.com	☐ localhost	☐ localhost.localdomain

Select all. | Invert selection. | Create master zone. | Create slave zone. | Create stub zone. | Create forward zone. | Create delegation zone. | Create zones from batch file.

| Delete Selected | Update Records in Selected | Add Record to Selected | Delete Records in Selected |

Fig. 46: Final Existing DNS Zone

We just completed a robust and fully functional virtual domain configuration!

Note: Contents of zone files are in: /var/named/

In this Part 5 of the hands-on guide lab manual, we just created the entry into the DNS server; however, we still have a couple of steps to go. If you do an **nslookup, it will not respond.** For this to work, we need to bind the IP address to the interface card and make it active in order to be used.

Part 6: Adding a Virtual IP and Virtual Domain (Virtual Host)

Binding an IP address to your NIC card, then getting Apache to use it for a virtual domain can be a pretty big headache. In this section we show you how to run through this process with our mighty Webmin and you'll see what a breeze it is.

Step 1: Binding a additional Virtual IP to your NIC

In this step we'll create an additional virtual IP address to bind to our virtual domain(s). The first thing that needs to be done in this case is to add additional IP address(es) to your NIC for every additional virtual domain added. It's very crucial to note that all virtual hosts (domains) use an IP address just as regular physical interfaces. Hence, if we don't bind the IP address to the interface, our virtual hosts will not work.

To do this, we're going to call upon our mighty Webmin to help us to do the job with ease, as follows:

1. Fire-up your browser and login to the Webmin.

2. From the left column, click **Networking > Network Configuration**, and from the right pane, click **Network Interfaces** icon/link.

3. Under the **Network Interfaces** page, you will see two tabs: "Active Now"' and "Activated at boot". The items listed under the "Active Now"' is/are the IP addresses that are currently active. You can add an IP address to this section, but it won't be active if you reboot, so you'll want to add the IP to the **Activated at Boot** section. This binds the IP address every time your machine boots.

4. Click the "Activated at boot" tab, followed by clicking "Add a new interface" link; you should be presented with the **"Create Bootup Interface"** page with required information to be filled-in, as shown in Fig. 47.

5. From Fig. 47, enter the required information as follows:

    - **Name** - Your main IP address is probably eth0. To add additional virtual ones that need to go in this sequence eth0:1, then eth0:2, etc. So if you haven't added an additional IP address before, then type in eth0:1.

    - **IP address** - This is the additional virtual IP address that you're going to bind to your NIC.

    - **Netmask** - This will be the same as your main IP address. Usually it's 255.255.255.0.

    - **Broadcast** - If you don't know this one go back one screen and copy down the one you have on eth0, e.g., in our case: 192.168.6.255.

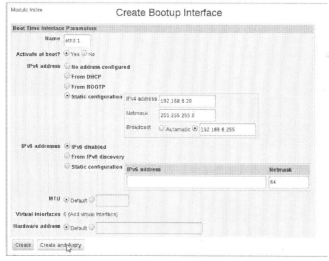

Fig. 47: The **Create Bootup Interface** page, enter the required information.

6. Once you're done entering the required information, click the **"Create and Apply"** button to complete the configuration, and it will take you back to the **Network Interfaces** screen.

   Note: We have assumed you want it activated right now, so we clicked on the **"Create and Apply"**. This will activate the IP address and you should now see it in the Interfaces **Active Now** section, see Fig. 48. Alternatively, you can click on the **"Create"** button, but it will not make the IP address active right-away.

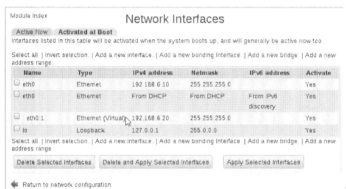

Fig. 48

7. Click the "Return to network configuration" link.

8. On the **Network Configuration** page, click on the "Apply Configuration" button to bind all the IP addresses and complete the configuration process.

9. Your new virtual IP address has now been added so it will bind when you start up.

   Note: Obviously, no other computer/devices in the network should be using the IP address **192.168.6.20!**

10. If you now issue the ifoconfig command, you should be able to see the output shown in Fig. 33 (Note: we have just shown the section of interest)

```
[root@centos7 ~]# ifconfig eth0:1
eth0:1: flags=4163<UP,BROADCAST,RUNNING,MULTICAST>  mtu 1500
        inet 192.168.6.20  netmask 255.255.255.0  broadcast 192.168.6.255
        ether 00:0c:29:82:bc:1a  txqueuelen 1000  (Ethernet)

[root@centos7 ~]#
```

Fig. 49: The `ifconfig` command, note our virtual network `eth0:1`.

Note. As we have noted earlier, for network infrastructure best practices, when you start adding virtual hosts, it's advisable to use a sequence number to bind IP address to the Interface card. For example, for your first virtual host, use: eth0:1 followed with eth0:2, eth0:3, eth0:4 and so on.

11. Remember to update your `/etc/hosts` file with `crmhostlabs.om` details:

```
192.168.6.10    centos7.govsystemlabs.com  centos7 www  ftp  mail
192.168.6.20    crmhostlabs.com  www  ftp  mail
127.0.0.1   localhost localhost.localdomain localhost4 localhost4.localdomain4
#::1        localhost localhost.localdomain localhost6 localhost6.localdomain6
```

Fig. 50

12. Remember to update your `/etc/resolve.conf` file with `crmhostlabs.om` details, as shown in Fig.51:

```
; generated by /usr/sbin/dhclient-script
search localdomain govsystemlabs.com
nameserver 192.168.6.20
nameserver 192.168.6.2
```

Fig. 51

13. Restart named service, type::

```
[root@contos7 ~]# systemctl restart named.service
```

14. Now issue the `dig` command to test our configuration, type:

```
[root@contos7 ~]# dig govhostlabs.com
```

```
[root@centos7 ~]# dig crmhostlabs.com

; <<>> DiG 9.9.4-RedHat-9.9.4-29.el7 <<>> crmhostlabs.com
;; global options: +cmd
;; Got answer:
;; ->>HEADER<<- opcode: QUERY, status: NOERROR, id: 29710
;; flags: qr aa rd ra; QUERY: 1, ANSWER: 1, AUTHORITY: 1, ADDITIONAL: 2

;; OPT PSEUDOSECTION:
; EDNS: version: 0, flags:; udp: 4096
;; QUESTION SECTION:
;crmhostlabs.com.                 IN      A

;; ANSWER SECTION:
crmhostlabs.com.          38400   IN      A       192.168.6.20

;; AUTHORITY SECTION:
crmhostlabs.com.          38400   IN      NS      centos7.govsystemlabs.com.

;; ADDITIONAL SECTION:
centos7.govsystemlabs.com. 38400 IN      A       192.168.6.10

;; Query time: 0 msec
;; SERVER: 192.168.6.20#53(192.168.6.20)
;; WHEN: Thu Dec 31 08:31:28 EST 2015
;; MSG SIZE  rcvd: 112

[root@centos7 ~]#
```

Fig. 52

15. Next, try the `nslookup` command now to test our new virtual domain; it should return the name servers, see Fig. 53. (Here on `"crmhostlabs.com"` and `"www.crmhostlabs.com"`) returns the correct result.

```
[root@centos7 ~]# nslookup crmhostlabs.com
Server:         192.168.6.20
Address:        192.168.6.20#53

Name:   crmhostlabs.com
Address: 192.168.6.20

[root@centos7 ~]#
[root@centos7 ~]# nslookup www.crmhostlabs.com
Server:         192.168.6.20
Address:        192.168.6.20#53

www.crmhostlabs.com     canonical name = crmhostlabs.com.
Name:   crmhostlabs.com
Address: 192.168.6.20

[root@centos7 ~]#
```
.... **Fig. 53**

Note: If you see this information returned, you are in business.

Note: we just completed a robust and fully functional DNS Server configuration and also added & configured a virtual domain (virtual Host)!

Step 2: Deploying Virtual Web Hosting in the Apache Server

A virtual host enables more than one website running on a single server to work seamlessly. A host represents a fully qualified domain name or IP address, such as www.website1.com and www.website2.com, etc.

Since we now have everything functional, we shouldn't miss the opportunity to serve virtual web sites. Hence, in this section we're going to deploy a virtual; web hosting running from our newly configured virtual domain.

To do this, we're going to call upon our mighty Webmin to help to the job with ease, as follows:

1. Again fire-up your browser and login to the Webmin

2. From the left column, click **Server** → **Apache Webserver**, to access Apache Webserver screen
   Note: The first time you click on Apache Webserver, it will ask you to re-configure known modules. It will list all of the modules in the httpd.conf file and have certain ones selected. Unless you know what you're doing with this area just leave it alone!

3. From the Apache Webserver screen, you should see three tabs: **"Global configuration"**, **"Existing virtual hosts"**, and **"Create virtual hosts"**, see Fig. 54.

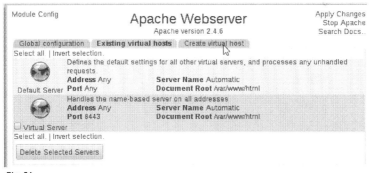

Fig. 54

4. From Fig. 54, click on the **"Create virtual hosts"** tab, to access the screen shown in Fig. 55.

298

Now let's fill in your virtual server (also known as virtual domain) information, see Fig. 55, as follows:

- **Address** –This is the IP address you want your virtual domain to use. Check "Specific address…", and enter the desired IP address. It should be the one you just added in the previous section, see Step 1, in our case: 192.168.6.20

- **Port** - By default, your browser uses port 80, unless you're doing something a little complex, just leave the default button checked.

- **Document Root** - This is where Apache Webserver will look for the web documents. You can type it in or click the button off to the right to browse your system.

- **Server Name** - You can leave this on automatic, or you can type something like e.g., "mydomain.com" off to the right. Keep in mind your Domain Name Server (DNS) determines what domain name is attached to your IP address, not this section.

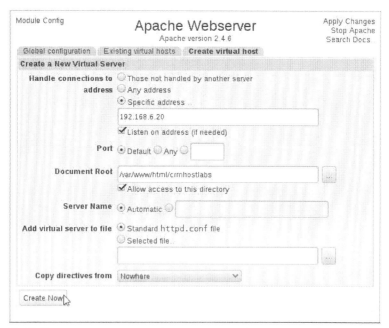

Fig. 55: The Create virtual host tab, enter the required information and click **Create Now** button.

5. After you've filled in and verified all of the information, click on the **"Create Now"** button. This will add the information to the httpd.conf file.

6. To activate the changes you've made, click on the "Apply Changes" on the top right corner of the screen, see Fig. 56.

Fig. 56: The Apache Web Server screen, showing our Virtual Server configuration..

Note. *Repeat this process for each additional virtual Domain.*

7. Just for curiosity let's check how our virtual host has been added to the httpd.conf file

8. Locate and edit httpd.conf file (mine is in /etc/httpd/conf/httpd.conf) on Linux CentOS 7 / RHEL 7.

9. Find Section between <VirtualHost *:80> and <VitualHost> at the very bottom of the page, and you should see our VirtualHost section listed as shown in Listing 1:

Listing 1: VirtualHost for our Virtual Web Host

```
# ServerName dummy-host.example.com
# ErrorLog logs/dummy-host.example.com-error_log
# CustomLog logs/dummy-host.example.com-access_log common
# </VirtualHost>
  <VirtualHost 192.168.6.20>
  DocumentRoot "/var/www/html/crmhostlabs"
  <Directory "/var/www/html/crmhostlabs">
  allow from all
  Options None
  Require all granted
  </Directory>
  </VirtualHost>
```

Note. Do this for each additional virtual Domain.

10. Time to put our good work to test.

11. Create a simple `index.html` page for demonstration purpose and place it under the Document Root "`/var/www/html/crmhostlabs`", type:

    `# nano /var/www/html/crmhostlabs/index.html`

12. Now if everything is setup right, you should be able to see your page through your web browser (assuming you've already registered the domain name and have DNS setup correctly if you serving pages live to the public using public IP address).

13. Now you can access your virtual Web hosting via your browser at: `http://crmhostlabs.com/`.

Fig. 57

Note 1: Please note that in this install guide lab manual, I used a Private IP address for demonstration and testing purposes. Once you're confident enough with your good work, you may want to go ahead and use your own Public IP addresses for your servers if you are going live online.

Note: 2: For redundancy, availability and security issues, you will need to setup the web server and the DNS server as different identities. Such that if the DNS sever goes down; the web server can be still reached through a different DNS (e.g., via slave DNS server).

Note 3: Remember to only use Webmin for all your Linux CentOS-7's Network Interface and DNS server administration

Part 7: Creating a Slave or Stub Zones

A slave DNS is simply a name server that copies zones files from a master DNS. For network infrastructure planning, designing and implementation and web deploying best practices, it's always recommended that additional DNS servers for redundancy purposes. This is very important to maintaining a 24/7 and 999.9 uptime availability of your web servers to your customers.

Slave and Stub zones are created in exactly the same way, and are quite similar in some ways though their purposes are very different. Slave zones keep a complete copy in memory, and sometimes also on disk, of a zone that it receives via a zone transfer from a master zone. A slave zone can answer any queries for a zone, and as long as network connectivity remains intact between the master and slave, and if the servers are configured correctly, it will stay in sync with the master server. A stub zone also syncs to a master server, however it only keeps NS and SOA record information from the master server. This allows BIND to keep up with delegation information automatically.

Therefore, once your DNS server resolves your zones correctly, it's important that you set up a slave DNS server for security purposes just in case your primary DNS server goes down. It's recommended that you should have this slave DNS as far as possible from your primary server, especially if you are offering services to the public, more-so if you're in the e-commerce services.

Step 1: Add the server to DNS master zone

Our Slave DNS server details:

Slave Server Name:	NS2.govsystemlabs.com
Slave IP address:	192.168.6.11
Master DNS Server:	192.168.6.10 (Master DNS Server IP address)

You /etc/hosts file on the Master DNS server should now look like:

```
192.168.6.10    centos7.govsystemlabs.com  centos7 www  ftp  mail
192.168.6.20    crmhostlabs.com  www  ftp  mail
192.168.6.12    NS2.govsystemlabs.com NS2
127.0.0.1   localhost localhost.localdomain localhost4 localhost4.localdomain4
#::1            localhost localhost.localdomain localhost6 localhost6.localdomain6
```

Fig. 58

Step 2: Create the Slave Server Forward Zone

To setup the slave DNS server, perform the following procedure:

302

1. Go back to the DNS master server so that we can add the "NS2.govsystemlabs.com" (for both forward and reverse) as one of the **Name Servers**.

2. From the **Existing DNS Zones**, click on the govsystemlabs.com icon, as shown in Fig. 59.

Existing DNS Zones

Select all. | Invert selection. | Create master zone. | Create slave zone. | Create stub zone. | Create forward zone | Create delegation zone. | Create zones from batch file.

Root zone   0   0000::1   127.0.0.1   192.168.6

192.168.6.20   crmhostlabs.com   govsystemlab.com   localhost   localhost.localdomain

Select all. | Invert selection. | Create master zone. | Create slave zone. | Create stub zone. | Create forward zone | Create delegation zone. | Create zones from batch file.

[Delete Selected]   [Update Records in Selected]   [Add Record to Selected]   [Delete Records in Selected]

Fig. 59

3. This should take you to the **Edit Master Zone** page. Next click on the **Address** icon, which should take you to the **Address Records** page. Now go ahead and complete the details as shown in Fig. 60, then click on **Create** button.

Module Index   Apply Zone
                                                                     Apply
Address Records   Configuration
                                                                  Stop BIND
In govsystemlabs.com

Add Address Record

Name	Time-To-Live ⊙ Default ◯
NS2.govsystemlabs.com.	
	seconds ∨

Address   192.168.6.12

Update reverse?   ⊙ Yes ◯ Yes (and replace existing) ◯ No

[Create]

Fig. 60

Note: the current setting plus the previous setting should now look like Fig. 61.

Name	TTL	Address
☐ govsystemlabs.com.	Default	192.168.6.10
☐ centos7.govsystemlabs.com.	Default	192.168.6.10
☐ NS2.govsystemlabs.com.	Default	192.168.6.12

Fig. 61

4. Next from the **Edit Master Zone** page. Click on the **Name Server** icon, which should take you to the **Name Server Records** page. Now go ahead and complete the details as shown in Fig. 62, then click on **Create** button..

Fig. 62

Note: the current setting plus the previous setting should now look like Fig. 63.

Name	TTL	Name Server
☐ govsystemlabs.com.	Default	centos7.govsystemlabs.com.
☐ govsystemlabs.com.	Default	NS2.govsystemlabs.com.

Fig. 63

5. You're done with this section.

Step 3: Create the Slave Server Reverse Zone

6. Now let's go ahead to set the Reverse Zone for the Slave DNS server on the Master DNS Server. To do this, from the **Existing DNS Zones** page, click on the "192.168.6" icon as shown Fig. 64.

Fig. 64

Note: follow the same procedure as before to add the Slave DNS server details Fig. 65, with finally detail shown in Fig. 65.

Module Index	Name Server Records	Apply Zone Apply Configuration Stop BIND

In 192.168.6

Add Name Server Record

Zone Name	6.168.192	**Time-To-Live** ● Default ○
		_____ seconds ∨

Name Server	NS2.govsystemlabs.com.	(Absolute names must end with a .)

Create

Fig. 65

Name	TTL	Name Server
☐ 6.168.192.in-addr.arpa.	Default	centos7.govsystemlabs.com.
☐ 6.168.192.6.168.192.in-addr.arpa.	Default	NS2.govsystemlabs.com.

Fig. 66

7. Finally, click on **Apply Configuration**, followed by restarting the `named` service.

Note: if you get the error `/etc/rndc.conf` file being missing, all you need to do is click the `'setup RNDC'` icon in the Webmin **'BIND DNS Server'** screen and confirm to do the setup. This creates the missing `rndc.conf` file.

Setup RNDC

Fig. 67

305

Step 3: Setup & Configure RNDC Key for Bind9 (DNS Server) on the Slave DNS Server (this may be necessary!)

An **RNDC** controls the operation of a name server. rndc uses tcp connection to communicate with bind server for sending commands authenticated with digital signatures. In the following steps we'll show how to configure the RNDC key for Bind9 on the Salve DNS server

3.1 Create RNDC and Configuration File

1. First step is to create the rndc key and configuration file. The **rndc** provides a command line too "rndc-confgen" to generate it, type:

```
# rndc-confgen
```

with following sample output:

```
[root@NS2 ~]# rndc-confgen
# Start of rndc.conf
key "rndc-key" {
    algorithm hmac-md5;
    secret "CYePhGn9bGe+LXAZ9oKvBA==";
};

options {
    default-key "rndc-key";
    default-server 127.0.0.1;
    default-port 953;
};
# End of rndc.conf

# Use with the following in named.conf, adjusting the allow list as
needed:
# key "rndc-key" {
#     algorithm hmac-md5;
#     secret "CYePhGn9bGe+LXAZ9oKvBA==";
# };
#
# controls {
#     inet 127.0.0.1 port 953
#         allow { 127.0.0.1; } keys { "rndc-key"; };
# };
# End of named.conf
```

2. You're done with this section.

3.2 Configure RNDC Key and Configuration

3. Now copy the entire output of the "rndc-confgen" and paste it into the "/etc/rndc.conf" file

```
[root@NS2 ~]# nano /etc/rndc.conf
```

4. Next, copy the key section of the output of the "rndc-confgen" and paste it into the "/etc/rndc.key"

```
key "rndc-key" {
   algorithm hmac-md5;
   secret "CYePhGn9bGe+LXAZ9oKvBA==";
};
```

5. You're done with this section.

3.3 Configure named.conf to use RNDC key

6. Finally, add at the following entry at the bottom of the "/etc/named.conf" file:

```
include "/etc/rndc.key";

controls {
        inet 127.0.0.1 allow { localhost; } keys { "rndc-key"; };
};
```

7. You're done with this section.

3.4 Restart Named (Bind) Service

8. First, for best practices before restarting named service, its recommended that you check the configuration file, enter;

```
# named-checkconf /etc/named.conf
```

and

```
# named-checkconf -t /var/named/chroot /etc/named.conf
```

Note: if there is no output from the above command, then the configuration is good.

9. Now restart named service, type:

```
# systemctl restart named.service
```

10. You're done with this section.

3.5 Test RNDC Setup

11. Now we need to test our **RNDC** setup, to do this run:

```
# rndc status
```

which should produce the following output:

```
[root@NS2 ~]# rndc status
WARNING:   key   file   (/etc/rndc.key)   exists,   but   using   default
configuration file (/etc/rndc.conf)
version: 9.9.4-RedHat-9.9.4-29.el7 <id:8f9657aa>
CPUs found: 2
worker threads: 2
UDP listeners per interface: 2
number of zones: 103
debug level: 0
xfers running: 0
xfers deferred: 0
soa queries in progress: 0
query logging is OFF
recursive clients: 0/0/1000
tcp clients: 0/100
server is up and running
```

12. You're done with this section.

Step 4: Updating Slave DNS Network Interface

In this section we're going to add the Slave DNS server's IP address to Network interface, as the **Secondary DNS** on both machines, which will be done in next section..

1. To do this, first we need to change to the directory as shown to update the "ifcfg-eth0", to static IP address, type:

```
# cd /etc/sysconfig/network-scripts/
# nano ifcfg-eth0
```

then set the configuration as follows:

```
TYPE="Ethernet"
BOOTPROTO="static"
NM_CONTROLLED=no
STARTMODE="auto"
IPADDR=192.168.6.12
BROADCAST=192.168.6.255
NETWORK=192.168.6.0
```

```
NETMASK=255.255.255.0
GATEWAY=192.168.6.2
DNS1=192.168.6.10
DNS2=192.168.6.12
IPV4_FAILURE_FATAL="no"
IPV6INIT=no
USERCTL=no
NAME="eth0"
UUID="60a16494-752d-4bbc-9cd1-4c83eac0b97b"
DEVICE="eth0"
ONBOOT="yes"
```

Note: update the Master DNS eth0 to reflect the same:

2. Next, update the `"/etc/resolv.conf"` file configuration as follows:

```
; generated by /usr/sbin/dhclient-script
search localdomain govsystemlabs.com
nameserver 192.168.6.10
nameserver 192.168.6.12
nameserver 192.168.6.2
```

3. Finally, update the `"/etc/hosts"` file configuration as follows:

```
192.168.6.12    NS2.govsystemlabs.com NS2
192.168.6.10    centos7.govsystemlabs.com  centos7 www  ftp   mail
192.168.6.20    crmhostlabs.com  www  ftp   mail
127.0.0.1   localhost localhost.localdomain localhost4 localhost4.localdomain4
#::1        localhost localhost.localdomain localhost6 localhost6.localdomain6
```

Fig. 68

4. You're done with this section.

Step 5: Install and Configure Slave DNS Server on Linux CentOS 7

1. Get hold of another physical server or fire-up another VMware virtual machine and install Linux CentOS 7, once installation is completed, then make sure that you update it with the latest patches and bug fixes, by issuing the following command:

```
# yum update -y
```

2. First we need to perform `"nslookup"` to check and verify that our Slave Server can see the Master Server, and correctly return the results, as shown in Fig. 69.

```
[root@NS2 ~]# nslookup govsystemlabs.com
Server:        192.168.6.10
Address:       192.168.6.10#53

Name:   govsystemlabs.com
Address: 192.168.6.10

[root@NS2 ~]#
[root@NS2 ~]# nslookup NS2.govsystemlabs.com
Server:        192.168.6.10
Address:       192.168.6.10#53

Name:   NS2.govsystemlabs.com
Address: 192.168.6.12

[root@NS2 ~]#
```
Fig. 68

3. Next, download and install Webmin

```
[root@NS2 Downloads]# rpm -ivh webmin-1.770-1.noarch.rpm
warning: webmin-1.770-1.noarch.rpm: Header V3 DSA/SHA1 Signature, key ID 11f63c5
1: NOKEY
Preparing...                     ################################# [100%]
Operating system is CentOS Linux
Updating / installing...
   1:webmin-1.770-1               ################################# [100%]
Webmin install complete. You can now login to https://NS2.govsystemlabs.com:1000
0/
as root with your root password.
[root@NS2 Downloads]# ▊
```
Fig. 69

4. You're done with section.

Step 6 Creating a Forward Zone on the Slave DNS Server

1. Install **Bind9** on the Slave Server

```
# yum install bind*  -y
```

2. Start and enable httpd service to automatically start on boot:

```
# systemctl start httpd.service
# systemctl enable httpd.service
```

3. Now point your browser to https://ns2.govsystemlabs.com:10000 and login to the Webmin admin page.

4. From the left pane, click **Servers > BIND DNS Server**, and then click "Create Primary Configuration File and Start Nameserver", as was done earlier in Fig. 6. You should see a Root Zone icon displayed under the **Existing DNS Zones** on the **BIND DNS Server** main page.

5. Next, under the **Existing DNS Zones**, click "Create slave zone" link, to access the **Create Slave Zone** page. Make sure that the "Forward (Names to Address) " is checked under the Zone type

6. Fill in the required information (replace with your information) as shown in Fig. 70:

Fig. 70

Note: creating a slave is extremely simple with Webmin. The only information required is the domain name or the network (as was used in the master zone i.e., the main DNS Server) earlier), and the addresses of one or more master nameservers. As with Master zones, you configure both a forward and reverse zone type for each zone. This server can then be used by clients just as the master zone is used, in fact whether it is a slave or master is transparent to the user.

7. When done entering the information, click on the **Create** button, and you should be taken automatically to the **Edit Slave Zone** page

8. From **Edit Slave Zone** page, click on the "Return to zone list" link. You should see our newly created "govsystemlabs.com" forward zone icon displayed under the **Existing DNS Zones** section.

9. You're done with this section.

Step 7: Creating a Reverse Zone on the Slave DNS Server

1. Again from the **Existing DNS Zones**, click "Create slave zone" link, to access the **Create Slave Zone** page, shown in Fig. 71. Make sure this time that the "Reverse (Names to Address)" is checked under the **Zone type** section.

2. Fill in the required information (replaced with your information):

Fig. 71

3. When done entering the information, click on the **Create** button, and you should be taken automatically to the **Edit Slave Zone** page

4. From **Edit Slave Zone** page, click on the "Return to zone list" link. You should see our newly created "192.168.6" revere zone icon displayed under the **Existing DNS Zones** section, as shown in Fig. 72.

312

Existing DNS Zones

Select all. | Invert selection. | Create master zone. | Create slave zone. | Create stub zone. | Create forward zone. | Create delegation zone. | Create zones from batch file.

Select all. | Invert selection. | Create master zone. | Create slave zone. | Create stub zone. | Create forward zone. | Create delegation zone. | Create zones from batch file.

Delete Selected   Update Records in Selected   Add Record to Selected   Delete Records in Selected

Fig. 72

Note: now scroll to the to of the page, and from the top right-hand corner, click **Start BIND**, if it isn't started yet, followed by clicking **Apply Configuration** to complete our creation of slave zone (or Slave DNS server), see Fig. 72.

5. Next scroll to the bottom (or Fig. 72 above), and click on the "`govsystemlabs.com`" forward zone icon/link, to access **Edit Slave Zone** page, and you should see that all our information from the **Master Zone** (Master DNS server) have been copied (replicated) to **Slave Zone**, see Fig. 73.

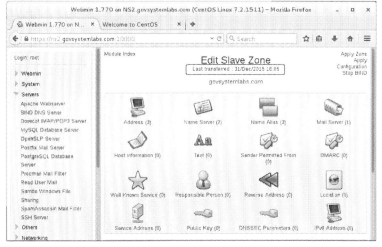

Fig. 73: The **Edit Slave Zone** screen, showing the replicated information from master DNS server.

313

6. You can now check and verify each & every information replicated from the master zone, e.g., click the `Address (3)` icon/link to see its content, see Fig. 74, which shows the correct information.

Fig. 74

7. Click on the "`Return to zone list`" link.

8. You're done with this section.

Step 8: Add Other DNS servers on the Slave DNS Server

1. From the **BIND DNS Server** main screen, under the **Global Server Options** heading, click "`Other DNS Servers`", to access Fig. 75. Add the IP address of the Slave DNS server "`192.168.6.12`", and then click **Save**, followed by "`Return to zone list`".

Fig. 75

2. You're done with this section.

Step 9: Configure Zone Transfers on the Slave DNS Server

The next task is to configure how our two zone replicates to each other. By default, zone transfers are not allowed. This is mainly for security reasons, for example, if a hostile machine can read your zone file, it can determine which machines are worth attacking. So the next step in configuring our Slave server is to permit them access to the zone file. This is achieved by performing the following task:

1. From the **Existing DNS** Zones, click on the "govsystemlabs.com" icon, which should take you to the **Edit Slave Zone** page.

govsystemlabs.com

2. From the **Edit Slave Zone** page, scroll down to the bottom of the page, and click "Edit Zone Options" icon/link.

3. Scroll down to section under **"Notify slaves of changes?"**, & enter the information shown in Fig. 76 (**Note: Master Servers** entry should already exist)

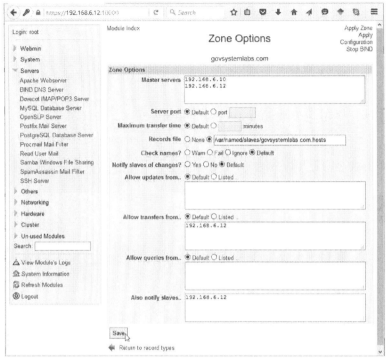

Fig. 76

4. When done, click on the **Save** button.

   Note: The zone transfer depends on the serial number. The serial number, in many cases will represent the year + date + hour. The slave will also check on the refresh interval to verify if the master has been updated, if the master has been updated the new information is transferred to the slave DNS to keep the database synchronized.

   For example, the verification will depend on the retry time in 3600 seconds (1hr) set as value on the retry option at the SOA of the zone (master server). If the slave DNS fails to contact the master server when it reaches the expired time 604800 seconds and it did not find the master server on each retry; the slave DNS server then removes the zone in its database and will no longer be a slave for that specific zone from the SOA.

5. Click on the "Return to record types" link.

316

6. Click on the "Return to zone list" link.

7. Logout of your Webmin on the slave server.

   Note 1: for ease of administering your slave DNS server, you can register it on the Master DNS server using Webmin.

   Note 2: Once you have perfected the testing stage, pilot testing stage, then you can move to the production phase with real public IP address and ICANN registered domain name.

Step 10: Test for DNS Redundancy Kick-in

In this section we're going to test how best our redundancy we put in place is able to cope with a sudden catastrophic failure of DNS Master Server.

To do so, perform the following procedure:

1. First and foremost, you should make sure that the Slave DNS server has the latest DNS master server database information. Click Apply Configuration to grab the latest database.

2. Today on Jan 01, 2016, as you can see from Fig. 77, our Slave DNS system is now working beautifully.

Fig. 77

3. Next, suddenly turn-off (simulate DNS master catastrophic failure) (on VMware just right-click on the DNS master virtual machine, and select **Suspend**). (**Note:** before suspending Master DNS Server the NSLOOKUP should be as shown in Fig. 78).

```
[root@NS2 ~]# nslookup govsystemlabs.com
Server:          192.168.6.10
Address:         192.168.6.10#53

Name:   govsystemlabs.com
Address: 192.168.6.10

[root@NS2 ~]#
[root@NS2 ~]# nslookup NS2.govsystemlabs.com
Server:          192.168.6.10
Address:         192.168.6.10#53

Name:   NS2.govsystemlabs.com
Address: 192.168.6.12

[root@NS2 ~]#
```
Fig. 78

Note: now, wait for a few minutes then check by issuing the "nslookup" command to test if Slave DNS was able to take over

4. Finally, issue the "NSLOOKUP" command, from our Slave DNS server, as shown below. And as can be observed, we're still to perform the "nslookup govsystemlabs.com", even though the master server is down.

```
[root@NS2 ~]# nslookup govsystemlabs.com
Server:          192.168.6.12
Address: 192.168.6.12#53

Name:   govsystemlabs.com
Address: 192.168.6.12
[root@NS2 ~]#
```

```
[root@NS2 ~]#
[root@NS2 ~]# nslookup NS2.govsystemlabs.com
Server:          192.168.6.12
Address: 192.168.6.12#53

Name:   NS2.govsystemlabs.com
Address: 192.168.6.12

[root@NS2 ~]#
```

5. Well done & congratulation, you're done with is great task – although the journey might have seemed complex and long – if you're still with me and all your setup is working correctly – then we can all pat our back for a job well done! You now have the most robust DNS server ever built. You deserve a good break, a bonus, a present a raise etc etc....

Part 9: ICT405 - Mastering CentOS 7 / RHEL 7 Server Administration and System Integration Training

Make a smart move, its time you reconfigure your skill-sets and move your career into the fastest moving high tech gravy train of the Linux Open Source world, join our Linux program today:

You can now register and take our superb Mastering CentOS-5/6 and /RHEL 5/6 Server Administration. This Training cover compete server installation, administration and system integration from simple task to cloud computing with Eucalyptus and OpenNebula cloud.

- ICT405 – Mastering RHEL 7 / CentOS 7 Training

Contact us today:

Email: info@globalopenversity.org   **URL:** www.globalopenversity.org

Part 10: Hands-on Labs Assignments

You're required to complete these assignments as part of class assignments and submit the results to your respective instructor. Continue assessment progress marks will be awarded as part of the grading systems:

7. Install Linux CentOS-7 / RHEL 7 server and ensure its updated with the latest patches and bug fixes.
8. Install and configure a Master DNS
9. Install and configure a Slave DNS
10. Configure and deploy multiple virtual hosting domains
11. Install & configure Zimbra or sendmail messaging server
12. Install and configure a web server
13. Install & configure OpenLDAP

Other Related Articles:

31. Using Webmin and Bind9 to Setup Enterprise DNS Server on Linux
32. Deploy Secure Messaging Solutions using Sendmail & Dovecot Servers with ClamAV on Linux
33. Install Guide Secure Postfix Messaging Server with Dovecot and ClamAV on Linux v1.2
34. Build and Deploy Enterprise sipXecs Integration with Openfire
35. Integrate MS Outlook 2007 Addressbook with SugarCRM Contacts on Windows
36. Build Private Clouds with Ubuntu 10.10 LTS Enterprise Cloud Platform
37. Build and Deploy Your Own Private PIAF-GOLD with Asterisk VoIP Telephony System

Chapter VI

Step-By-Step Guide Fedora 23 Server Installation & Administration

Introduction

Fedora (formerly **Fedora Core**) is an operating system based on the Linux kernel, developed by the community-supported Fedora Project and sponsored by Red Hat. Fedora contains software distributed under a free and open source license and aims to be on the leading edge of such technologies. Fedora Server is a powerful, flexible operating system that includes the best and latest datacenter technologies. It puts you in control of all your infrastructure and service. Finally, Fedora Cloud provides a minimal image of Fedora for use in public and private cloud environments. It includes just the bare essentials making it very light on resources, but you get enough to run your cloud application.

Fedora Workstation is a polished, easy to use operating system for laptop and desktop computers, with a complete set of tools for developers and makers of all kinds. It's a reliable, user-friendly, and powerful operating system for your laptop or desktop computer. It supports a wide range of developers, from hobbyists and students to professionals in corporate environments. The latest release includes quite a few improvements thanks to GNOME and other upstream projects. Fedora's developers are also on the cusp of switching to the new Wayland graphical server by default, with a stable, optional Wayland session available in Fedora 23.

Finally, Fedora 23 provides you with the balance most tech and ICT infrastructure designers looks for – a leading edge operating system with enterprise-level tools for fast provisioning and configuration.

Hands-on Lab Session

In this Hands-on lab session, you will learn how to install Fedora 23 server. You'll also learn how to perform post-installation configuration e.g., upgrade the system with new patches and bug fixes, configure static IP address from dynamic one, change the computer hostname, modify hosts file, perform ping test among others. You'll also show you how to install and administer LAMP stack, phpMyAdmin etc. Setup RPM Fusion and Fedy tools to enhance your multimedia solutions (VLC, Adobe Flash etc.). Install & configure Plex media server for cloud hosting multimedia offerings. Upon completion of this Hands-on training you should have gained enough skill to deploy, maintain and administer Fedora 23 server with ability to extend it to deploy mainstream applications like webhosting etc.

Part 1: Installing and Updating Fedora 23 Server

Step 1: Install Fedora 23 Server

50. Point your browser to Fedora 23 and download DVD ISO Server
51. Once you have downloaded the Fedora 23 ISO specific to your distribution, you have the option of burning it into CD/DVD or just by using the ISO package to install it from your virtual machine, in our case VMware.

52. Fire-up a new virtual machine and perform the initial configuration and setup to use ISO package.

53. Start the virtual machine, and you should be able to see the first Fedora 23 installation screen., as shown in Fig. 1, hit the **Enter** key to start installation.

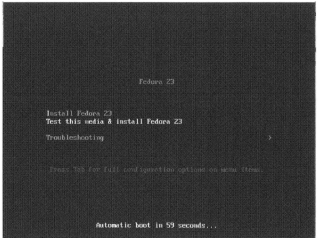
Fig. 1a

Fig. 1: Hit the <ENETER> key to start loading & installing Fedora 23.

```
[    9.033931] dracut-pre-trigger[462]: cat: /tmp/dd_disk: No such file or direc
tory
[  OK  ] Started Show Plymouth Boot Screen.
[  OK  ] Reached target Paths.
[  OK  ] Reached target Basic System.
    9.913054] dracut-initqueue[559]: mount: /dev/sr0 is write-protected, mounti
ng read-only
[  OK  ] Started Show Plymouth Boot Screen.
[  OK  ] Reached target Paths.
[  OK  ] Reached target Basic System.
    9.913054] dracut-initqueue[559]: mount: /dev/sr0 is write-protected, mounti
ng read-only
[  OK  ] Created slice system-checkisomd5.slice.
         Starting Media check on /dev/sr0...
/dev/sr0:    1cd120922a791d03e82939Za2b6b2107
Fragment sums: fba28f6826a9387e92a28d3eb8b199a8ac73726f57c8d7ed6eaff6bed1ac
Fragment count: 20
Supported ISO: no
Press [Esc] to abort check.
Checking: 005.5%_
```

Fig. 1b

54. From Fig. 2, **WELCOME TO Fedora 23** screen, accept the default selection, or change as desired and then click **Continue** button.

Fig. 2

55. From Fig. 3, **INSTALLATION SUMMARY** screen, here you can customize your installation by using other **Installation Sources** other than your local DVD/USB media, such as a network locations using **HTTP**, **HTTPS**, **FTP** or **NFS** protocols and even add some additional repositories, but use this methods only if you know what you're doing. So leave the default **Auto-detected installation media** and hit on **Done** to continue

323

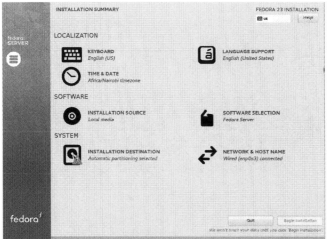

Fig. 3

56. From Fig. 3, **INSTALLATION SUMMARY** screen, click on the SOFTWARE to take you to the **INSTALLATION SOURCE** screen, accept the default selection "Auto-detected instillation media" or change as desired, click on **Done** to continue. (**Note**: you can also click on the **Verify** button to check on the media status), see Fig. 4.

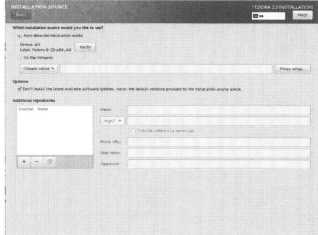

Fig. 4

57. From Fig. 3, **INSTALLATION SUMMARY** screen, click on the INSTALLATION DESTINATION to take you to the **INSTALLATION DESTINATION** screen, accept the default selection "Auto-configure partitioning" or change as desired, click on **Done** to continue, see Fig. 5

Fig. 5

58. From Fig. 3, **INSTALLATION SUMMARY** screen, click on the INSTALLATION DESTINATION to take you to the **NETWORK & HOST NAME** screen, type hostname, in our case "**f23.govhostinglabs.com**" change as desired, click on **Done** to continue, see Fig. 6.

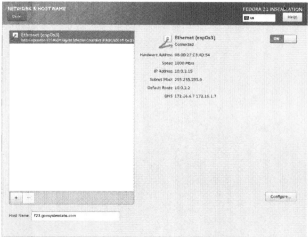

Fig. 6

325

59. From Fig. 7, **INSTALLATION SUMMARY** screen, you're now ready to begin installation once you're satisfied with your settings, click on **Continue** to continue.

Fig. 7

60. From Fig. 8, **CONFIGURATION** screen, here we're required to set the root password and also add the user as shown, when done with installation you can set them up.

Fig. 8

61. From Fig. 9, **CONFIGURATION** screen, Click on the ROOT PAASWORD to set it as shown, click Done to continue.

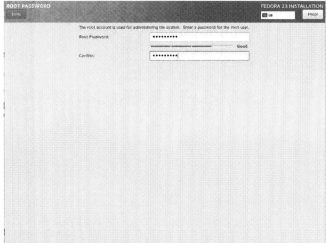
Fig. 9

62. From Fig. 10, **CREATE USER** screen, add the desired user as shown, click Done to continue.

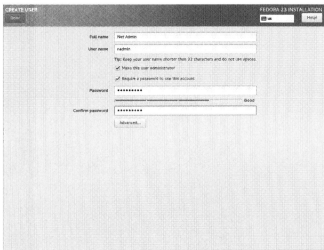
Fig. 10

63. From Fig. 11, **CONFIGURATION** screen, wait for the system to configure root user password and the adding of user.

Fig. 11

64. From Fig. 12, **CONFIGURATION** screen, when done click on **Finish Configuration** to continue.

Fig. 12

65. From Fig. 13, **CONFIGURATION** screen, wait for the systems to complete the task, when done click on **Reboot** button to continue. (Note: the license agreement notification)

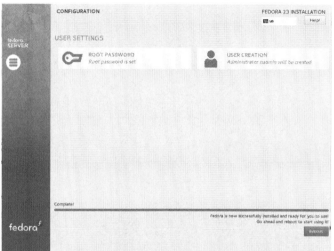

Fig. 13

66. From Fig. 14, the system will go through rebooting process, just relax for it to take you to the login screen.

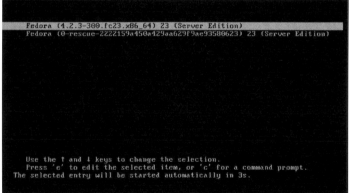

Fig. 14

67. The system will go through a rebooting process, as shown in Fig. 15. Wait for it to complete the process.

Fig. 15

68. From Fig. 16. you should be presented with the login screen, login with the credentials created earlier during the installation:

```
Fedora 23 (Server Edition)
Kernel 4.2.3-300.fc23.x86_64 on an x86_64 (tty1)

Admin Console: https://10.0.2.15:9090/ or https://[fe80::a00:27ff:fe01:c3e1]:909
0/

localhost login: root
Password:
[root@localhost ~]#  _
```

Fig. 16

69. You're done with this section.

Step 2: A Quick Note about DNF vs YUM, Updating Packages to Latest Versions, and Rebooting

As from Fedora 22, the YUM package-manager was replaced by DNF. DNF is highly backward-compatible, and uses a nearly (but not completely) identical command syntax. All is, however, not lost – you can still choose to either continue typing in 'yum' commands (which are passed off transparently to dnf), or use "dnf" commands directly. In this hands-on standardizes on using "dnf", but you may choose 'yum' instead if you prefer.

1. Perform a full update of all installed packages (including the kernel if necessary).

```
sudo dnf update
```

2. When you're ready, reboot the system after these steps have completed for changes to take effect (especially any Kernel updates that may have happened).

```
sudo systemctl reboot
```

3. You're done with section.

Step 3: Install Gnome GUI on F23

1. Fedora 23 does not come with GUI, so we need to install it, enter:

```
dnf groupinstall "Fedora Workstation"
```

2. We need to enable the graphical to start automatically on boot, type:

```
systemctl enable gdm.service
```

3. To start the graphic interface, enter:

```
# systemctl start gdm.service
```

OR

```
# startx
```

4. You should be presented with the GUI login screen shown in Fig. 17.

Fig. 17

5. You can login with Net Admin (`nadmin`) credentials as set during the initial installation.

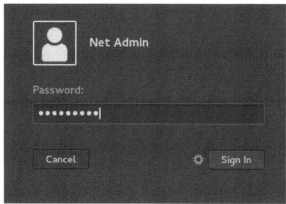

Fig. 18

6. Now you should be presented with the Fedora 23 Desktop screen, as shown in Fig. 19.

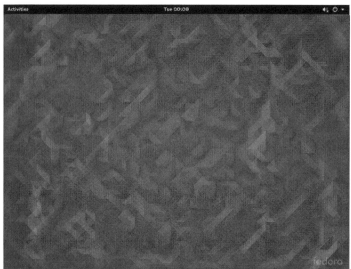
Fig. 19

7. Click on the **Activities** tab at the top lest hand corner to access other functionality, see Fig. 20.

Fig. 20

8. You're done with this section.

Step 4: Managing SELinux and Firewalld

1. Managing SELinux
SELinux is part of the kernel that enforces access control over many parts of the system, including filesystems, processes, sockets, etc., it can be trouble-some especially when installing and working with applications which require some access to e.g., ports etc. especially when its in enforcing state.

1. To change the SELinux policy from enforcing to disabled, type:

```
sudo sed --in-place=.bak 's/^SELINUX\=enforcing/SELINUX\=disabled/g'
/etc/selinux/config
```

2. You'll need to reboot the system for the changes to take effect, run:

```
sudo systemctl reboot
```

2. Managing Firewalld
Firewalld is the local firewall daemon that is included by-default with recent CentOS/ RHEL / Fedora releases. Because it can interfere with things such as uPnP, file-sharing, remote-control apps, etc., `firewalld` when necessary you will learn how to allow ports and services through firewalld. In some cases, you may also feel the need to disable or terminate it, however, such action do present a great risk when system is Internet facing!.

3. You can terminate `firewalld` if it is running, and then remove it from the system permanently.

```
sudo systemctl stop firewalld
```

or remove it:

```
sudo dnf remove firewalld
```

WARNING! **DO NOT REMOVE** firewalld in case your system is in any way exposed to the internet or other untrusted zones – it is highly recommended that you ensure those zones are adequately protected by their own firewalls before disabling the system's local firewalld.

4. You're done with this section/

Part 2: Post Installation Configurations.

Step 1: Perform System Upgrade

For best practices in IT, it's important to always perform systems upgrade after initial installation is completed. To do this, perform the following procedures:

3. From Fig. 20 above click on **Activities → Show applications → Terminal**.

4. From Fig. 22, you should be presented with Terminal window, type "ifconfig" command and hit Enter, you should be able Network card information. Note here "eth0" is shown as "eno16777736" with IP address "192.168.6.130". Go ahead and ping it to check if its active.

```
[root@localhost ~]# ifconfig
eno16777736: flags=4163<UP,BROADCAST,RUNNING,MULTICAST>  mtu 1500
        inet 192.168.6.130  netmask 255.255.255.0  broadcast 192.168.6.255
        inet6 fe80::20c:29ff:fe03:56b6  prefixlen 64  scopeid 0x20<link>
        ether 00:0c:29:03:56:b6  txqueuelen 1000  (Ethernet)
        RX packets 52160  bytes 71848355 (68.5 MiB)
        RX errors 0  dropped 0  overruns 0  frame 0
        TX packets 23474  bytes 1878259 (1.7 MiB)
        TX errors 0  dropped 0 overruns 0  carrier 0  collisions 0

lo: flags=73<UP,LOOPBACK,RUNNING>  mtu 65536
        inet 127.0.0.1  netmask 255.0.0.0
        inet6 ::1  prefixlen 128  scopeid 0x10<host>
        loop  txqueuelen 0  (Local Loopback)
        RX packets 1544  bytes 1064878 (1.0 MiB)
        RX errors 0  dropped 0  overruns 0  frame 0
        TX packets 1544  bytes 1064878 (1.0 MiB)
        TX errors 0  dropped 0 overruns 0  carrier 0  collisions 0

virbr0: flags=4099<UP,BROADCAST,MULTICAST>  mtu 1500
        inet 192.168.122.1  netmask 255.255.255.0  broadcast 192.168.122.255
        ether 52:54:00:42:31:b6  txqueuelen 0  (Ethernet)
        RX packets 0  bytes 0 (0.0 B)
        RX errors 0  dropped 0  overruns 0  frame 0
        TX packets 0  bytes 0 (0.0 B)
        TX errors 0  dropped 0 overruns 0  carrier 0  collisions 0

[root@localhost ~]#
```
Fig. 22a

```
[root@localhost ~]# ping 192.168.6.130
PING 192.168.6.130 (192.168.6.130) 56(84) bytes of data.
64 bytes from 192.168.6.130: icmp_seq=1 ttl=64 time=0.185 ms
64 bytes from 192.168.6.130: icmp_seq=2 ttl=64 time=0.100 ms
^C
--- 192.168.6.130 ping statistics ---
2 packets transmitted, 2 received, 0% packet loss, time 999ms
rtt min/avg/max/mdev = 0.100/0.142/0.185/0.044 ms
[root@localhost ~]#
```
Fig. 22b

9. From **Terminal** window, issue the command "`dnf update -y`" as shown in Fig. 23: This enables the system to get the latest patches and bug fixes.

```
dnf update -y
```

10. You're now down with system update. In the next section we're going to learn how to change NIC adapter configuration from dynamic IP address to static IP address.

Step 3: Check Computer Hostname

Note 1: The old way of changing hostname by modifying the "`/etc/sysconfig/network`"; no longer works and if you do so, it did not take an effect of the modification. That is, even do so, after you reboot the server, the hostname will still remains "`localhost.localdomain`". The procedure to change the hostname in RHEL 7 is now totally different from the previous version, this section will help you to setup the hostname on both the RHEL 7 / CentOS 7.

Note 2: Fedora 23 Supports three class of Hostnames

7. **Static** - The static hostname is the traditional host which can chosen by the user and is stored in "`/etc/hostname`" file

8. **Transient** - The transient hostname is maintained by the kernel and can be changed by DHCP and mDNS.

9. **Pretty** - It is a free UTF-8 hostname for the presentation to the user.

Note 3: Hostname can be
- 64 character in length
- Recommend to have FQDN
- Consists of: $a-z$, $A-Z$, $0-9$, "-", and "." only.

In this section we're going to change the computer hostname. But first let's check the current hostname.

14. To check the hostname issue "`hostname`" command, as shown in Fig. 24. which shows the current hostname is: : "`localhost.localdomain`"

```
[root@localhost ~]# hostname
localhost.localdomain
[root@localhost ~]#
```
———————— Fig. 31

15. You're done with this section.

2. Using nmtui tool to Change Hostname on F23

16. The NetworkManager tool is used to set the static hostname in "/etc/hostname". From the Terminal window issue the command "nmtui" to ass the NetworkManager dialogue box as shown in Fig. 32. From here you can do three things: Edit a connection; Activate a connection, and Set system hostname. Move to Set system hostname and hit **Enter** key or OK.

Fig. 25

17. Now in case, for example, you're interested in changing the hostname to, say: "server01.mydomain.org". In our case, "f23.govsystemlabs.com" Now you can modify your hostname as desired and then hit **Enter** key followed by **OK** and Enter key.

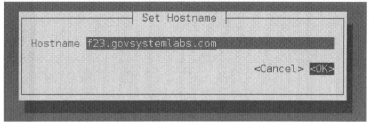

Fig. 26

18. You can verify the change in the hostname as shown in Fig. 27:

```
[root@localhost ~]# hostname
f23.govsystemlabs.com
[root@localhost ~]# cat /etc/hostname
f23.govsystemlabs.com
[root@localhost ~]#
```
Fig. 27

337

19. You're done with this section.

3. Using `hostnamedctl` command to Change Hostname on Fedora 23

Hostnamectl is used to change the hostname. With this tool we can change all three classes of hostname, however, here we are only interested with the static hostname.

9. First, and as usual, we need to check the current hostname, as shown in Fig. 28:

```
# hostnamectl status

[root@localhost ~]# hostnamectl status
   Static hostname: f23.govsystemlabs.com
         Icon name: computer-vm
           Chassis: vm
        Machine ID: 58e935488c7041678fbd11602c1582e6
           Boot ID: cd1be6370e3d436ca452e96e17787603
     Virtualization: vmware
  Operating System: Fedora 23 (Workstation Edition)
       CPE OS Name: cpe:/o:fedoraproject:fedora:23
            Kernel: Linux 4.2.3-300.fc23.x86_64
      Architecture: x86-64
[root@localhost ~]#
```
Fig. 28

10. Next, if desired, you can change the hostname, as follows:

```
#  hostnamectl set-hostname server01.mydomain.com
```

11. You can also use the hostnamectl command on its own.

```
[root@f23 ~]# hostnamectl
```

12. You're done with this section.

3. Using `nmcli` tool to Change Hostname on Fedora 23

The nmcli tool can be used to query and setup the static hostname in "/etc/hostname" file.

8. To check the hostname:

```
# nmcli general hostname
```

9. To change the hostname:

338

```
# nmcli general hostname server01.mydomain.com
```

10. You're done with this section.

4. Edit "/etc/hostname" to Change Hostname on Fedora 23
Note: this is the simplest but requires a reboot of the server to in order to take effect

11. You are done with this section.

4. Modify "/etc/hosts" to take effect of the changes
1. Using your favorite text editor, change the /etc/hosts file to reflect the changes, change desired.

```
127.0.0.1      localhost localhost.localdomain localhost4 localhost4.localdomain4
192.168.6.130  f23.govsystemlabs.com f23
::1            localhost localhost.localdomain localhost6 localhost6.localdomain6
```

12. Save and exit.

13. You are done with this section.

Step 4: Changing the Interface from the "eno16777736" to the old "eth0" if using VMware 12 Pro

The VMware 12 Pro, now installs the system with "eno16777736", which will want to change back to the old "eth0".

Step 1: Change Interface from the "eno16777736" to "eth0"
8. The first step is to check the current setting by type "ifconfig" command:

```
[root@f23 ~]# ifconfig
eno16777736: flags=4163<UP,BROADCAST,RUNNING,MULTICAST>  mtu 1500
        inet 192.168.6.130  netmask 255.255.255.0  broadcast 192.168.6.255
        inet6 fe80::20c:29ff:fe9c:b595  prefixlen 64  scopeid 0x20<link>
        ether 00:0c:29:9c:b5:95  txqueuelen 1000  (Ethernet)
        RX packets 1913  bytes 128626 (125.6 KiB)
        RX errors 0  dropped 0  overruns 0  frame 0
        TX packets 218  bytes 22031 (21.5 KiB)
        TX errors 0  dropped 0 overruns 0  carrier 0  collisions 0
```

```
lo: flags=73<UP,LOOPBACK,RUNNING>  mtu 65536
        inet 127.0.0.1  netmask 255.0.0.0
        inet6 ::1  prefixlen 128  scopeid 0x10<host>
        loop  txqueuelen 0  (Local Loopback)
        RX packets 6  bytes 436 (436.0 B)
        RX errors 0  dropped 0  overruns 0  frame 0
        TX packets 6  bytes 436 (436.0 B)
        TX errors 0  dropped 0 overruns 0  carrier 0  collisions 0

virbr0: flags=4099<UP,BROADCAST,MULTICAST>  mtu 1500
        inet 192.168.122.1  netmask 255.255.255.0  broadcast 192.168.122.255
        ether 52:54:00:49:5d:71  txqueuelen 0  (Ethernet)
        RX packets 0  bytes 0 (0.0 B)
        RX errors 0  dropped 0  overruns 0  frame 0
        TX packets 0  bytes 0 (0.0 B)
        TX errors 0  dropped 0 overruns 0  carrier 0  collisions 0
```

Note: you can also check the same using `"ip addr show"`

9. We now need to edit the `"/etc/default/grub"` file to update it:

```
[root@f23 ~]# nano /etc/default/grub
```

```
GRUB_TIMEOUT=5
GRUB_DISTRIBUTOR="$(sed 's, release .*$,,g' /etc/system-release)"
GRUB_DEFAULT=saved
GRUB_DISABLE_SUBMENU=true
GRUB_TERMINAL_OUTPUT="console"
GRUB_CMDLINE_LINUX="rd.lvm.lv=rootvg/usrlv rd.lvm.lv=rootvg/swaplv
crashkernel=auto vconsole.keymap=us rd.lvm.lv=rootvg/rootlv
vconsole.font=latarcyrheb-sun16 rhgb quiet"
GRUB_DISABLE_RECOVERY="true"
```

Now look for the line `"GRUB_CMDLINE_LINUX"` and add the following: `"net.ifnames=0 biosdevname=0"`

And which should now look like:

```
GRUB_CMDLINE_LINUX="rd.lvm.lv=rootvg/usrlv rd.lvm.lv=rootvg/swaplv
crashkernel=auto vconsole.keymap=us rd.lvm.lv=rootvg/rootlv
vconsole.font=latarcyrheb-sun16 rhgb quiet net.ifnames=0
biosdevname=0"
```

10. Next run the following command:

```
[root@f23 ~]# grub2-mkconfig -o /boot/grub2/grub.cfg
Generating grub configuration file ...
Found linux image: /boot/vmlinuz-4.2.3-300.fc23.x86_64
Found initrd image: /boot/initramfs-4.2.3-300.fc23.x86_64.img
Found linux image: /boot/vmlinuz-0-rescue-58e935488c7041678fbd11602c1582e6
Found           initrd           image:           /boot/initramfs-0-rescue-
58e935488c7041678fbd11602c1582e6.img
done
[root@f23 ~]#
```

Note: if you didn't put any names during the initial installation, you'll need to rename the interface file by renaming the file "/etc/sysconfig/network-scripts/ifcfg*".

```
[root@f23 ~]# mv /etc/sysconfig/network-scripts/ifcfg-eno16777736
/etc/sysconfig/network-scripts/ifcfg-eth0
```

11. Reboot the system:

```
# shutdown -r now
```

12. After system reboot, run:

```
# ifconfig
```

```
[root@f23 ~]# ifconfig eth0
eth0: flags=4163<UP,BROADCAST,RUNNING,MULTICAST>  mtu 1500
        inet 192.168.6.129  netmask 255.255.255.0  broadcast 192.168.6.255
        inet6 fe80::20c:29ff:fe03:56b6  prefixlen 64  scopeid 0x20<link>
        ether 00:0c:29:03:56:b6  txqueuelen 1000  (Ethernet)
        RX packets 49  bytes 7235 (7.0 KiB)
        RX errors 0  dropped 0  overruns 0  frame 0
        TX packets 71  bytes 7288 (7.1 KiB)
        TX errors 0  dropped 0 overruns 0  carrier 0  collisions 0

[root@f23 ~]#
```

Step 1: Disable Network Manager

13. Disable Network Manager, type:

```
# systemctl disable NetworkManager.service
```

14. You're done with this section.

Part 3: Installing LAMP Stack: Linux, Apache, Mariadb (MySQL), PHP on Fedora 23 Server

The LAMP stack forms the basic core components for a dynamic, database-driven web site. We'll use "dnf" to handle all the required packages. LAMP stack is nothing but software bundle or a platform consisting of Linux operating system, Apache web-server, MySQL (now MariaDB) database server and PHP (or Perl/Python) scripting language. The LAMP stack is used for building heavy duty dynamic websites entirely out of free and open-source software. In this section of the Hands-on guide, we are going to go through on how to install and run LAMP stack.

This section will present us the opportunity to install Apache2 (httpd), PHP, MySQL (server and client), and the component that allows PHP to talk to MySQL database.

Step 1: Install Apache on Fedora 23 Server

1. From the Terminal window, run the following dnf command to install Apache web-server:

```
sudo dnf install httpd -y
```

Note: Troubleshooting: In case you encounter dependencies problem, then you can perform yum command with "-skip-broken" option, as follows:

20. Next, we now need to enable the httpd service to start automatically at the boot time, type:

```
sudo systemctl enable httpd.service
```

Note: to disable the httpd service at boot time, issue:

```
sudo systemctl disable httpd.service
```

21. Now, we need to start the httpd service, type:

```
sudo systemctl start httpd.service
```

22. Test your httpd functionality, go to http://localhost or http://your-domain or http://ip-address, and if all works well, it should display **Fedora 23 Test Page,** as shown in Fig. 21.

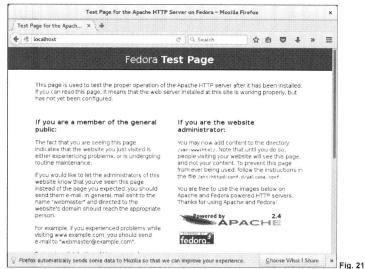

Fig. 21

Note: to stop `httpd` service, run:

```
sudo systemctl stop httpd.service
```

23. To restart `httpd` service, run:

```
sudo systemctl restart httpd.service
```

24. To verify the `httpd` service status, enter:

```
sudo systemctl is-active httpd.service
```

25. To gracefully restart `httpd` service status, enter:

```
sudo apachectl graceful
```

26. To test `httpd` configuration file for errors, enter:

```
sudo apachectl configtest
```

Sample output:

```
Syntax OK
```

27. You're done with Apache2 server setup and testing.

28. You're with this section.

1. The httpd (Apache) service default configuration
- Default config file: `/etc/httpd/conf/httpd.conf`
- Configuration files which load modules: "`/etc/httpd/conf.modules.d/`" directory (e.g., PHP).
- Select MPMs (Processing Model) as loadable modules [worker, prefolk (default)] and event
  "`/etc/httpd/conf.module.d/00-mpm.conf`
- Default ports: `80` and `443` (SSL)
- Default log files: "`/var/log/httpd/{access_log, error_log}`"

29. You're with this section.

Step 2: Install MariaDB (MySQL) Database Server on F23

MariaDB is an enhanced, drop-in replacement for MySQL server. Fedora 23 has shift from MySQL to MariaDB for its database management systems needs.

1. Install MariaDB on F23
11. To install MariaDB run the `yum` command as follows:

```
sudo dnf install mariadb-server maraidb -y
```

12. Start Mariadb (`mariadb`) daemon service, if you haven't done so, run:

```
sudo systemctl start mariadb.service
```

13. To make sure Mariadb (`mariadb`) daemon service start automatically at boot time, type:

```
sudo systemctl enable mariadb.service
```

14. To stop/start and disable mariadb service use the following commands:

```
sudo systemctl stop mariadb.service       # Stop mariadb server
sudo systemctl restart mariadb.service    # Restart mariadb server
sudo systemctl disable mariadb.service    # Disable mariadb server
```

```
sudo systemctl is-active mariadb.service    # Is mariadb server
running
```

15. You're done with this section.

2. Securing MariaDB

IMPORTANT! Set up the MySQL database root password. Without a password, ANY user on the box can login to mysql as database root. The mysql root account is a separate password from the machine root account.

Now that our MySQL (Mariadb) database is running, we want to run a simple security script that will remove some of the dangerous defaults and also allow us to lock down access to our database a little bit. To do this, from the Terminal window type:

```
sudo mysql_secure_installation
```

The prompt will ask you for your current root password. However, since we have just installed MySQL, you most likely won't have one, so leave it blank by pressing enter. On the next prompt you will be asked if you want to set a root password. Go ahead and enter Y, and follow the instructions as below:

```
Enter current password for root (enter for none):
OK, successfully used password, moving on...

Setting the root password ensures that nobody can log into the MariaDB
root user without the proper authorization.

New password: password
Re-enter new password: password
Password updated successfully!
Reloading privilege tables..
... Success!
```

Note: for the rest of the questions, you should simply hit **"ENTER"** key through each prompt to accept default values, or change as desired. This will remove some of the sample users and databases, disable remote root logins, and load these rules, so that MySQL immediately respects the changes we have made. However, since this is a non production server, which are only using for training, we have left some of the settings as is. (**Note:** for production server please do ensure that the server full locked-down).

29. We can now login into our database as follows (enter the password set above):

```
$ mysql -u root -p

$ mysql -u root -p
```

```
password:
Welcome to the MariaDB monitor.  Commands end with ; or \g.
Your MariaDB connection id is 3
Server version: 10.0.20-MariaDB MariaDB Server

Copyright (c) 2000, 2015, Oracle, MariaDB Corporation Ab and others.

Type 'help;' or '\h' for help. Type '\c' to clear the current input statement.

MariaDB [(none)]>
```

30. You're with this section.

3: Creating a Test Database

10. Now we need to create a sample database and database user for a sample application. You will use this database and username in your database connection string. The "GRANT" statement actually creates a new MYSQL user account.

```
MariaDB> GREATE DATABASE webdb;
MariaDB> GRANT ALL PRIVILEGES ON webdb.* TO 'webuser'@'localhost'
IDENTIFIED BY 'webpass';
MariaDB> FLUSH PRIVILEGES;
MariaDB>exit
```

```
MariaDB [(none)]> CREATE DATABASE webdb;
Query OK, 1 row affected (0.00 sec)

MariaDB [(none)]> GRANT ALL PRIVILEGES ON webdb.* TO 'webuser'@'localhost' IDENT
IFIED BY 'webpass';
Query OK, 0 rows affected (0.03 sec)

MariaDB [(none)]> FLUSH PRIVILEGES;
Query OK, 0 rows affected (0.41 sec)

MariaDB [(none)]>
```
Fig. 30

11. You can check if your "webdb" database has been successfully created, using "show databases" command.

```
MariaDB [(none)]> SHOW DATABASES;
+--------------------+
| Database           |
+--------------------+
| information_schema |
| mysql              |
| performance_schema |
| webdb              |
+--------------------+
4 rows in set (0.12 sec)

MariaDB [(none)]>
```
————————————————————————— Fig. 31

12. You're done with MySQL (MariaDB) setup, configuration and testing.

13. You're done with this section

Step 3: Install PostgreSQL Database on Fedora 23 Server

This will install the PostgreSQL database server and the component required to write PHP scripts that communicate with postgresql. Do this if you didn't initially install it. We use yum to handle dependencies and gather all of the required packages. For more information on PostgreSQL, see http://www.postgresql.org

14. To install PostgreSQL and the component that allows PHP to talk to it, run:

```
# dnf -y install postgresql postgresql-server php-pgsql
```

15. We need to initialize PostgreSQL database, Run:

```
# service postgresql initdb

root@f23 ~]# service postgresql initdb
Hint: the preferred way to do this is now "/usr/bin/postgresql-setup --initdb
--unit postgresql"
 * Initializing database in '/var/lib/pgsql/data'
 * Initialized, logs are in /var/lib/pgsql/initdb_postgresql.log
[root@f23 ~]#
```

16. Configure the new service to start automatically on boot:

```
# systemctl enable postgresql.service
# systemctl start postgresql.service
```

Note: when you start postgresql for the first time, it'll initialize the database.

347

17. Start the `postgresql` interactive shell and create your first user and database.

```
# su - postgres          \\The dash "-" is important!
```

4. Next, issue the command, `"psql template1"`, to enter the default postgresql database

```
-bash-3.2$ psql template1
```

The whole sequence is as shown in Fig. 34.

```
[root@localhost ~]# su - postgres
-bash-4.3$
-bash-4.3$ psql template1
psql (9.4.5)
Type "help" for help.

template1=# help
You are using psql, the command-line interface to PostgreSQL.
Type:  \copyright for distribution terms
       \h for help with SQL commands
       \? for help with psql commands
       \g or terminate with semicolon to execute query
       \q to quit
template1=#
```
Fig. 34

Note: `"template1"`is the database that is included by default with PostgreSQL.

18. Check the `version` of your `postgresql` database:

```
template1=# select version();
                    version
----------------------------------------------------------------
PostgreSQL 9.4.5 on x86_64-redhat-linux-gnu, compiled by
GCC gcc (GCC) 5.1.1 20150681 (Red Hat 5.1.1-4), 64-bit
(1 row)
template1=# \q
-bash-4.2$ exit
```

19. Now create dbase user `"webadmin"` and make him a superuser:

```
-bash-4.2$ createuser -P webadmin
Enter password for new role:
```

```
Enter it again:
Shall the new role be a superuser? (y/n) y
-bash-4.2$
```

20. Next create the database `"webdb"`

```
-bash-4.2$
-bash-4.2$ createdb -O webadmin webdb
-bash-4.2$
```

21. Now connect into your newly created database:

```
-bash-4.2$ psql webdb
Psql (9.2.13)
Type "help" for help.
web_db=#
```

22. Logout of your dbase:

```
webdb=# \q
-bash-42$ logout
[root@rhel7 ~]#
```

23. Edit the **postgres** host based access `"pg_hba"` configuration file:

```
# vi /var/lib/pgsql/data/pg_hba.conf
```

24. Modify the local line to use `"md5"` based authentication rather than `"peer"`. Please review the PostgreSQL documentation before making this change and take the security

```
local          all          all                    md5
```

25. Restart the postgresql database service.

```
# /sbin/service postgresql reload             \\ restarts postgresql
```

26. Log back into the server

```
# su - postgres
```

27. Test your connection.

```
# psql -U webadmin webdb          \\ or psql webdb
```

28. You're on installing and configuring PostgreSQL database.

29. Hooray! – Enjoy LAMP + PostgreSQL

Step 4: Install & Test PHP Install on Fedora 23 Server

31. To install PHP and modules such as gd/myql type the following `yum` command:

```
sudo dnf install php php-mysql php-pgsql php-gd php-peer -y
```

32. Next you must restart the httpd (Apache) service, type:

```
sudo systemctl restart httpd.service
```

33. Following the above steps for Apaache2 setup, the document root for Apache is `"/var/www/hmtl/"`

34. Create a test PHP script file called `"/var/www/html/test.php"` and place it in the documents root. A useful test script sample:

```
sudo vi /var/www/html/test.php
```

and appended the following code:

```
<?php
    phpinfo(INFO_GENERAL);
?>
```

35. Now fire-up your browser and point it to: http://localhost/test.php and you should the browser rendered as shown in Fig. 35.

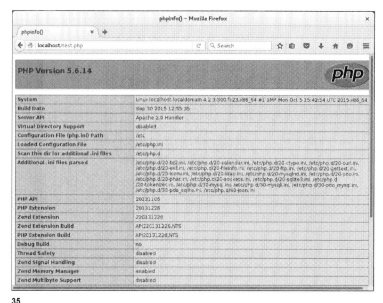

Fig.

36. You're done with PHP5 setup and testing.

Step 5: Install & Configure phpMyAdmin on F23

phpMyAdmin 4.5 Released. It is web-based client written in php for managing MySQL and MariaDB databases. It provides a user friendly web interface to access and manage your databases. To ease usage to a wide range of people, phpMyAdmin is being translated into 72 languages and supports both LTR and RTL languages

1. Install phpMyAdmin on F23

Now, we are ready to install the phpMyAdmin package., to do this type:

10. After accepting the new repository, you can install the `phpMyAdmin` package by typing:

```
sudo dnf install phpmyadmin  -y
```

11. When done with installation, we need to restart Apache service to reload new settings.

```
# systemctl restart httpd.service
```

12. You're done with this section.

2. Accessing phpMyAdmin in Browser

13. Now you can access phpMyAdmin by pointing your browser http://mydomain.com/phpadmin or with your server IP/FQDN, as shown in Fig. 38

Fig. 38

14. Login with same credential you use to login to MariaDB database, see Fig. 39.

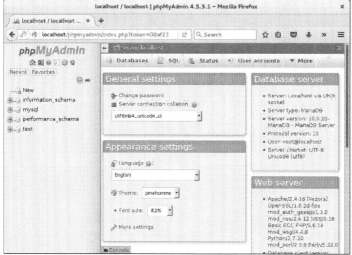

Fig. 39

15. You're done with this section.

37. Hooray! – Enjoy working with LAMP server.

Part 4: Add RPM Fusion repositories

Since most of my multimedia experience has moved to my Plex Server and for those who consume movies and music through digital media players like Chromecast and Amazon Fire TV (both powered by Linux), you'll no longer have the requirement to get all codecs and drivers. But oftentimes you may need to play something locally and for that you will need drivers and codecs.

1. Install RPM Fusion Repos

It's important to note, that Fedora, like many other distributions, can't ship such packages through official repositories so you'll need to add RPM Fusion repos to your system. You can achieve this via command line way of doing it or you can open a browser, go to the RPM Fusion site and enable RPM Fusion Free and RPM Fusion Non-Free repositories, by clicking on those links.

1. To use the CLI option then run the following command in the terminal app:

   su -c 'dnf install http://download1.rpmfusion.org/free/fedora/rpmfusion-free-release-$(rpm -E %fedora).noarch.rpm http://download1.rpmfusion.org/nonfree/fedora/rpmfusion-nonfree-release-$(rpm -E %fedora).noarch.rpm'

   Note: once the repositories are enabled you can the go ahead and install packages like VLC which can play almost every possible media file.

2. Install VLC

2. To install VLC, run the following command:

   sudo dnf install vlc -y

3. In case you don't use Plex for your multimedia needs (which you should, then you can install Clementine for music playback.

   sudo dnf install clementine -y

4. You're done with this section.

3. Install Fedy Tools

There is a nifty tool that lets you install codecs and other software called Fedy which can do wonders on your system. Fedy is a must have tool for Fedora users including the new Fedora 23. Fedy provide a simple way to install third party applications which are not included on Fedora installation. You may install Google Chrome, Adobe Flash Plugin, Dropbox, Oracle Java JRE and many more. It comes with a simple user interface. Simply click Install button close to the application you want to install. Fedy will do the rest.

To install Fedy tool, perform the following procedures:

5. First download Fedy install script from **Here** and save it to your Download directory

6. From the terminal change to your Download directory, and do the following tasks:

```
cd /home/nadmin/Downloads
su
chmod +x fedy-installer
./fedy-installer
```

Note: once the tool is installed, open it and then install all that you need on your Fedora system, including the Chrome browser to watch Netflix and Amazon Prime.

1. When done, you should find Fedy application listed on your Applications menu, click on it to access Fig. 40.

Fig. 40

2. Enjoy the fun and power of Fedy tools to manage & enhance your power to watch some nifty multimedia on Amazon & Netflix.

3. You're done with this section.

Part 5: How to Create a Streaming Media Server using Plex on Fedora 23 Server

Step 1: Download & Install Plex Server

You will be surprised to find out that installation is the easiest piece of the Plex puzzle in any Linux distro. Let's walk through the steps.

1. Point your web browser to and <u>download the installer</u> that meets your needs, for our case, RPM files for Fedora server (for this lab, `plexmediaserver-0.9.14.6.1620-e0b7243.x86_64.rpm`)

2. Change to the download directory where you downloaded the file

2. Now, double-click on the downloaded installer, or type:

```
sudo rpm -ivh plexmediaserver-0.9.14.6.1620-e0b7243.x86_64.rpm
```

Note: alternatively, you can also use port number to allow port 32400 through instead as follows:

```
sudo firewall-cmd --permanent --add-port=32400/tcp
sudo firewall-cmd --reload
```

3. Allow the installation to complete. That's it! The installation of the Plex media server is done.

Step2: Starting the Plex server

1. Now we need to start up the Plex server and also enable it to automatically start on boot, type:

```
sudo systemctl enable plexmediaserver
sudo systemctl start plexmediaserver
```

2. The Plex server will start running in the background and you can connect to the web-based interface to set up your server.

3. Now start your browser and point it to <u>http://localhost:32400/web</u>, http://ip-address:32400/web, or http://mydomian:32400/web You will be presented with the Plex web-based administration

355

tool, as shown in Fig. 41. Read and then click on the **Agree** button to accept the **Plex Terms of Service**.

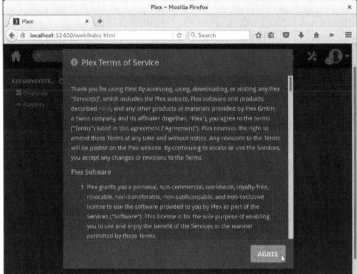

Fig. 41

4. You should be presented with the Plex admin console as shown in Fig. 42.

Fig. 42a

5. From Fig. 42 above, click on the drop-down menu to access the Sign In link.

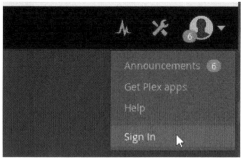

Fig. 42b

6. You should be presented with the login page as shown in Fig. 43.

Note: the first thing you should do is to sign up for a Plex account (even the free account) so you are able to take advantage of some of the extra features. You can sign-up here. Once you have your account created, you're ready to go. Use the credentials to now login to your server.

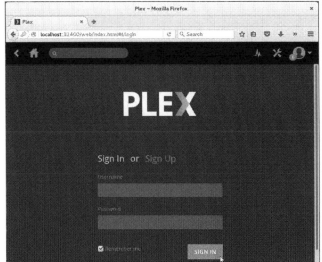
Fig. 43a

Fig. 43b

7. From Fig. 42 above, click on the **Channels** link to access the Fig. 44, and then click on Install Channels link. You can also click on he CHECK UPDATES to update your Plex server.

358

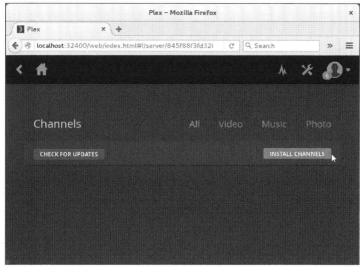

Fig. 44

8. Next click on 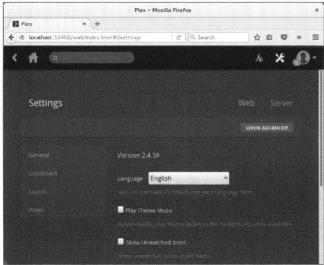 icon at the top right-hand corner to access Fig. 45.

Fig. 45

9. From Fig. 45 above, click on the **Server** link to access Fig. 46.

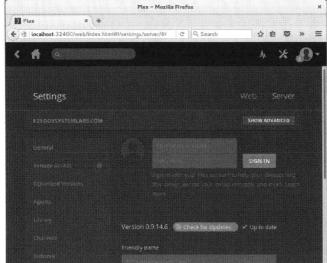

Fig. 46

10. You're done with section.

Step 2: Install and Configure Samba Share on Fedora 23

In this section you'll learn how to install and configure Samba server on separate Fedora 23 box and create a Samba share store. To do this, you'll need to perform the following procedure:

Step 1: Install and Configure Samba Share

17. The first step is to install samba (if not already installed), type:

```
# yum install samba -y
```

18. Once installed, overwrite the default "/etc/samba/smb.config" file with the following:

```
[global]
workgroup = WORKGROUP
server string = %h server
encrypt passwords = true
passdb backend = tdbsam
```

```
obey pam restrictions = yes

[MOVIES]
comment = Movies Library
path = /store/movies/
browseable = yes
public = yes
read only = yes

[MUSIC]
comment = Music Library
path = /store/music/
browseable = yes
public = yes
read only = yes

[PHOTOS]
comment = Photos Library
path = /store/photos/
browseable = yes
public = yes
read only = yes

[HOME_VIDEOS]
comment = Home Videos Library
path = /store/homevideos/
browseable = yes
public = yes
read only = yes

[TV_SHOWS]
comment = TV Shows Library
path = /store/tvshows/
browseable = yes
public = yes
read only = yes
```

Warning! You should only create a completely open share like the one here if you trust the people who have access to your Samba PDC server; open FTP servers, for example, have been compromised in the past and abused as drop boxes for pirated software.

19. After you've added these shares to your `"smb.conf"` configuration file, remember to either restart Samba or tell it to reload its configuration files, however, before doing that run the : `"testparm"` command.

20. Save your changes and run `"testparm"` command to test your samba configuration:

```
# testparm
```

if all is ok, a sample output should look like:

```
[root@f23 ~]# testparm
Load smb config files from /etc/samba/smb.conf
rlimit_max: increasing rlimit_max (1024) to minimum Windows limit
(16384)
Processing section "[MOVIES]"
Processing section "[MUSIC]"
Processing section "[PHOTOS]"
Processing section "[HOME_VIDEOS]"
Processing section "[TV_SHOWS]"
Loaded services file OK.
Server role: ROLE_STANDALONE

Press enter to see a dump of your service definitions

# Global parameters
[global]
    server string = %h server
    obey pam restrictions = Yes
    idmap config * : backend = tdb

[MOVIES]
    comment = Movies Library
    path = /store/movies/
    guest ok = Yes

[MUSIC]
    comment = Music Library
    path = /store/music/
    guest ok = Yes

[PHOTOS]
    comment = Photos Library
    path = /store/photos/
    guest ok = Yes

[HOME_VIDEOS]
    comment = Home Videos Library
```

```
    path = /store/homevideos/
    guest ok = Yes

[TV_SHOWS]
    comment = TV Shows Library
    path = /store/tvshows/
    guest ok = Yes
[root@f23 ~]#
```

Note: this checks "`smb.conf`" for syntax errors. Any errors must be corrected before moving on. Once all is OK, you can start-up and enable Samba to start automatically on boot, as follows:

```
# systemctl enable smb.service
# systemctl start smb.service
```

21. Set `firewall-cmd` to allow samba service, type:

```
firewall-cmd --permanent --add-service=samba
firewall-cmd --permanent --add-service=samba-client
firewall-cmd --reload
```

22. You're done with this section.

Step 2: Create Shared Folders

The next step is to create the appropriate users and folders. To do this, perform the following steps:

23. Create our directories, type

```
sudo mkdir -p /store/movies/
sudo mkdir -p /store/music/
sudo mkdir -p /store/photos/
sudo mkdir -p /store/homevideos/
sudo mkdir -p /store/tvshows/
```

24. You're done with this section.

Step 3: Adding your own Multimedia Folders

1. From your server, let's access the `/store/music/` directory add some music files to share, as shown in Fig. 47.

Fig. 47

2. Next, open your Plex management console and click on + icon to access the **Add Library** page, as shown in Fig.

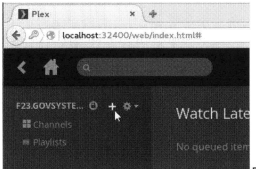
Fig. 48

3. From the **Add Library** page, Fig. 49, click on the **Music** tab, enter the Name of your library and choose the language. Click Next to continue.

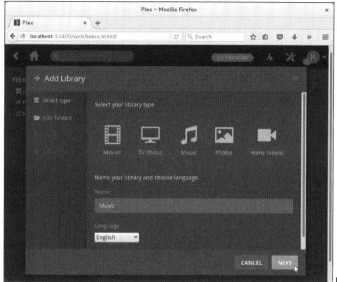
Fig. 49

4. From the next dialogue box, click on the **BROWSE FOR MEDIA FOLDER** to select the desired folder to share, as shown in Fig. 50.

Fig. 50

5. From Fig. 51, browse to select the desired media and then click on the **Add** button to continue.

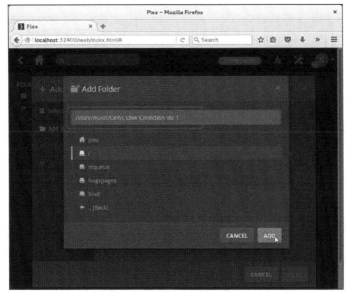

Fig. 50

6. You should now be presented with Fig. 51 with your selected music folder being listed under **Music** with additional information **Recently Added**

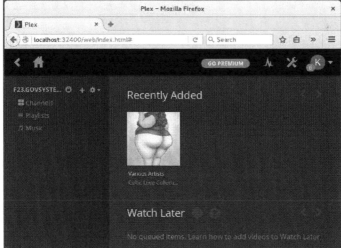

Fig. 51

7. You're done and you can now easily enjoy your shared music from anywhere anytime if you're connected to a public IP address. From Fig. 52 you can observe our playlist to choose from.

Fig. 52

8. Repeat the same for all the multimedia options you wish to add to the Plex server e.g., movie, TV series etc.

9. You're done with this section and the Hands-on lab - good luck.

Part 6: Need More Training on Mastering ICT Infrastructure Development & Deployment

Are you having trouble understanding or comprehending ICT infrastructure planning, design and deployment projects with Microsoft Windows Server, Linux (CentOS, RHEL etc.), DNS servers provisioning, IPA (Identity Management) provisioning, Application Servers (WildFly, JBoss, GlassFish, Joomla CMS, Moodle LMS), Public, private to personal cloud provisioning with ownCloud, Seafile secure cloud storage, eyesCloud, Eucalyptus cloud, OpenNebula, FastStack etc.), if so, then check out some of our top ICT skills enhancement training courses at: Global Open Versity, Vancouver Canada.

Mastering RHEL 7 / CentOS 7 Server Administration and System Integration Training - ICT405

You can now register and take our superb Mastering RHEL 7 / CentOS 7 Server Administration. This Training cover compete server installation, administration and system integration from simple task to cloud computing with ownCloud and Seafile Secure Cloud Storage and virtualization skills enhancement with VirtualBox integrated with phpVirtualBox web management console.

- ICT405 – Mastering RHEL 7 / CentOS 7 Training

Contact us today: Email: info@globalopenversity.org   **URL:** www.globalopenversity.org

Part 7: Hands-on Labs Assignments

You're required to complete these assignments as part of class assignments and submit the results to your respective instructor. Continue assessment progress marks will be awarded as part of the grading systems:

1. Install Linux Fedora 23 server and ensure it's updated with the latest patches and bug fixes.
2. Install and configure Linux Fedora 23 and install DNS Server, LAMP Stack, WildFly, Bacula Backup, JBoos-Portal
3. Install and configure Linux Fedora 23 and install and configure FreeIPA (Identity Management) server
4. Install and configure virtualization with VirtualBox with phpVirtualBox on your Fedora 23
5. Install and configure virtualization with ownCloud private cloud on your Fedora 23
6. Install and configure virtualization with Seafile Secure Cloud Storage on your Fedora 23

Other Related Articles:
1. Install Guide Secure Postfix Messaging Server with Dovecot and ClamAV on Linux v1.2
2. Build and Deploy Enterprise sipXecs Integration with Openfire
3. Step-By-Step Build & Deploy Citrix XenServer and XenCenter v1.0
4. Step-By-Step Install Guide Xen Hypervisor on Linux Server v1.1
5. Step-By-Step Build & Deploy Citrix XenServer and XenCenter v1.2
6. Step-by-step Install Guide for Moodle with Dimdim Web Meeting
7. Step-By-Step Install Guide Alfresco Community 3.3g on RHEL5 Server v1.0

Chapter VII

Install & Setup Astaro Security Gateway to Protect Corporate Network

Project: *Deploy secure enterprise network defense solution using Astaro Security Gateway (ASG).* (Astaro Security Gateway is Trademark of <u>Astaro AG</u>.) The ASG is all in One – The Unified Threat Management (UTM) appliance that brings enterprise-class Network, Web and Mail Security to organizations for all sizes. You have the option to use Home Use Edition, fully free for home use; the Essential Edition, fully free for Business Use; and the Professional Edition, which you can purchase for commercial use; however, you have the possibility to test it free for 30 day trial. In this IT Security & Network Defense Hands-on Training session, we're going to use the Professional edition for training purposes.

7.0 Introduction

Information security is commonly thought of as a process and not a product. However, standard security implementations usually employ some form of dedicated mechanism to control access privileges and restrict network resources to users who are authorized, identifiable, and traceable.

As attacks on enterprise grow more sophisticated and diverse; companies need to rethink their network defense and entire enterprise risk management strategies. Security for that matter is not only about protecting the network, but also the data. That requires a combination of tactics, from securing the network perimeter to encrypting data on mobile and storage devices. Today, many enterprises look at network as taking a layered approach. As security become more complex, businesses increasingly see a need for enterprise security strategies, as well as ways to collate information from the various tools and evaluate their performance. And they are grappling with new issues created by growing mobility and anywhere anyplace anytime access – making the remote users the "new perimeter" frontier and not the firewall – thus increasing risk to enterprise resources. Therefore, in this respect, the network security gateway defense systems must be configured correctly to allow internal users and road-warriors access to the private network – is very critical. Not to mention business partners who often while on the company premises also require network access.

The Perimeter Security
An organization's perimeter defense is the oldest and, some would say, the most cluttered security layer. Firewalls have kept watch for over two decades at the frontier where corporate networks reach the public network, the Internet. A firewall blocks questionable network packet from reaching internal networks, denying passage based on the IP address of the packet's source or destination service – such as File Transfer Protocol (FTP) – the packet is attempting to reach. Intrusion detection systems (IDS) followed firewalls into the fray, detecting malicious worms and other attacks

that would get past a firewall. Intrusion prevention systems both detect and block attacks. Also on the network boarder: secure messaging gateways designed to prevent spam and e-mail-borne viruses.

In reaction to those mounting lines of perimeter defense consolidation, some organizations, have began to replace traditional, single-purpose devices with a hardware-software combination called a Unified Threat Management (UTM) appliance. The device combines the firewall typical of perimeter defenses with intrusion prevention systems, anti-spam and antivirus software, and Web filtering. That is, the implementation of UTM technology, is expected to lead to real benefits e.g., consolidated specialized devices thereby reducing management complexity which in turn reduces support and upgrade costs. The negative side, UTM is CPU intensive – for example – the Web and spam filtering are the two greatest consumers of CPU and memory resources, and hence, will definitely impact the hardware more than anything else. Therefore, for IT best practices; watch out for CPU-intensive appliances such as Web filtering. *Solution*: use load balancing to achieve best performance and prevent one appliance from becoming a single point of failure.

In this respect, today, almost all major network Security Appliances vendors integrate a broad range of advanced firewall services to protect businesses from the constant barrage of threats on the Internet and in many business network environments. There are also software based network security solutions that one can acquire and install on a relatively low cost computer but with more RAM. Astaro Security Gateway, for example, provides you with full UTM perimeter coverage on your platform of your choice. Whether as hardware, software or as a virtual appliance, all deployment methods feature the same functionality, have an identical user interface and can be deployed in multiple configurations.

As a secure foundation, these Security Appliances provide rich stateful inspection firewall services, tracking the state of all network communications and preventing unauthorized network access. Building upon those services, these Security Appliances deliver strong application layer security, application-aware inspection engines that examine network flows at various layers. To defend networks from application layer attacks and to give businesses more control over applications and protocols used in their environment, these inspection engines incorporate extensive application and protocol knowledge and employ security enforcement technologies that include protocol anomaly detection, application and protocol state tracking, Network Address Translation (NAT) services, and attack detection and mitigation techniques such as application/protocol command filtering, content verification, and URL deobfuscation. These inspection engines also give businesses control over instant messaging, peer-to-peer file sharing, and tunneling applications, enabling businesses to enforce usage policies and protect network bandwidth for legitimate business applications.

In opting for Astaro's unified threat management offering UTM, for example, an organization would be in a position to do away with several stand-alone pieces of gears, e.g., Cisco System PIX firewalls and Internet Security Systems intrusion detection systems. Furthermore, the Astaro product's anti-spam and Web filtering capabilities would enable an organization to jettison individual stand-alone security elements e.g., GFI Software's MailEssentials anti-spam filter, SurfControl's Web filtering application and many others. This type of simplification is expected to lower corporate security costs by a few thousand dollars a year in reduced software licensing and support expenditures.

However, all is not rosy in the integrated IT perimeter security front. Still, organizations seeking the benefits of integrated perimeter security face implementation challenges with unified threat management. In this respect, one of the main issues you're going to have with UTM is the fact that you are doing so much in one box, and therefore, one has to be careful about scalability. In reality, although, these appliances are pretty powerful device – one would still be careful to take great care during planning, designing and implementation stages with closer look at requirements and usage, more-so during peak times – as it is estimated that it would take a real performance hit during busy time of the day. The product's Web filtering function, in particular, is extremely CPU-intensive. When in action, the product scans for viruses on each user's Internet connection, so CPU demand mounts as the number of concurrent Web surfers' rises.

However, it's important to note that this kind of problems can easily be alleviated by using load balancing technique, by shifting CPU intensive tasks – e.g., spam filtering – to a second appliance. That appliance, for example, would actually be another Astaro's software loaded onto the company's own hardware. However, we believe that smaller organizations can probably get by with one appliance. But as a best practice, it is expected that midsize and enterprise size organizations should split the load between two boxes via load balancing. This would prevent one appliance from becoming a single point of failure.

For this lab training session, we are going to use Astaro Security Gateway (ASG), the Professional Edition which comes with a 30 day free trial. The ASG comes in three options as stated elsewhere. Astaro Security Appliances and Software supports an optimized and hardened version of Linux Kernel 2.6. The RPM system is built on the reliable SUSE SLES v9 packaging. Astaro's framework is based on a variety of open source projects. Astaro Security Gateway Software powered by Astaro Security Linux is a complete network security solution that protects organizations against a wide range of threats to security and productivity. It provides nine critical security applications grouped into three main groups: i) Web Security (Spyware protection, Virus protection for the Web, Content filtering); ii) E-mail Security (Virus protection for email, Spam protection, Phishing protection); iii) Network Security (Intrusion detection, Firewall, Virtual private network gateway).

A Case for Multi-Layered Enterprise IT Security Network Defense

The existence of myriad layers in the typically IT security strategy begs the question: can they interact? The various security technologies have mostly acted in isolation over the years and continue to do so to a considerable degree even to-date. Currently, the main emphasis and struggle is being able to integrate and manage all those technologies as a unified defense as opposed to so many different point solutions in the enterprise. As explained above, integration can be found within layers. At the perimeter, unified threat management (UTM) appliances fill the role, combining firewall and intrusion prevention, among other functions.

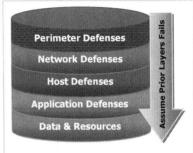

Fig. 1: Enterprise Security – Defense-In-Depth

In IT speak; security is a many-layered thing for most IT managers. This is basically because attacks may target network, workstation, server or application vulnerabilities. Blended threats combine multiple attack vectors – Trojan horses, spyware, worms and viruses, for example – in an attempt to outflank an organization's defenses. And over the years, starting from the mid 80s and the birth of PCs, the attack tools have been growing in sophistication, which require almost no technical skills to use, as depicted in Fig. 2. In response, enterprise erected a series of barriers on the principle that an attack that beats one security measure won't get past other protections. This approach goes by several names: layered security, defense-in-depth – but the underlying premise is the same, see Fig. 1

The traditional thinking view of layered security places firewall at the outermost ring of the protection – guarding the corporate network from public network (the Internet) borne incursions, see Figs. 1 & 2. After the firewall, attention turns to network-based intrusion detection/prevention systems that aim to snuff out attacks that sneak through the firewall. Antivirus software and host-based intrusion detection/prevention systems protect servers and client PCs, providing still another layer.

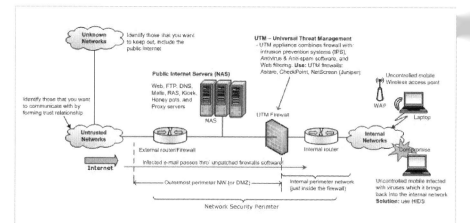

Fig. 2: Typical Secure Internal Network Infrastructure

Firewall – via filter rules (TCP, UDP, & ports) must be the gateway for all communications between trusted and untrusted and unknown networks (NWs). It is the choke point where all communication must pass through

Perimeter network (NW) or DMZ which is put in place using: *firewalls & routers* – on the *NW edge*, permits secure communications between corporate NW and third-parties. It includes: *DMZ, extranet, & intranets.* Perimeter network is the key that enables many mission-critical NW services. It also offers a layer of protection for the internal NW in the event that one of Internet accessible servers is compromised

Bastion Hosts: cannot initiate, on its own, a session request back to the private NW. Implies it can only forward packets that have already been requested by clients from internal private NW. To maintain secure communication and Private network protection, bastion hosts should have **all** appropriate up-to-date **service packs (SP), hot fixes**, and **patches** installed. System/network admins must also ensure that **logging** of all security-related **events** should also be enabled and **regularly reviewed/analyzed** to track both successful and unsuccessful security events.

While emerging classes of tools may fend off attacks at multiple layers, there are pitfalls if the tools are not properly configured, managed or integrated with existing systems. In effect, chief information and security officers have to be jack of all trades to implement an effective layered security strategy. In overall, a layered security strategy – built around numerous preventive controls – requires good perimeter defenses – i.e., you need to have host- and network-based intrusion detection integrated with other security solutions all the way down to the desktop level, also known as end-point. Current statistics indicate that a typical enterprise spends more than 5% of its IT budget on security, with expected growth in annual spending pegged at 9%, compared to 4% to 5% for IT overall.

Today, most IT network security strategists prefer to define layers in terms of critical security processes – tasks such as vulnerability management and intrusion prevention. Process-based definitions like these don't commit IT managers to a specific technology approach and also guard against redundant technology. For example, anti-spyware products entered the market a few years ago – as a product set distinct from antivirus; however, both support the same process. In this respect, one may wonder "what is so different about process of blocking spyware from the process of blocking viruses". Currently, vendors such as Symantec have since consolidated anti-spyware and antivirus on the same desktop. This new approach, has given rise to increased emphasis on host security for so-called end-points such as servers and PCs so that these devices can defend themselves. These technologies include host-based intrusion protection systems (HIDS). For information more read: Developing IT Security Risk Management Plan from Docstoc.com.

In this IT Security & Network Defense Hands-on Training session, we're going to use the Professional edition for training purposes.

ASG Minimum Hardware Pre-requisite
ASG installation generally runs for 25 minutes, and you can complete it with relatively modest hardware requirements such as a 386 processor (or compatible CPU) with 512MB RAM, 10G IDE or SCSI hard drive, Bootable CD-ROM drive, and 3 Network Cards (2 if there is no need for a DMZ). If you plan to utilize caching proxy, IDS or other add-ons, consider additional horsepower in terms of RAM/Processor.

Hands-on Solution:
In this Hands-on Lab session, you'll learn how to setup virtual network on VMware (you may also use any other virtual machines like MS VirtualPC, Linux Xen, or VirtualBox from Sun). Next you will learn how to initialize a virtual machine with three NIC adapters, which we'll use to install & configure ASG. You'll also learn how to install & configure a second virtual machine with WinXP to use for configuring and testing your ASG functionality via WebAdmin running at port 4444. Finally, you'll have an opportunity to do the Hands-on Labs assignments to test what you have learned in this session. You'll also learn how to setup Astaro SSL VPN to allow road warriors secure remote access to the corporate network reources and applications. Once you're done with this labs session you should have gained an experience and capability to enable you to plan design implement and deploy a simple but secure medium enterprise network infrastructure.

Network Diagram Configuration

It's assumed that you have a good understanding of Linux operating system and its working environment. It's also assumed that you know how to install windows XP on VMware.

Figure 3 shows our network setup for pilot lab training session of our private enterprise LAN, which we have configured using VMware with three NIC adapters attached to Astaro Security Gateway (Virtual Machine 1). The `eth1` is attached to the public side of the network and is receiving its IP address from Internet modem DHCP server. The `eth0` is configured with static IP address and is also the NIC that is attached to DHCP server which feeds the dynamic IP address to the devices located within the private LAN via the `VMnet2` virtual switch. The third NIC adapter, `eth2` is attached to DMZ network side. Virtual Machine 1 is running Linux based Astaro Security Gateway, Internal PC (Virtual machine 2) is running WinXP, however, you can also use any Linux distro.

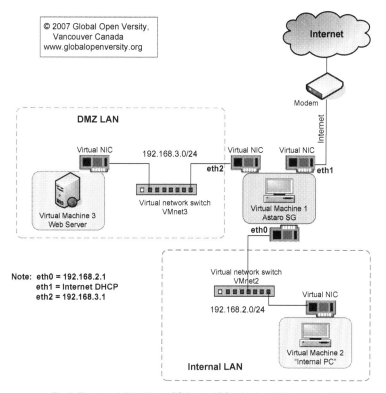

Fig. 3: Enterprise LAN, with test PC (Internal PC) added, and Web server in DMZ

Note: once you're done with pilot testing and all is working great then you can migrate your setup to your production environment.

Part 1: Install & Configure Astaro Firewall

To understand Astaro or any other Firewall let's take a look at a very common scenario for medium to large enterprise network. We need to provide internet access to all computers in the network and yet we want them all to be protected from outside access. The best access is transparent where the users' behind firewall or UTM appliance doesn't feel the presence of firewall when they access the internet. However, external access must be blocked except where specifically allowed, and that's via VPN server. Astaro shines in such setup. You can setup this configuration in just about over an hour. And the best part of all is that the client machines need nothing more than a simple configuration during setup wherein you specify that the IP address etc. information will be provided by DHCP.

Step 1: Install Astaro Security Gateway (ASG)

As you may recall, there are three options for anyone who intends to install and use Astaro Security Gateway (ASG) Editions: i) Home Edition, free for home use; ii) Essential Edition, free for business use, iii) the Professional Edition, free for 30 day trial, thereafter, you must purchase the license. Here we're going to download and use the Professional Edition for a 30 day trial, as we're just using it only for training purposes.

To install Astaro SG, perform the following procedure:

1. Hope over to Astaro.com website and download the latest package, which at the time of writing this lab manual was "ASG v7"
2. Once you have downloaded the ASG ISO specific to your need, you have the option of burning it into CD or just by using the ISO package to install it from your virtual machine, in our case VMware.
3. Fire-up a new virtual machine and perform the initial configuration and setup to use ISO package, ensure to give the virtual machine three NIC adapters
4. Start the virtual machine, and you should be able to see the first ASG installation screen as shown in Fig. 4. Hit the **Enter** key to commence installation.

Fig.4

5. From Fig. 5, Press **<Enter>** to start Installation, or **<ESC>** to abort.

Fig. 5

6. From Fig. 6, Press **F8** to proceed.

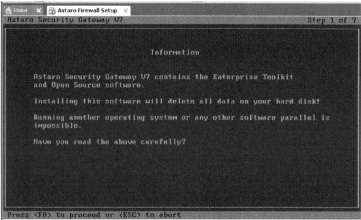

Fig. 6

7. From Fig. 7, select the **Keyboard layout** and then hit **Enter** to continue.

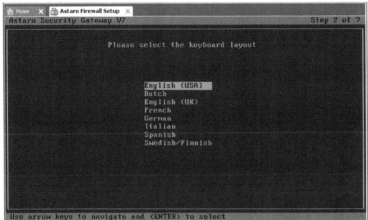

Fig. 7

8. From Fig. 8, the **Detected Hardware** screen, press **F8** to accept the information and continue.

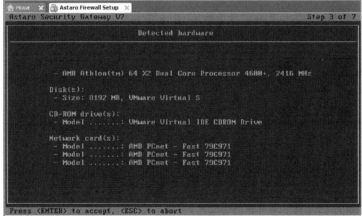

Fig. 8

Note: that we have three NICs detected as we had initially configured during the virtual machine setup.

9. From Fig. 9, use the arrow keys to navigate and then hit **Enter** to select your area.

Fig. 9

10. From Fig. 10, use the arrow keys to navigate and then hit **Enter** to select your time zone.

Fig. 10

11. From Fig. 11, accept the default current date and time, or modify as desired, and then hit **Enter** to continue.

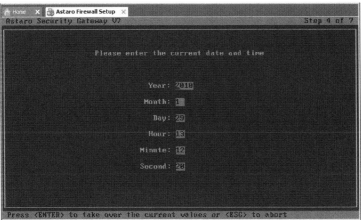

Please enter the current date and time

Year: 2010
Month: 1
Day: 29
Hour: 13
Minute: 12
Second: 29

Press <ENTER> to take over the current values or <ESG> to abort

Fig. 11

12. From Fig. 12, as can be seen, ASG has detected the first NIC card for the Private LAN interface and which is also used for administrative purpose. Hit **Enter** to continue.

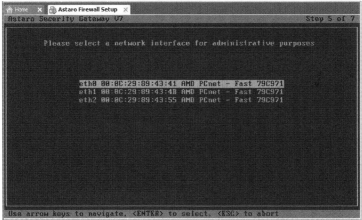

Please select a network interface for administrative purposes

eth0 00:0C:29:89:43:41 AMD PCnet - Fast 79C971
eth1 00:0C:29:89:43:4B AMD PCnet - Fast 79C971
eth2 00:0C:29:89:43:55 AMD PCnet - Fast 79C971

Use arrow keys to navigate, <ENTER> to select, <ESG> to abort

Fig. 12

13. From Fig. 13, accept the default the IP address for the administrative network interface, and then hit **Enter** to continue.

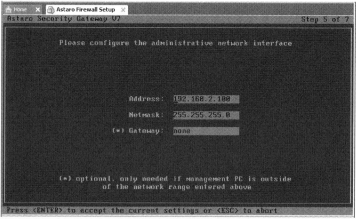
Fig. 13

14. From Fig. 14, carefully read and comply with the license regulations, and then hit **Enter** to accept and continue with the installation, or hit **ESC** to abort.

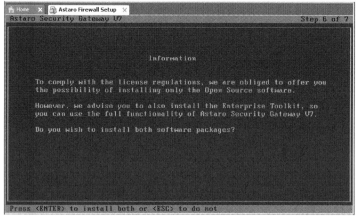
Fig. 14

15. From Fig. 15, carefully read the WARNING! The next step will "Erase all the data from your first harddisk". When certified, hit **F8** to accept and continue with the installation, or hit **ESC** to abort.

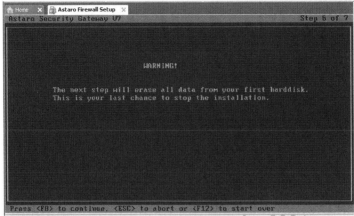

Fig. 15

16. From Fig. 16, the installation process will first go through a Checksum verification, and then proceed to start the Installation.

Fig. 16

17. From Fig. 17, note the secure administrative URL: https://192.168.2.100:4444/, which we're going to browse to complete the configuration once the machine reboots. Reboot the system.

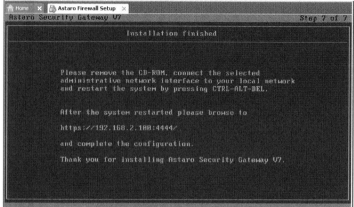

Fig. 17

18. From Fig. 18, you can hit the **F2** key to view the details of systems bootup process.

Fig. 18

19. From Fig. 19, we nee to reset the default root user password before we can proceed, as follows: enter the **login:** "`root`", and the **Old Password:** "`Password`", and then enter the new password as desired.

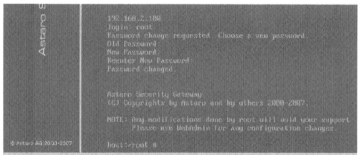

Fig. 19

20. Now, fire-up the Internal PC (virtual machine 2), if you don't have one then go ahead setup one.

21. Next, login to the Internal PC. Fire-up your favorite browser, type: https://192.168.2.100:4444/, as shown in Fig. 20. In the **Basic System Setup** window, enter the Administrator Contact & the

password for the ASG. Read the license agreement & then check **"I accept the license agreement"**. Finally, click **Perform basics system setup** button to continue.

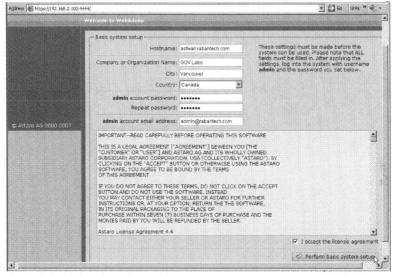

Fig. 20: Enter Admin contact and password.

22. Enter the admin credentials and then click **Login**, as shown in Fig. 21.

Fig. 21

23. From Fig. 22, accept the default selection **"Continue with this wizard"**, or choose as desired. Click **Next** to continue.

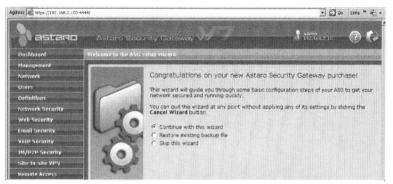

Fig. 22

24. From Fig. 23, the "License installation" screen, we're using the 30 day trial license for lab training purposes. Click **Next** to continue.

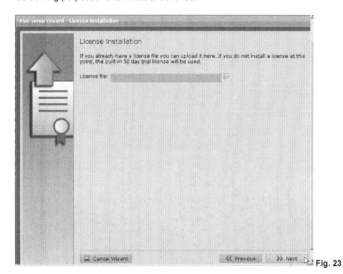

Fig. 23

25. From Fig. 24, the **Internal (LAN) Network settings**, accept the default, & then click **Next** to continue.

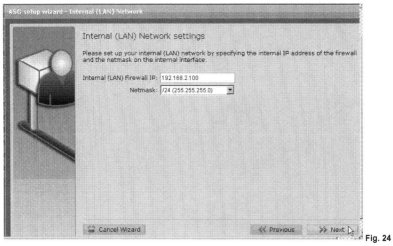

Internal (LAN) Network settings

Please set up your internal (LAN) network by specifying the internal IP address of the firewall and the netmask on the internal interface.

Internal (LAN) Firewall IP: 192.168.2.100

Netmask: /24 (255.255.255.0)

Cancel Wizard   Previous   Next   Fig. 24

26. From Fig. 25, accept the default selection "Address Settings", and then click **Next** to continue.

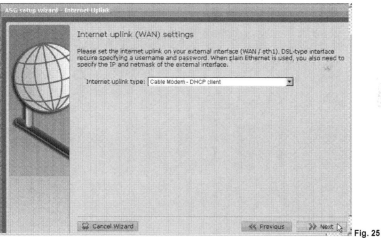

Internet uplink (WAN) settings

Please set the internet uplink on your external interface (WAN / eth1). DSL-type interface require specifying a username and password. When plain Ethernet is used, you also need to specify the IP and netmask of the external interface.

Internet uplink type: Cable Modem - DHCP client

Cancel Wizard   Previous   Next   Fig. 25

27. From Fig. 26, the **Firewall settings**, select the options as desired, and then click **Next** to continue.

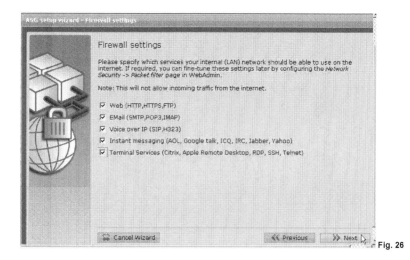

Fig. 26

28. From Fig. 27, the **Intrusion prevention settings,** select the options as desired, and then click **Next**.

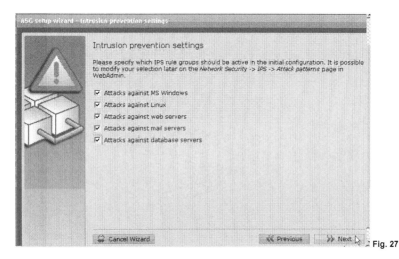

Fig. 27

29. From Fig. 28, the **instant messaging and Peer-to-Peer settings,** select the options as desired, and then click **Next**.

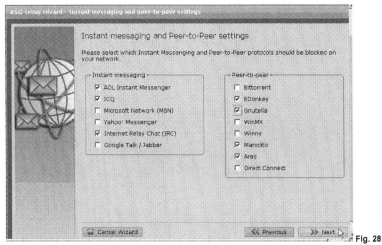

Fig. 28

30. From Fig. 29, the **Web Security settings,** select the options as desired, and then click **Next**.

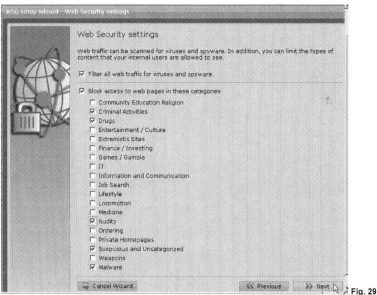

Fig. 29

31. From Fig. 30, the **Email Security settings,** select the options as desired. Next, enter the **Internal mail server IP address** and **Routed SMTP domains**; and then click **Next**.

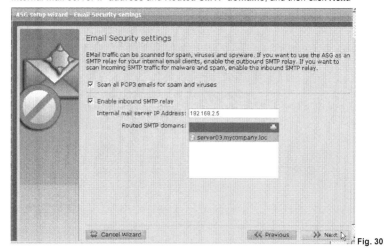

Fig. 30

32. From Fig. 31, the **Thank you for completing the ASG setup wizard!** Click **Next** to complete. Then click the Apply and Finish button.

Fig. 31

33. From Fig. 32, shows **Dashboard** of the as-completed ASG installation using wizard.

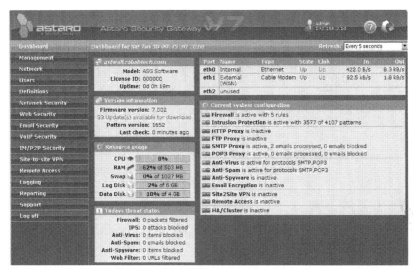

Fig. 32: shows Dashboard of the as-completed ASG installation using wizard.

Step 2: Install System and Virus Scanner Updates

Following IT security best practices, it's very imperative and critical that you update your systems and any other third party applications running on your immediately you have completed initial systems setup.

As for ASG, by default, the Firmware and Pattern Up2Dates will be downloaded automatically from the Up2Date server. To keep the system safe, please install a new Firmware Up2Date shortly after the download. Now, the initial configuration is complete, from Fig. 32, and as can be observed we've 33 updates to process, therefore, we'll go ahead and install these updates.

1. To do this, click **Management** directory,

2. Next, select **Up2Date** menu, and from **Overview** tab, click Update to latest version now, as shown in Fig. 33.

390

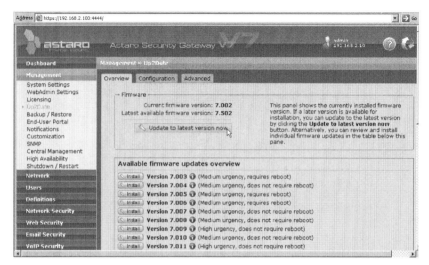

Fig. 33: Updating system and virus scanner updates

3. You should an Alert window pops-up, as shown below. Click **OK**, and wait for update to complete.

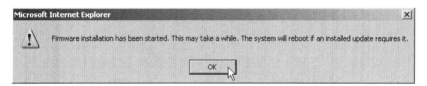

4. You're done with the initial setup of the Astaro Security Gateway network defense system.

Step 3: Configure the HTTP Proxy

In IT networks, a **HTTP Proxy server** is a server (a computer system or an application program) that acts as an intermediary for requests from clients seeking resources from other servers. A client connects to the proxy server, requesting some service, such as a file, connection, web page, or other resource, available from a different server. The proxy server evaluates the request according to its filtering rules. For example, it may filter traffic by IP address or protocol. If the request is validated by the filter, the proxy provides the resource by connecting to the relevant server and requesting the service on behalf of the client. A proxy server may optionally alter the client's request or the server's response, and sometimes it may serve the request without contacting the specified server. In this case, it "caches" responses from the remote server, and returns subsequent requests for the same content directly. A proxy server that passes requests and replies unmodified is usually called a gateway or sometimes tunneling proxy.

A proxy server has many potential purposes, including:

- To speed up access to resources (using caching). Web proxies are commonly used to cache web pages from a web server.

- To keep machines behind it anonymous (mainly for security)

- To apply access policy to network services or content, e.g. to block undesired sites.

- To log / audit usage, i.e., to provide company employee Internet usage reporting.

- To bypass security/ parental controls.

- To scan outbound content, e.g., for data leak protection.

- To scan transmitted content for malware before delivery.

- To circumvent regional restrictions.

To configure HTTP Proxy, perform the following procedure:

1. From Fig. 32 above, click **Web Security** directory,

2. Next, select **HTTP** menu and then click the Enable button, a shown Fig. 34

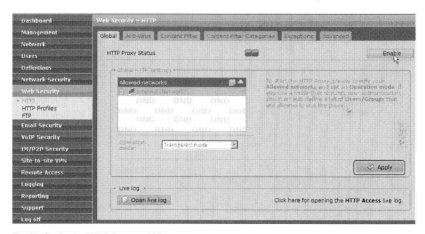

Fig. 34: Configuring HTTP Proxy on ASG

3. Finally, click the Apply button to effect the changes, and you should see the information printout as shown below indicating the http proxy was completed successfully.

Global HTTP settings saved successfully

392

4. You're done with this section.

Part 2: Setup and Configure SSL VPN

Remote access to corporate network data from any location at any time is a necessity for mobile or home workers in many businesses. However, setting up these clients on individual PCs often becomes a huge administrative burden, and in many cases the technology used only provides limited access to certain private network resources and applications. Astaro VPN clients offer flexible remote access for any type of network environment and operating system with minimal administrative effort.

Astaro provides two VPN Client applications, offering mobile workers with easy-to-manage secure remote access to corporate networks:

- **Astaro Secure Client:** Powerful and feature rich client for IPSec based remote access for businesses seeking to connect their road warriors or for connecting branch offices Also includes a personal firewall for additional protection of the local client. Protects access from Windows 2000/XP/Vista/7.
- **Astaro SSL Client:** Easy-to-use platform independent client for transparent SSL access to all company applications. Available free of charge. Installs on Windows, Linux, MacOS and UNIX operating systems.

Step 1: Setup SSL VPN

By default SSL VPN is set to inactive, therefore, before setting up SSL VPN you need to enable it. To do this, perform the following procedure.
1. Login to the ASG WebAdmin with Admin credentials via https://192.168.2.100:4444/
2. Click **Remote Access** and then choose **SSL** and from the left pane click from the **Global** tab click the `Enable` button to enable SSL VPN

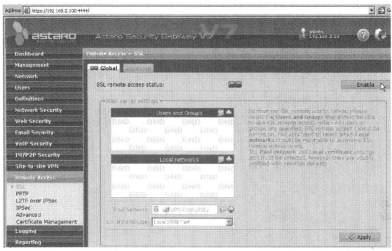

Fig. 35: Setting up SSL VPN

3. Next, we need to setup users/groups from the **Users and Groups** that should be able to use SSL VPN remote access (RA). Click the icon to add the remote access user, and from the **Add User** dialog box as shown in Fig. 36, complete the information required. For example let's add user:

   Username: iwong
   Full Name: Irene Wong
   Email: iwong@mycompany.loc
   Password: xxxxx

4. Click **Save**

5. Again, from Fig. 35, from the **Local networks**, click the icon, and drag and drop ✎ Internal (Network), which allows the remote access user to access the entire range of internal IP addresses and hence the whole internal network resources and applications.

6. Click the **Apply** button to effect the changes.

7. The final setup should look like shown in Fig. 37.

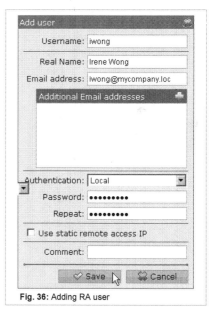

Fig. 36: Adding RA user

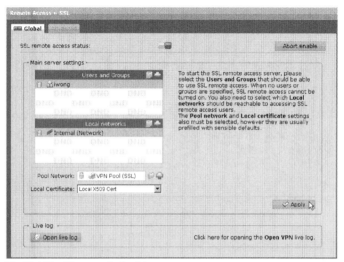

Fig. 37: Adding RA user and network to access

8. From Fig. 37, click the **Advance** tab, and under the **Encryption settings** heading; we need to beef up our encryption parameters, as follows:

    Encryption algorithm: `AES-192-CBC`
    Key size: `2048 bit`

9. Click the **Apply** button to save the changes, as shown in Fig. 38.

Fig. 38: Under **Advance** tab → **Encryption settings**, change as desired.

Step 2: Setup End-User Portal (EUP)

Here we need to setup the EUP, which allows the remote access (RA) users to securely login via Web interface without the need to use the Admin credentials from anywhere anyplace anytime. In this case RA use will need to use the ISP provided public IP address to setup his SSL VPN connection to private corporate network.

To do this, perform the following procedure:

10. From the left hand side click the **Management** link and then choose `End-User Portal`

11. Next, under **Global** tab, click the `Enable` button to enable EUP, see Fig. 39.

12. Now we need to setup the network that is allowed to access EUP. From the **Allowed network** section, click the ▣ icon, and drag and drop ⊘Any i.e., any network from the Internet. This will allow our remote access users to securely access the whole internal network resources and applications from any IP address over the entire Internet.

13. From the lower section, under **Global** tab, choose "`Allow only specific users`" option, and then click the ▣ icon, and drag and drop the user ⊘iwong, or change as desired.

14. Finally click the **Apply** button to effect the changes, as shown in Fig. 39.

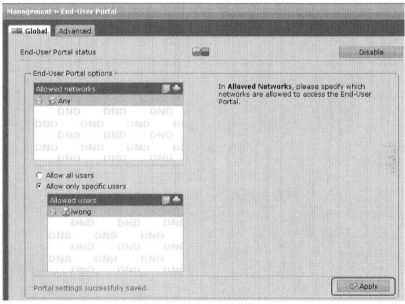

Fig. 39: Under **Global** tab, under EUP options, configure as desired.

Step 3: Setup ASG VPN Client

Astaro VPN Clients are easy to install with just a few simple mouse clicks. They offer secure and unlimited remote access to any type of network environment, including native applications not offering a web based interface.

To setup ASG VPN Client, perform the following procedure:

1. Login to the ASG End User Portal (EUP), using `iwong` credentials via https://192.168.83.213/, this in our case, is the IP address provided by the ISP. Make sure to change to your IP address given to you by your ISP.

2. Accept the Certificate warning by Adding Exception if it's self-issued certificate!

3. From Fig. 40, click **SSL-VPN** tab and depending on your OS, click the respective download. In our case we're using Windows XP, so I'll click the first `Download` button on the list. Alternatively, if you're not installing the entire package then click the second download button.

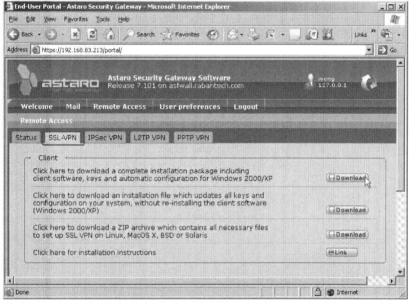

Fig. 40: Click the download button to download the SSL VPN client package

4. Unzip the downloaded package, and then under unzipped folder, double-click the `setup.exe` file to start installing the ASG VPN Client.

397

5. From Fig. 41, the **Astaro SSL VPN Client Setup Wizard**, click the **Next** button.

Welcome to the Astaro SSL VPN Client Setup Wizard

This wizard will guide you through the installation of Astaro SSL VPN Client

Next >   Cancel

Fig. 41

6. From Fig. 42, read and accept the license

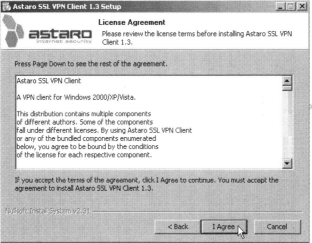

astaro
internet security

License Agreement

Please review the license terms before installing Astaro SSL VPN Client 1.3.

Press Page Down to see the rest of the agreement.

Astaro SSL VPN Client

A VPN client for Windows 2000/XP/Vista.

This distribution contains multiple components
of different authors. Some of the components
fall under different licenses. By using Astaro SSL VPN Client
or any of the bundled components enumerated
below, you agree to be bound by the conditions
of the license for each respective component.

If you accept the terms of the agreement, click I Agree to continue. You must accept the agreement to install Astaro SSL VPN Client 1.3.

Nullsoft Install System v2.31

< Back   I Agree   Cancel

Fig. 42

7. On the next screen, **Choose the install Location**, accept the default or change as desired, and then click the **Install** button
8. On the next screen, **Installation Complete**, click the **Next** button
9. From Fig. 43, the **Completing the Astaro SSL VPN Client 1.3 Setup Wizard**, click the **Finish** button to complete installation.

Fig. 43

10. You, should now see additional icons added to your Windows Tasks bar, as shown below:

11. Now double click, the traffic light █ icon, to access the **Astaro SSL VPN Client** dialog box, as shown in Fig. 44.

12. Enter RA user `iwong`, whom we had setup earlier, and then click the **OK** button to connect securely using SSL VPN to the private network.

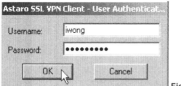
Fig. 44

13. Now the traffic light █ icon should change to █ to indicate that the **Astaro SSL VPN Client** connection was successful.

14. You should now to able to browse and access securely all the corporate private network resources and applications just like you're within the private network.

15. You're done with ASG SSL VPN client setup and configuration.

399

Part 3: Hands-on Lab Assignments

Use Figs. 3 and 45 to help you with your Hands-on labs:

1. Install and configure DNS master server and Slave DNS server for your private network placed within the DMZ LAN
2. Install configure a messaging server for your network placed within the private LAN with mail relay place in DMZ.
3. Install and configure a LAMP server for your network placed within the private LAN
4. Using Load Balancing, install and configure a Web server for your network placed within the DMZ LAN
5. Install and configure a SugarCRM server for your network placed within the private LAN. Integrate SugarCRM with MS Outlook 2007 using Kinamu Connector for Outlook.
6. Install and configure a Moodle LMS server for your network placed within the private LAN to be used for staff training
7. Finally ensure that all systems are able to connect and communicate seamlessly.
8. Enable & Configure SSL VPN access for company road warriors to securely access the private network resources and applications.

Fig. 45: A more practical network

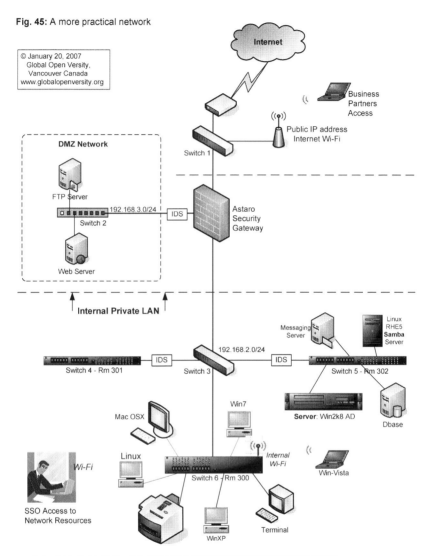

Note: Add network devices to switches 3 & 4 or any other part of the network as desired.

Other Related Articles & Hands-on Lab Manuals:

You may grab these articles from Docstoc.com:

1. Build and Run your own iSCSI SAN with OpenFiler v1.0
2. Step-By-Step Install Guide eyeOS Cloud Computing Operating System
3. Building and Running Private Cloud With Eucalyptus Systems v1.0
4. Step-By-Step Build and Deploy Xen Hypervisor Virtualization on Linux OpenSUSE 11.3 Server
5. Build your Own Private Cloud using Ubuntu 10.04 Eucalyptus Enterprise Cloud Computing Platform
6. Step-By-Step Install Guide Linux CentOS-5 VM on Citrix XenServer v1.0
7. Step-By-Step Build & Deploy Citrix XenServer and XenCenter v1.2
8. Step-By-Step Install Guide Windows Server 2008 R2 Virtualization With Hyper-V v1.0
9. Step-By-Step Install Guide OpenEMR on Ubuntu 10.04 LTS
10. Edit Step-by-Step Install Guide OSCAR McMaster CMS on Linux Ubuntu 10.04 LTS v1.4
11. Step-By-Step Install Guide Mandriva Enterprise Server 5 v1.0
12. Step-By-Step Install Guide eHealth OpenEMR on Debian 5 Server
13. Install Guide OpenLDAP for Enterprise Identity Management and SSO
14. Install Guide Linux Samba as Primary DC and SSO Identity Management
15. Build Private Clouds with Ubuntu 10.10 LTS Enterprise Cloud Platform
16. Step-By-Step Install Guide Openfire Jabber Server on Linux v1.0
17. Using Webmin and Bind9 to Setup DNS Server on Linux
18. Build your own ISP Hosting using EHCP on Ubuntu 10.04 LTS Server
19. Build your own ISP Hosting using ISPConfig on Ubuntu Server v1.0
20. Step-By-Step Install Guide DTC on Linux CentOS5 Server v1.0
21. Install Guide Secure Sendmail with Dovecot & Roundcube Webmail v1.0
22. Build your Own Private Data Center Backup Solutions using Ubuntu Powered RESTORE Backup Server v1.0
23. Install & Setup Astaro Security Gateway to Protect Corporate Network v1.1

Index

Made in the USA
Middletown, DE
18 October 2016